THREE FUNNELLED BASTARD

DID SHE CHANGE THE COURSE OF WORLD WAR II?

A TRUE STORY

WALLY MULLER

Published by

**MELROSE
BOOKS**

An Imprint of Melrose Press Limited
St Thomas Place, Ely
Cambridgeshire
CB7 4GG, UK
www.melrosebooks.co.uk

FIRST EDITION

Cover designed by Melrose Books

ISBN 978-1-908645-51-7

Printed and bound in Great Britain by:
Mimeo Ltd, Huntingdon, Cambridgeshire

FSC
www.fsc.org
MIX
From responsible
sources
FSC® C019549

DEDICATION

TO ALL WHO LOST THEIR LIVES DURING OR FOLLOWING
UPON OPERATIONS AT SEA IN THE SECOND WORLD WAR
– FRIEND, FOE AND NON-COMBATANT ALIKE. THEY ALL
PAID THE HIGHEST PRICE.
MAY THEY REST IN PEACE.

They went with songs to the battle
They were young
Straight of limb, true of eye, steady and aglow.
They were staunch to the end against odds uncounted;
They fell with their faces to the foe.
They shall grow not old, as we that are left grow old;
Age shall not weary them nor the years condemn
At the going down of the sun and in the morning
We will remember them

Laurence Binyon

ILLUSTRATIONS

PHOTOGRAPHS

DIAGRAMS

CONTENTS

AUTHOR'S PREFACE

Probably the first question that will come to mind is: Why another book about HMS *Cornwall?* The saga of this World War II British warship has already been the focus of at least two excellent, well researched books – *Turns of Fate* by Ken Dimbleby and *In Deep and Troubled Waters* by Tony Large, besides featuring prominently in others (not always accurately) and, one may well ask, is there anything more to be said? Of this I am uneasily aware and it was not without trepidation that I embarked upon yet another book on the same theme, knowing, in addition, that I do not have the literary and narrative skills of Dimbleby and Large, both former shipmates of mine whom I am privileged to value as personal friends.

The author, circa 1942

Nevertheless I believe, for several reasons, that the

Cornwall chronicles have not yet reached satiation and that there is indeed more to tell. On the one hand a number of minor events and anecdotes do not feature in the books mentioned while, in regard to others that do, some elaboration or different slants are worth relating. But it is the main, central happening – the sinking of HMS *Cornwall,* its special circumstances and far-reaching consequences – that merit greater attention and scrutiny, factors which impact meaning to the subtitle of this book: 'Did she change the course of World War II?' Startling as that hypothesis may seem, there were abundant other occurrences during the war which can also conceivably be identified as critical to the war's outcome, situations where one might say "If only that had then happened" or "Had this not been done", etcetera – *Turns of Fate*, as aptly entitled by Dimbleby.

The Second World War was in almost every respect the greatest armed conflict of all time. It lasted for six years and a day, measured from the date Germany invaded Poland in 1939 to the formal surrender of Japan on board USS *Missouri* in 1945, was waged by 56 nations and cost more than 55 million lives. More has been written about it than about any othe, and undoubtedly much more will be written for generations to come, often by authors who at the pertinent period had not yet been born, but with each passing year the true portrayal of events by upcoming writers will tend to slip further into the mists of uncertainty and scepticism. Indeed, even some present-day accounts proffered by the media might invite Malcolm Muggeridge's quip: "Everything true except the facts", or Mark Twain's *bon mot*: "When I was younger I could remember everything, whether it happened or not". Those who can still narrate at first hand, who personally participated in WWII, are diminishing apace and for the most part have already lived beyond eighty-five summers. Therefore they of this dwindling vintage who are able to contribute something to the tale should do so soon while, as was explained to me, "You still have all your marbles" (or most of them) and before the curtain finally comes down. I must emphasize here that whether or not the death of *Cornwall* affected the course of WWII she was not the only contender for that distinction because another cruiser, HMS *Dorsetshire,* was steaming in company at the time and was also sunk in the same encounter with the enemy. Therefore, if plausibility is found in the subtitle of this book, then both ships share therein equally.

· The history of World War II may strategically be divided into two halves, the first in which the fortunes of conflict largely favoured Germany, Italy and Japan while the second, from 1943 onwards, saw ascendancy steadily passing to Britain and Commonwealth, the United States and Soviet Russia. Astride both halves, however, there were, I believe, eight turning points or junctures at which, according to its own dimension, the tide of fortune was irrevocably reversed. These, in roughly chronological sequence, were:

1. Battle of Britain, May–September 1941, when the Royal Air Force prevented conquest by the Luftwaffe of daylight skies over England (Churchill: "Never in the field of human conflict was so much owed by so many to so few.") This put paid to German invasion designs.
2. Repulse of German armies before Moscow and Leningrad, October 1941 and succeeding months, by Soviet defenders aided by extreme winter conditions.
3. Battle of Midway, 4 June 1942, when the Japanese First Carrier Fleet was defeated by the US Navy in central Pacific. (Fuchida: "The battle that doomed Japan.")
4. El Alamein in the Western Desert some 70 miles west of Alexandria, November 1942, where Rommel's Axis forces were halted and subsequently forced into headlong retreat. (Churchill: "Before Alamein our armies never had a victory. After Alamein we never had a defeat.")

5. Guadalcanal in the Solomon Islands, the furthest Japanese advance southwards, intended to isolate Australasia from the United States, finally retaken by US marines January 1943 after five months' ferocious fighting on land and sea.
6. Stalingrad on the lower Volga, February 1943, when the German salient thrusting towards the Caspian Sea to 'amputate' the Ukrainian granary, Black Sea maritime facilities and the Caucasian oilfields was, after six months of bloody slaughter, trapped and destroyed.
7. Imphal and Kohima on India's north-eastern border when British and Indian forces finally, in June 1944, broke Japanese investment and foiled their invasion of the subcontinent.
8. Battle of the Atlantic. This raged virtually from Britain's declaration of war until Germany's surrender five years and eight months later. The main focus was on the U-boat peril (Churchill: "The only thing that really frightened me during the war."), the climax occurring about July/August 1943.

Analysts may differ in assessment and detail but few, I think, would refute the thesis that the foregoing eight were episodes of clear-cut watershed consequence. Nonetheless I would, with relevance to the subtitle of this book, confidently add to the list a ninth, namely:

9. Deliverance of the Eastern Fleet from annihilation by the Japanese on 5/6 April 1942, thanks to the deviatory intervention of cruisers *Cornwall* and *Dorsetshire,* unintentionally 'thrown to the wolves'.

The book's main title derives from the design of a line of heavy cruisers generally identified as 'County' class with their distinctive three funnels, sardonically referred to by the lower deck as 'three funnelled bastards' especially when the flow of liquor evoked boisterous singing in canteens, bars and other places of imbibition. If the book merits any tribute it will be because it is totally true and authentic concerning the ship while, by the same token, references made to occurrences in other settings are drawn from authoritative sources. (In upholding this claim I think I should, to be meticulous, qualify 'totally true' insofar as it applies to the spoken word, that is to say to wherever I have enclosed in quotation marks something that was said. It will be appreciated that with the effluxion of time I may not remember exactly what words were used on such occasions but I do give the assurance that everything quoted is to the best of my belief a true reflection of what was actually expressed at the time.)

Names, where given, of shipmates and others are actual and in this regard I make special mention of *Cornwall's* commanding officer, Captain Mainwaring. His name, where it appears in post-war books, is invariably spelt Manwaring, as apparently inscribed in the official Navy lists (which one would assume to be correct) but aboard *Cornwall* the spelling was certainly known to all as Mainwaring (pronounced Mannering) and as such it appeared in published reports and communiqués at that time. The official communiqué from the Admiralty announcing the sinking of the cruisers *Cornwall* and *Dorsetshire*, as received by teleprinter in South Africa (and presumably elsewhere), spelt the *Cornwall* captain's name as 'Mainwaring'. I have chosen to adhere to names and spellings as were *then* commonly accepted, including Mainwaring; Simonstown, instead of today's Simon's Town; Ceylon, as the island of Sri Lanka then was; and Bombay for Mumbai. Language on the lower deck (while on the subject of words) was frequently rough, as is chronic among sailors, but I have, when relating what was said, endeavoured to avoid the lewd and profane, or the worst of it. However, in two or three instances I have indeed recorded speech that strays somewhat on the crude side (yet tame by modern literary standards), but this was done merely to impart some small perceptions of lower-deck utterances. I apologise, therefor.

In commenting on international activities I have had the temerity (to use a kinder term than the more exact 'damn cheek') to look critically at some of the most prominent, powerful, notorious leaders and potentates of the twentieth century. Who am I to do this? What are my wartime credentials? Well, I scrubbed decks, polished brasswork and slapped on grey paint as directed, with, I fear, sub-average dexterity and ardour. But, as the saying goes, "A cat can look at a king!"

There is an added reason for writing another book on HMS *Cornwall*: as with everyone who served on her, I loved the old three funnelled bastard.

She deserves another.

PRELUDE

1

MONDAY NIGHT SAILOR

Now the fun begins

It all began with poison gas.

January 1938 saw me fresh out of school, measuring from keel to topmast 1 fathom, or about 6 feet 2 inches, but weighing a paltry 145 lb, with a string-bean physique which, I was informed, would not, if standing sideways on, cast a shadow. Another tribulation was hay fever. This, which on average made my life a misery once or twice a week, my mother blamed on the flowering gum trees in our street in East London and which my father, with good intent, sought to cure with cough lozenges. Otherwise I was fit and healthy.

I was commencing my 18th year, the stipulated age when young white males were required by the government of the Union of South Africa to register for peacetime National Service in the Active Citizen Force (ACF), in times of national necessity it was intended to support the Permanent Force (PF). The registration form invited the reluctant candidate to indicate in which arm of the ACF he would prefer to serve – army, navy, air force or medical corps –without any assurance that his preference would at call-up be gratified. Indeed, as the system worked on a quota basis, he might not be called up at all, which eventuality was the fervent hope of the majority.

I dismissed without ado any inclination towards the air force and medical corps, soberly aware that my maladroit propensities would in the case of the former ensure the destruction of any aircraft, even before it left the ground and, as for the latter, only exacerbate existing health hazards. My choice, therefore, lay between army and navy. I had no firm preconceptions in this regard and in a noncommittal way sought to compare what I imagined the pros and cons of the two services would be under warring conditions. There was of course talk of war at that time but I knew and cared little about international affairs. I had heard distantly on the radio or noted vaguely in the *Daily Dispatch*, our local newspaper, as I skimmed through to the sports pages, names such as Blum, Daladier, Hitler of course, Chamberlain and Dollfuss; and occurrences such as the Rhineland coup, something called an Anschluss in Austria, civil war in Spain, Italian invasion of Abyssinia, and the League of Nations, but none of these meant much to me, did not seem to concern us here, 6,000 miles away at the bottom end of Africa. What was of prime importance was the scheduled tour of the All Blacks in 1940.

Nevertheless, if there was to be a war and I was involved, which would be the lesser of two evils – army or navy? Neither held out much appeal, quite apart from the prospect of both being shot or blown to pieces. The army called to mind waterlogged trench warfare, tank battles and hand-to-hand bayonet combat, while the navy evoked visions of being trapped in a sinking ship. Which was worse? Should I toss a coin? Then I remembered poison gas, vividly described in a book I had read, and starkly portrayed in a movie I had once seen of gassed casualties on the Western Front during the 1914–1918 War. That swung it; gas warfare was an army peril, so I would opt for the navy. Poison gas was the deciding factor yet ironically, of all the fearful implements of destruction available during the global conflict that soon followed, gas was never used.

I completed the registration form and sent it off, hoping for the best – namely exemption by quota or, failing that, second best – the navy.

In my case a call-up to the army meant, in all probability, the Kaffrarian Rifles, the local infantry regiment established in 1883, while navy, on the other hand, implied the South African division of the Royal Naval Volunteers Reserve, or RNVR(SA). Under an agreement between the governments of the Union and Britain, brokered by a committee of Imperial Defence, the Royal Naval Africa Station controlled the administration and training of RNVR(SA), with bases established at Simonstown, Port Elizabeth, East London and Durban. Active service in the RNVR in peacetime generally entailed weekly evening training involving parade ground drill and instruction in seamanship, spread over a period of three to four years with, at the end of each year, a month's intensive training in Simonstown, including sea time on a Royal Naval vessel.

If my name came up through the enlistment process I could expect to be part of the 1939 intake, but that seemed far away at the time – a whole year ahead almost – and I hardly thought about it. But having taken the first enrolment step and being conscious of increasing public concern about the possibility of war, I did begin to take slightly more interest in the world's trouble spots, listened somewhat more attentively to news broadcasts, and turned over the front pages of the *Daily Dispatch* less cursorily than before. I noted that in February Hitler annexed Austria to the German Reich and then focussed his avarice on Czechoslovakia, which in September, following the pact contrived at Munich by prime ministers Chamberlain of Britain and Daladier of France with Duce Mussolini of Italy and Chancellor Hitler, was compelled to cede Sudetenland, the territory along its northern border with Germany. Thus, I learned, had the Third Reich in 1938 increased its population by more than 10 million, acquired a vast expanse of territory and, among much else, the gigantic Skoda munitions arsenal. Gradually I, and thousands of other young greenhorns, began to take closer notice of the vociferous German with his slanting hairline and Charlie Chaplin moustache. He had, I seemed to recall, written a book titled *Mein Kampf* which raised hackles in some quarters. But otherwise life went on unperturbed as usual, our preoccupations being rugby, cricket and other pleasurable pursuits, and humming and whistling the hits of the day: 'South of the Border', 'Penny Serenade' and Judy Garland's 'Over the Rainbow'.

My call-up for peacetime training in the ACF, naval division, arrived in January 1939 and I reported on the stipulated date to the RNVR base in lower Fleet Street near the upper reaches of the Buffalo Harbour, along with a large number of other raw young men of about my age – a motley bunch from all walks of life. After introductory formalities we were each issued with a large canvas kitbag; two blue, one white and two heavy-duty drill uniforms; two caps and cap ribbons; shirts, or 'dickies'; blue-jean collars; shoes; heavy-duty UDF (Union Defence Force) boots; belt; a cumbersome oilskin coat; and various accessories which included a sailor's heavy clasp knife with single blade and spike, and a thick, official *Manual of Seamanship*, 'published by authority of the Lords Commissioners of the Admiralty'.

Uniforms were thrust at us by indifferent stores personnel who inexpertly decided size at a glance, so a decent fit was exceptional and in the case of my skinny physique the jumpers or upper half of the uniforms could comfortably have doubled as maternity jackets. We were then put to name-marking our kit, which was done with paint and applied with large wooden letter blocks – white paint on dark articles and black paint on lighter coloured items. Such was our induction as 'Monday night sailors'. The dominating figure at the base was Chief Gunnery Instructor Tom Vincent. An unforgettable character, he radiated the pride of the Royal Navy in every way – deportment, what he said and did, all-round efficiency, instilment of discipline and, not least, an infectious deadpan sense of humour. When in charge he would keep up an ongoing stream of salty jibes and invective, though never with malice or hurtfulness, which had the men frequently hard put to suppress their mirth. As instructor, guide and mentor to young sailors in the making, he had unsurpassed credentials. He had been at Jutland in 1916 as a boy seaman and, twenty years later, at the funeral of King George V, had been in charge of the gun carriage bearing the royal casket. Vincent's first task was to knock our ragtag bunch of new recruits into some sort of shape and eventually into a reasonably smart and disciplined body. In the early stages he concentrated on parade ground drill, starting from scratch – how to wear our uniforms, don our caps, when and how to salute, how to march, stand to attention, stand at ease – making us go through the motions over and over again.

After several weeks, when the Chief Gunnery Instructor (CGI) judged our performance to have progressed sufficiently, he would march us out of the base and up Fleet Street to the market square, where at that time of night there was ample space and few obstructions. There we paraded, marched and drilled in obedience to Vincent's stentorian commands liberally interspersed with derisive admonishments which attracted townsfolk passing by and amused them immensely. Generally, I think, we acquitted ourselves on the square in the public eye fairly well but occasional blunders were inevitable. One evening as the CGI marched us across in single file he bawled out, 'Right wheel'. The man in the head of the file wheeled left and the two immediately behind followed him blindly to the left. The fourth man in line of file, more alert and noting the faux pas committed by the first three, wheeled right and marched off in the opposite direction, the rest of the column following on behind. Vincent, moving with panther-like agility, ran to the front of the main column, motioned it to halt and stood the men at ease to watch and enjoy the unfolding spectacle.

Meanwhile the three who had wrongly wheeled left, blissfully unaware that anything was amiss, continued marching towards the far side of the square, heads and shoulders erect, arms swinging in best regulation style. Eventually they reached a line of parked motor cars and, unable to proceed further, and having received no further command, commenced marking time on the spot, knees rising high, until suddenly, sensing something strange, they discovered to their extreme mortification the predicament they were in, whereupon everyone else on and around the square erupted in exuberant laughter that continued until well after the red-faced trio had doubled back to rejoin their company.

As the weeks passed the 'square bashing' diminished and instruction in the basics of seamanship began, using the seamanship manual as guide. Frequently the men were divided for this purpose into smaller groups under supervision of Petty Officers or senior hands. We learned about ships: "A ship has two sides, called Port and Star'bd. Port is the side on your left when you're facing the bows with your arse towards the stern. The bows is the sharp end of the ship"; about upper and lower deck, fo'c'sle and quarterdeck, bridge, helm and compass platform; "…and you'll be serving on ships, not boats. Get that into your thick skulls. Your granny will ask what boat are you on. Boats are the small stuff carried aboard ships, with oars and sails and the like, and motorboats. The only naval vessels what we call boats are submarines. And while we're at it, warships have guns, not cannons."

We were introduced into the world of ropes and cordage, wire hawsers, bends and hitches, knots and splices, blocks and purchases, anchors and cables, shackles, Blake screw stoppers, bollards and bitts, capstans, hawse pipes and fairleads, masts and rigging, buoys and mooring, and so much more. We were lectured on elementary navigation, steering and compass reading, the 'Rule of the Road' (the basic principle of which is 'keep to the right'), navigation lights, loglines and depth sounding. Practical instructions in depth sounding invariably gave cause for apprehension because Vincent loved to inflict on us the age-old procedure of 'heaving the lead'. Simply put, this involved ascertaining the sea depth by dropping a lead weight attached to a line into the water, the line bearing measurements marked with strips of leather and coloured bunting. In actuality at sea, however, the exercise is much more complex, requiring a high degree of skill because the ship would usually be underway, albeit slowly, and the lead would need to be hove well ahead in the direction that the ship is moving so that by the time the lead touches the bottom and the line goes slack the ship will be almost perpendicularly above it, allowing the leadsman or his assistant to sing out the depth as indicated by the measurement marked on the line. For this purpose ships were fitted with small platforms called 'chains' on either side of the fo'c'sle and the leadsman would stand on the platform when heaving the lead, which was shaped like a thick bar, about a foot in length and weighing approximately 14 lb. The bottom end of the lead was hollow to permit 'crowning' with tallow which, when the lead was hauled back inboard, was expected to indicate the nature of the seabed, for example sandy or rocky.

Heaving the lead - in shallow water

To heave the lead the leadsman, standing on the platform and leaning outboard, would ease the lead down towards the water until it hung at a suitable distance from hand – perhaps two fathoms – having previously secured the other end of the line to a stanchion as a safety measure. He would then start swinging the lead, pendulum fashion, until sufficient momentum was gained to swing the lead up and around in full wide circles. After two or three such revolutions the leadsman would let the line and lead go, timing the release so as to propel the lead as far as possible for'ard into the water to sink. When the line slackened it was assumed that the lead had reached sea-bottom and the depth at that point could be determined from the markings on the line.

For training purposes in heaving the lead at the base, a makeshift platform had been constructed, projecting outwards from the edge of the corrugated-iron roof of the main building and, as volunteers were scarce, Vincent would detail a few fearful ratings to try their hand up in the 'chains' at heaving the lead, which exercise, if efficiently executed, would propel the lead and line in an arc through the air to land some thirty yards away in a disused flowerbed. If, as was most frequently the case, expertise in the heave was lacking, then a number of probabilities resulted, including decapitation of anyone within range. One evening the leadsman, struggling to control the whirling lead, released it a split second too late, sending it obliquely up skywards to come crashing down on the corrugated-iron roof with a reverberating boom that must have put pigeons to flight half a mile away. The occupants of the building came pouring out wide-eyed with alarm, the duty officer leading the charge.

"Sorry, Sir," forestalled Vincent quickly. "The line slipped out of 'is hand," then turning at once with a twinkle in his eye, he berated the hapless leadsman for his ineptitude. The duty officer stood glaring at the offender for three or four seconds, but failing to find words adequate to the occasion, turned about and re-entered the building.

When the officer was out of earshot Vincent said to the leadsman in a subdued tone, "Shame on you; you woke 'im up."

There was, of course, much more to be learned and many more skills to be acquired but under the expert, exacting, wisecracking tutelage of Chief GI Vincent there was, as the saying goes, never a dull moment, and for us Monday night sailors the first weeks and months of 1939 passed pleasantly enough. But on the international stage, events were taking place that penetrated even my politically detached consciousness. Britain and France, despite a clear assemblage of war clouds, still clung to the belief that Hitler would honour his assurance given at Munich in September 1938 that Germany's annexation of the Czech Sudetenland was his last territorial claim in Europe, but already in the January following, evidence seeped through that both Hitler and Mussolini held the view that, at the crunch, neither Britain under Chamberlain nor France under Daladier would fight. There were indications that Hitler's aspirations that Czechoslovakia had not sated his appetite for conquest and occupation and that, in the northeast, recovery of territory ceded under the Treaty of Versailles: the Polish corridor, Danzig and Upper Silesia, was assuming ominous implications.

The month of March brought heightened tension, with reports of large-scale German troop movements in the Austrian/Bavarian region, and on the 10th German divisions crossed unresisted into Czechoslovakia, which four days later was incorporated into the Reich. This flagrant breach of the Munich Agreement finally dispelled any lingering optimism and trust on the part of Britain and France, whose attitude towards Hitler's regime changed abruptly from that day forward. On the 23rd our radio announced that German troops had occupied Memel on the Baltic, which had been ceded to Lithuania. This news puzzled me momentarily as I had thought the name Memel was exclusive to a village in the Orange Free State, but a significant counter stride towards confrontation was taken on the 31st when Chamberlain told parliament that the governments of Britain and France, outraged at Hitler's persistent territorial pillaging, and anticipating that Poland was next on schedule, had assured the Polish government of all support in their power in the event of action which threatened that country's independence – in effect a guarantee in that contingency to take up arms on their behalf.

On 7th April Mussolini, emboldened by the accomplishments of his Aryan counterpart, ordered Italian forces across the Adriatic into Albania, which soon succumbed, thus providing the dictator with a launching pad for the future invasion of Greece. On the 27th Chamberlain introduced conscription from age 20 – an unprecedented step in Britain – yet even at that stage many observers still believed that by exercising mutual restraint and allowing the dust to settle, war would be averted and, indeed, a short period of relative calm did then follow, giving support to that belief. For some time a number of European countries, fearing the stronger powers, had sought a measure of protection in alliances, the majority of which had little value, prompting Churchill's droll scepticism as to whether a small nation seeking alliance with the Soviet Union as protection from Nazi Germany had more to fear from German aggression than from Soviet rescue.

Notable within the purview of alliances was a formal proposal by the Soviets for a tripartite agreement with Britain and France, which was still on the negotiation table when a thunderbolt struck which reverberated around the world. On 23rd August, Germany and Russia, historically bitter enemies, announced that they had entered into a non-aggression pact between themselves. While an incredulous world foresaw only grave consequences in this development, their alarm would have been greatly intensified had they known that, apart from the pact disclosed, a secret agreement had also been reached covering the division of Poland and the Baltic states. Churchill wrote subsequently that "only totalitarian despotism in both countries could have faced the odium of such an unnatural act".

In considering the pact, each of the two dictators had his own agenda: Stalin to play for time to mobilise his defences; and Hitler to ensure the conquest of Poland without Russian intervention and, hopefully, influence Britain and France to reconsider their commitment to the Poles. Britain and France, however, were quick to disillusion him, declaring that the new development would in no way affect their obligations, which they were determined to fulfil if the need arose.

At dawn on 1st September 1939 the German Wehrmacht crossed the border into Poland, and the Second World War commenced. Tom Vincent at the next Monday parade said tersely, "Now the fun begins." He spoke from experience.

* * * * *

2

CALL-UP SAILOR

We are
We are
The RNVR
And we're here to do our bit

A new mood now pervaded the Monday night parades – an undercurrent of expectation and excitement. War was in the air. Britain and France, having delivered an ultimatum without response, declared war on Germany on 3 September 1939, and in Cape Town on the following day in parliament, which by chance had been assembled for a different reason, Prime Minister Hertzog's motion of 'non-belligerence' was defeated, thereby precipitating his resignation. Thereupon the Governor General called upon General Smuts to form a new government, which on 6 September declared war, ranging South Africa on the side of Britain, France and the Commonwealth.

The country was alarmingly unprepared for war, particularly from the naval perspective. Its navy, at the time still designated 'SA Naval Service', had no real naval vessels, while its personnel boasted only three officers and three lower ranks – six in total. On the other hand, RNVR(SA) numbered about 800 men of all ranks, either presently serving, as I then was, or in reserve. These were generally earmarked for probable service in the Royal Navy, which was responsible for their training, but they were not contractually bound thereto. Most of us indeed were thinking and talking in terms of being drafted to Royal Navy cruisers or other warships calling at Simonstown, and rejoiced at the prospect of 'joining the navy and seeing the world'. And there was something special about the navy: the uniform perhaps – something that also seemed to draw added attention and appreciation in the public eye. Strangers would greet us in the street with a cheery "Hello Jack," and we became more conscious of the old song 'All the nice girls love a sailor, all the nice girls love a tar'. But for the time being we would have to await 'developments'. They were not long in coming.

It was at the close of a Monday night parade very soon afterwards that the Commanding Officer addressed us. Crews, he announced, were required for minesweeping and any volunteers amongst us should hand in their names at the office after the parade had been dismissed. The men stood for a few seconds in silence, somewhat nonplussed: this was not quite what they had expected. Then the CO added, "You must understand, of course, that minesweeping can be very dangerous." That seemed to break the spell and when, after dismissal, a number of men stepped forward and proceeded towards the office, I found myself following. Bravery is not my strong suit, so I suspect that my action was purely adrenaline driven. Anyway, I duly signed on 'for four years or the duration of hostilities, whichever is the shorter'. We were informed that we would be called up as and when circumstances required and that in the meantime we should arrange accordingly with our employers, and hold ourselves in readiness. As I journeyed home later that evening I pondered whether I had, when opting for the navy a year earlier, ascribed too much weight to the notoriety of poison gas.

All men and women enlisted for war service throughout the South African forces were volunteers. The government never imposed conscription although, had the country faced invasion, that policy would no doubt have changed. There was a strong anti-war component within the white population, mainly amongst the Afrikaner community, and even a very small pro-Nazi element, yet, interestingly, more than 70 per cent of all men and women who volunteered were Afrikaans speaking.

My call-up came on 22 January 1940 along with seven other ratings, and after undergoing the customary medical examination, which included eyesight, urinary test and prancing around a room in the nude to the jeers of sundry onlookers, we were drafted to entrain the following day for Cape Town. The other seven on draft were Sandy Stephenson, Norman Hardwich, Charlie Wilhelm, Timmins, Fisher, St Clair-Whicker and Tickey Howard. We were a little hazy about what lay ahead but assumed that we would still be serving in the Royal Navy without preclusion from transfer to other RN ships at a future time. However, dynamic developments had been taking place on the South African war front since 6 September. General Smuts, ever the man of action, had lost no time in addressing the enormous shortcomings in the Union Defence Force, mustering behind him an exceptionally competent team of high-ranking achievers, headed by his brilliant Chief of General Staff, General Sir Pierre van Ryneveld. On 15 January, just one week prior to our call-up, the S A Naval Service was transformed into the new Seaward Defence Force (SDF), already with 15 requisitioned little ships and a personnel of 420 under the command of Rear-Admiral Halifax as director, recalled from retirement in the Royal Navy at the personal invitation of General Smuts. The SDF now relieved the Royal Navy of responsibility for minesweeping, antisubmarine patrols and other related naval duties at all South African harbours and this, our draft soon discovered, was to be our destiny. Suddenly, it seemed, our dreams of 'seeing the world' were reduced to observing the South African coastline.

The train journey to Cape Town was, to me, memorable for one reason. Shortly after departure from East London my mates suggested that we go to the dining saloon, and there I drank the first, in my life, pint of beer. It went straight to my head and presently when someone proposed a second round I excused myself and returned unsteadily to my compartment to sober up. I had occasion to recall that first pint when war ended nearly six years later.

Upon arrival in Cape Town we were transported to the Castle of Good Hope, the massive pentagonal fortification built by the Dutch East India Company and completed in 1679. A naval training base had been established outside and against the rampart facing Table Mountain, and there we joined up with men from other units to commence our war service in the navy. Most of us, including myself, were assigned to a seaman gunner's course under the tutelage of Chief Gunnery Instructor Dick Whittington, another tough martinet with a long RN background. His job was to knock us into shape to take charge of the entire armament on minesweepers and antisubmarine patrol ships, whose number had by now increased, at least on paper, to 29. They were converted trawlers and whale catchers commandeered from fishing companies and were to be armed with a 12-pounder gun (approximately 3 inch calibre) mounted on a platform on the fo'c'sle, depth charges on a roll-off chute on the stern, Lewis automatic machineguns, rifles, .45 revolvers, Very signal pistols and distress rockets. Ammunition was stored in a magazine in the bows on or below the waterline.

The gunnery course was intensive and Whittington gave us little respite – physical training to start the day, followed by parade ground drill, often with rifles, and much of it executed at the double. Then came gunnery instruction and practice, ranging from 6-inch down to 12-pounder, with gun crews changing positions constantly; simulating battle situations; and coping with casualties. "Every number on the gun," he would bellow, "must be able to do every other job, and sometimes two or three jobs at the same time. If the gunlayer cops it, don't fret over 'im; leave that to the medics. Toss 'is body out of the way and jump into 'is seat and do 'is job as well. The gun must keep firing – except if there is a serious problem, like if the gun misfires when the gunlayer squeezes the trigger, when he will immediately shout the order: 'Still, misfire, carry on', whereupon the gun's crew will carry out the misfire drill as laid down. Could be a broken striker that must be replaced. Or when the breech is closed and the breech worker sees that this 'ere red mark on the breechblock is not exactly opposite that red mark on the back side of the gun – that means that the breechblock hasn't fully turned and engaged, probably because the projectile weren't rammed home far enough and if the gun is fired in that faulty position the charge will likely blow out backwards instead of out the muzzle, wiping out the whole gun's crew and anyone else nearby, as happened in a gun turret in the last war."

Typical minesweeper - S A Navy 1940

We had team competitions on the 6-inch practice loader, hefting 100 lb dummy projectiles and imitation charges on to the loading tray, and then ramming them up the chute to see how many rounds per minute we could fire. "Watch it, you clumsy jackasses. Drop that projie on your foot and you'll be off to the shipwright for a wooden leg." We learned the theory of engaging an enemy, of range, elevation, deflection, trajectory, plotting the fall of shot. We had instruction on the care and handling of small arms, in particular the Lewis machine-gun, air-cooled and magazine fed, how to strip it down completely and then reassemble it "as quick as 'ell, without leavin' any parts over. You might have to do that if the gun jams, and your life could depend on how quick you are."

Special attention was devoted to depth charges (the standard, cylindrical roll-off type), how to install the primer, adjust the depth setting and, more importantly, how to arm the pistol with a detonator for insertion into the primer. "Detonators," growled Whittington with great emphasis, "are the most dangerous explosives in the Navy. These 'ere are dummies for training," indicating small crayon-shaped objects arranged separately and upright in a wooden box, "but you'll be in charge of the real thing aboard ship and you'll need to treat them with utmost care and respect at all times. Drop one of 'em and it's likely to go bang and blow your foot off. Keep well away from your chums when you're 'andling detonators, so's you don't get bumped, and stay focussed on what you're doing. Leave the skylark-ing for later. 'Andling detonators is the one time you don't jump to attention when approached or spoken to by an officer, not even an admiral, or by the King 'imself. You stay put attending to the detona-tors, and finish the job. That's laid down in KR and AI. What's that? King's Regulations and Admiralty Instructions, sonny."

One day they loaded us on to a truck and drove us, with rifles, bayonets and service revolvers out to a shooting range. We did target firing from 200 yards in different positions – lying prone, kneeling on one knee, and standing upright – Chief Whittington striding up and down behind the firing line dispensing advice liberally sprinkled with caustic admonishment. "Gawd, come on! Call yourselves marks-men? My Aunt Sarah can do better than that," and "If it depends on you lot, Jerry's got nothing to worry about." When we moved back to 600 yards our accuracy, such as it was, deteriorated drastically, especially when, in addition, we had to fire with bayonets fixed, aggravated by a brisk crosswind. Whittington had a ball. "I dunno. Never mind the bull's-eye; you bunch couldn't 'it a cow on the arse with a banjo." Eventually one man had his eyebrow gashed open by the butt of his recoiling Lee Enfield and had to pull out with blood trickling down his cheek. "Best call it a day," said Whittington with feigned despondency, "before you all land up in 'ospital, without the enemy needing to fire a shot."

An elderly white-haired British soldier of high rank, who wore a red band around his cap and an array of ribbons on his breast, addressed us one day. Recalled from retirement, he had been deputed, it seemed, to lecture recruits on matters of discipline and morale. He spoke with the quiet assurance and unpretentiousness of one who had really been there and done that, who had experienced the ordeals and horrors of the First World War, who knew exactly what he was talk-ing about. He stressed the importance of obeying orders, especially in an emergency, and down to the smallest detail. "You can question them later if necessary, provided this is done in an orderly manner through the proper channels." He spoke of maintaining composure, particularly if one is in a position of authority over others, citing as an example his experience of fighting in built-up areas where men needed to cross a street under threat of sniper fire. The officer would, gauging the moment, have his men dash across the street in batches, bent over low, to take cover on the far side. Then, following last of all, the officer would often, to gain the respect and confidence of his men, walk across in an upright manner.

"Comradeship is very important for morale as it creates a strong spirit of sharing and togetherness," he said. "But beware of agitators. We all grumble at times; we wouldn't be human if we never did and, make no mistake, there will be plenty to grumble about before this war is over. But the agitator is something else. He's a troublemaker, urging insubordination, disobedience, sometimes even mutiny. He likes to tell you your rights. In the Navy he is often called a 'sea lawyer' by his shipmates, but he is not your friend, and if you let him he'll land you in big trouble, but usually manages to worm out of it himself. He will want *you* to do his dirty work, and carry the can back. Have nothing to do with agitators.

"But getting back to obeying orders and following regulations – do so to the smallest detail, because failure in this regard can have the gravest consequences. For instance, imagine you as sailors are members of a gun's crew during a naval battle. The gun cannot fire because the man on ammunition supply panicked and so failed to place a shell on the loading tray in time, so the enemy got their shot in first and hit one of your magazines, so your ship was sunk, so the battle was lost, so the war was lost – and all because the least important member of your gun's crew didn't do a simple job as taught. All right, laugh if you will; perhaps that story is a bit far-fetched. But there again, is it? The point I ask you to remember at all times is: the smallest fault can cause the greatest calamity. Never forget it."

At that time we were billeted at Wynberg Military Camp, a vast establishment that accommodated servicemen of every kind and nationality, and that same evening we were at supper in a large mess hall tucking in with the gusto of healthy young men after a long day. As I recall, the main fare was some kind of stew – hot, palatable and plentiful. At another table a short distance away was a group of Royal Air Force personnel, and presently one of them strode purposefully over to us. "Look, lads," he burst forth, "we could be here in this damned hole for a long time. Are we going to put up with this swill that they're dishing up for us to eat? We've got to do something about it, don't you agree?"

We were completely taken aback because to us the food was good and the only response he got was a few tentative grunts. The RAF guy waited a second or two, eyeing us each in turn then, obviously miffed by our lack of enthusiasm, added, "Well, anyway, think about it. We can talk again later," and, turning, he walked back to his table. When he was safely beyond earshot one of our group said in a low voice, "Agitator." We all laughed.

Our final exercise before passing out was a practice shoot far out in Table Bay aboard HMSAS *Africana,* one of the first "little ships" to be fitted with minesweeping gear and a 12-pounder gun on the fo'c'sle. This was, as it were, our baptism of fire and I clearly recall my shock, as a member of the gun's crew, when the 12-pounder was fired for the first time. I and the rest of the crew, completely inexperienced in gunnery at close quarters, had not expected such an ear-splitting crack, and that right next to us. Nevertheless the shoot, with dummy shells, was carried out satisfactorily although, in the absence of targets, no standards of accuracy could be established. A day or two later a passing out parade was held at the Castle.

Strangely, of the original draft of eight from East London, I was the only one at that stage who was posted as Seaman Gunner to a ship. Sandy Stephenson, who had completed several years in the RNVR, had negotiated some move in higher places, and left us. Norman Hardwich and Charlie Wilhelm, both provincial rugby players for Border, were moved somewhere else and later that year they both also played for Western Province. Wilhelm was elevated to commission rank as sub-lieutenant and a year or two later found himself in Scotland, which country he also represented on the rugby field. Hardwich in due time was drafted as Seaman Gunner to one of the newly converted whale catchers, aboard which, in the Mediterranean, he won the Distinguished Service Medal for gallantry. Tickey Howard transferred to the signalling branch and found the means to decamp from the SDF and regain eligibility for service in the Royal Navy. Later he was drafted to HMS *Neptune* and died when that ship struck mines off Tripoli on 19 December 1941 and was lost with all hands but one. Timmins and Fisher were drafted elsewhere and I lost all contact with them. St Clair-Whicker, who was not physically robust, requested, and was granted, an appointment as officers' steward. He died of natural causes before the war ended.

I was posted as Seaman Gunner to HMSAS *Babiana*, a coal-burning trawler commandeered from Irvin and Johnson, the dominant sea fisheries company, and since converted and commissioned as a minesweeper. My introduction to my first ship was anything but encouraging. When I found her in the late afternoon she was moored in the old Victoria Basin in Cape Town harbour, filthy and black with coal dust, litter abounding, electric cables running from ship to wharf. The commanding officer was Lieutenant W. Taylor, a lean and weathered trawler skipper and highly competent seaman. He sent me for'ard to find accommodation in the fo'c'sle mess, which was down a narrow stairway, below deck in the bows which, trundling my kitbag, I reached with some difficulty and found myself in cramped quarters bounded on two sides by double-decker bunks, lockers against the bulkhead and a large table in the middle secured to the deck. It looked most uninviting but, worse than that, I discovered, in the dim shore-supplied lighting, that I had seemingly landed amid eight of the toughest, most villainous looking scoundrels I had ever had the misfortune to behold. Begrimed and unshaven, clad in a motley accumulation of dirty, smelly clothing – overalls, pants, vests and neckcloths – they were attacking their evening meal with the collaboration of chipped and dented plates and mugs, old jam tins and an assortment of utensils which, I noted with deepening apprehension, included wicked looking trawlermen's knives commonly used for gutting fish. None of them, seen through a haze of tobacco smoke, conveyed the impression of having signed a pledge of abstinence from liquor.

"Hello," I ventured timidly, to be riveted immediately by eight murderous pairs of eyes, "I'm the new gunner."

After an ominous silence of several seconds a barrel-chested, bull-necked individual who, I soon gathered, went by the not uncommon name of Smith, said gutturally through a mouth full of food,

"Just in time for supper. Take a seat over there," indicating with a bent fork a narrow aperture between two other burly buccaneers on the opposite side of the table, "and help yourself. You can have that empty bunk up there and this locker down here without a knob." He pushed over a spare chipped plate and a black-stained spoon while I wedged in. "It's a bit rough right now," he continued, "but should get better tomorrow or the next day when stores come aboard and we get cleaned up."

One of the others, with four front teeth missing, piped in with, "We're all trawlermen, deckhands and stokers. You're lucky; you've joined a good ship with a good crew."

"I'm glad about that," I said, hoping to sound in sincere agreement and, manipulating the plate and spoon as best I could, I helped myself to some boiled potatoes and rice from a pot in the centre of the table, and commenced my first meal afloat.

Later, when I lay on my bunk in the darkened mess, listening to the lapping of water against the ship's side a few inches from my head, and to the creak of fenders between ship and wharf, and various uninspiring noises emanating from noses and throats of men sleeping in the confined space, I was again beset by concerns as to whether I had taken too harsh a view of poison gas.

It is said that first impressions are most important. However, it is also held that there is an exception to every rule, which I think is true of my first impressions on joining *Babiana* because, notwithstanding my misgivings on that occasion, I soon took a brighter view of the situation in the days that followed. Hose and brooms quickly cleaned up the decks; litter was cleared away; buckets, scrubbers and bars of yellow soap brought a fair degree of respectability to our mess; new mugs, plates and eating utensils did indeed come aboard and the cook, once he had organised his galley, produced commendable if plain meals. On putting to sea for trials I became conscious of intriguing new perceptions: spray over the fo'c'sle and gunnels, the appealing tang of ozone, the murmur of wind in the rigging, the pitch and roll and, above all, a growing affection for that superbly seaworthy little ship.

Chief Whittaker came out with us one morning to supervise a practice shoot with the 12-pounder, organising a gun's crew of trawlermen and giving rudimentary instruction. As gunlayer in charge of the gun – the one who aimed, elevated, trained and fired it – I felt suddenly upgraded to a position of some stature on board and was accorded the nickname of "Guns". I was also agreeably surprised to discover that those pirate lookalikes who on my first evening had filled me with foreboding were in no way unfriendly. In fact they went out of their way to show me the ropes. Reflecting at the time on these rough-hewn shipmates with their tousled hair and calloused hands I was reminded of Dickens' huge, hairy Mr Peggotty telling the young David Copperfield, "You'll find us rough, sir, but you'll find us ready."

Very soon I too had callouses on my hands and, as a most welcome bonus, my bodyweight shot up within weeks from 145 to 175 lbs while the detested attacks of hay fever vanished, never to return.

* * * * *

3

MINESWEEPING SAILOR

... see how it rolled

The Seaward Defence Force, from its inception, embarked energetically upon sweeping the approaches to South African harbours, commencing with Cape Town and then extending operations to Durban, Port Elizabeth and East London as more trawlers and whale catchers became available for conversion. *Babiana* started her naval service in Cape Town and on a daily basis routinely left harbour shortly after dawn in company with another minesweeper to clear a prescribed channel for use by shipping approaching or departing from the port. The usual procedure was to execute what was termed an 'A sweep', whereby the sweep wire was spanned between two ships. Immediately upon clearing the breakwater the two minesweepers, steaming abreast, would close to about 25 yards. A heaving line would then be thrown from one minesweeper to the other, the retained end having been tied by bowline to the eye splice at the end of the sweep wire, which would then be played out through a stern fairlead and hauled across to the other sweeper and made fast there to a stern bollard. Thereupon the two sweepers would move about one cable apart (approximately 200 yards) and proceed on a parallel course abreast to clear the specified channel, the sweep wire held to the required depth below the surface by heavy rectangular frames of louvred steel called 'kites'. The channel extended out to sea to a point where the depth of water was considered too great for the effective laying of moored mines. Having reached that point, the minesweepers would swing about and sweep a return leg back to port along a line adjacent to that completed on the outward leg, thereby, in theory at least, doubling the width area cleared of mines on the day.

The minesweepers could also operate singly, using the oropesa method whereby the end of the sweep wire was carried out sideways in an arc by a large wooden device called an 'otter board', the wire and the board being likewise maintained at the correct depth by kites. Attached to the otter board by means of a thin wire rope was the oropesa float, cigar shaped, about 10 feet long and 2 feet thick, which rode on the surface indicating the end position of the sweep wire beneath it. The float was usually nicknamed 'Donald Duck' and invariably painted yellow to enhance visibility, for which purpose it also had on top a short staff displaying brightly coloured bunting. It was expected that if the mooring wire of a mine was snagged it would, if not severed by the sweep wire, be drawn along the sweep into hardened metal cutters affixed to the otter board. When its mooring wire was cut the mine would spring to the surface and be despatched by small arms fire from the sweepers.

At that early stage of the war enemy mines sown off the South African coast and other localities far distant from Europe were still of the standard, moored and horned type which detonated if one of the horns was fractured, as by contact with a ship's hull, but which, if not detonated, automatically defused themselves upon severance of the mooring wire. However, the more devilish contraptions, notably the magnetic and acoustic mines, had already caused havoc in the European zone. They lay flat on the seabed and could therefore not be swept by standard procedures. Numerous magnetic mines were parachute-dropped by German aircraft off the English east coast and in November 1939 alone 27 merchant ships and a destroyer, HMS *Blanche,* were sunk by this means while many more, including the cruiser HMS *Belfast,* were damaged. These actions almost resulted in the closure of the port of London. Fortunately on 22 November one ill-directed parachute deposited its mine on mudflats, where experts were able to recover and dismantle the device and establish countermeasures.

Our problems in South Africa during early 1940 were, however, confined to moored mines. The sweep wire used was four-stranded and extremely tough and knobbly, very difficult to manipulate and to splice. It was housed aboard the sweepers on large, winch-driven drums. Our mine clearance routine was generally pleasant enough and in the weeks that followed *Babiana* did duty at several ports, putting to sea in the early morning and returning at any time from midday to mid-afternoon depending upon the distance covered as dictated by the topography and declivity of the seabed environing each port. If the sea was very rough, sweeping would be regarded as impracticable and would be dispensed with for the day.

The ship's company was nominally 19, comprising the lieutenant in command, a sub-lieutenant, a chief and assistant Engineer, four stokers, a bosun, a Leading Seaman, five Able or ordinary seamen including myself, a wireless telegraphist, a signalman, a cook and an officers' steward. Chores for seamen, apart from handling the sweeping gear, included the usual cleaning, scrubbing, painting, doing a trick on the helm and jettisoning ash hauled up from the stokehold. In harbour I, as seaman gunner, devoted my time to maintenance and cleaning of the 12-pounder gun on the fo'c'sle platform, the Lewis machinegun which at sea was mounted on the "monkey island" above the wheelhouse, rifles, revolvers, ammunition, fireworks and depth charges housed on a chute above the stern.

Shore leave for half the crew was every alternate day from about 1600 hours unless unusual circumstances obtained, expiring at midnight or, if the situation allowed, at 06.00 the following morning. When operating out of East London it was for me particularly agreeable because I could go home every second afternoon and, among other things, indulge in the luxury of a hot bath. Indeed most of the ex-trawlermen aboard also had homes in East London and enjoyed the same pleasure and, as line fishing was for them a regular off-duty pursuit, they usually took home with them a handsome pelagic contribution to the dinner table.

One day a depth charge was test-fired off East London and a number of officers and other ranks from the Port Station came out with us to witness the exercise. This engendered considerable excitement and, one may add, some concern because of the shallowness of the sea at the designated spot, which meant a shallow gauge setting on the firing mechanism, resulting in a shorter span in time between dropping the charge and its detonation, which necessitated maximum speed by the trawler in order to attain a safe distance from the explosion. *Babiana's* maximum at the time was not much in excess of 10 knots, which would place it approximately 60 yards clear – rather close for comfort or, as the Chief Engineer wryly remarked, "Near enough to have our arse blown off." Even a slight malfunction in the firing mechanism could seriously aggravate the risk.

In the event, however, everything went spectacularly well – a sudden shock and a muffled crack simultaneously with a shimmer across the surface astern followed a split second later by an enormous eruption of discoloured water. Everybody was pleased, although those in the engine-room and stokehold below the waterline were visibly shaken, causing them to cast anxious glances around for signs of popped rivets, broken instruments or leaks. On the brighter side, a profusion of fish of all sorts rose stunned to the surface, and soon *Babiana's* foredeck was full, crewmen not otherwise engaged having gone to work briskly with spear and gaff. Her sister ship, *Bluff,* also reaped bountifully of the harvest, she having come out to grandstand the proceedings and, as they taunted us, "to pick up survivors".

My closest friend aboard at that time was a tough, square-jawed signalman named Luden, whose two abiding passions were the Royal Navy and Deanna Durbin, Hollywood's teenage golden girl of song. Hailing from Cape Town he, like me, was RNVR and also under a misrepresentation had volunteered for minesweepers and found himself not in His Majesty's Royal Navy but in the Seaward Defence Force or, as the rank and file frequently called it, the 'Seaweed Expense Farce'. Luden yearned to get 'where the action is' and away from 'these daily pleasure trips'.

"Perhaps you're safer where you are," I chaffed him.

"To hell with safety," he retorted. "I joined up to fight. If that means that at the end of the war my name will be on a roll of honour or belong to some unknown warrior memorial, then that's too bad."

Luden's off-the-cuff speculation was self-fulfilling. He was later drafted to one of four large Antarctic whale catchers newly converted as antisubmarine patrol vessels, which proceeded to the Mediterranean to operate under Royal Naval control. His ship, the *Southern Floe*, struck a mine off Tobruk on 11 February 1941 and, apart from one survivor, was lost with all hands, Luden among them. He would have died bravely.

Many yarns and anecdotes can be related about *Babiana*, the tough little ship and her diverse rough-hewn crew during those early months of the war, operating as she did from Saldanha Bay to Durban but, being of relatively lesser importance, they must, perforce, largely be passed by, and give way to an account of the foremost happening in my minesweeping experience. This was set in motion about two and a half months after I joined the ship.

On the European war front a period of calm had followed the German conquest of Poland in September 1939 – a six-month interval of relative inaction widely referred to as the 'phoney war' – but disturbed eventually by the invasion and subjugation of Denmark and Norway in April the following year. The calm was completely shattered on 10 May when the full might of the German armed forces stormed across their western frontier into Holland, Belgium and Luxembourg and, by coincidence it may be said, Germany opened its offensive against South Africa on the same date because during the night of 10 May their armed commerce raider *Atlantis* entered South African waters and laid 92 mines across the shipping lanes off Cape Agulhas.

The Agulhas bank covers a large area stretching more than 50 miles out to sea and is, due to relatively shallow depth, a select locality for laying moored mines. In addition it was at that time of great strategic importance, not only because of heavy coastwise shipping but, more ominously, because four of the largest vessels afloat were at sea heading for Cape Town and Simonstown from Australia en route to Britain. These ships – luxury liners converted into troopships – were expected to approach the African coast at that point to take bearings on the loom of the Agulhas lighthouse, the coastal blackout not having yet been implemented. The lighthouse at that southernmost point of Africa threw a very strong beam and although the *Atlantis* laid mines to within approximately 5 miles from the shore she was fortunate to accomplish her mission without detection. Good fortune smiled on her adversaries even more benignly because three nights later one of her mines close inshore exploded, for whatever reason, and the flash was observed by the lighthouse keeper who immediately reported to Cape Town, from whence a warning was transmitted to all shipping.

The troopships were the *Queen Mary, Mauritania, Aquitania* and *Empress of Britain*, packed with Australian servicemen, and had any of these been sunk in the Agulhas minefield it would have been a catastrophe of greatest magnitude. In the event the troopships advisedly avoided the danger area and reached their South African destinations by the end of May.

Admiral Halifax, Director of the SDF, swiftly took steps to neutralize the threat, and when a probing sweep on the Agulhas bank confirmed the presence of mines there he summoned *Babiana* and *Bluff* urgently from East London, where they were operating at the time, to form part of a special mine clearance flotilla. We had time only to telephone our families to say we were leaving, and sailed in the late afternoon for Cape Town on what was to be the roughest voyage that I personally experienced in all my years afloat. Immediately on rounding the breakwater we turned westwards into the teeth of a strong headwind and foam-crested waves which sent clouds of spray over the fo'c'sle. The weather deteriorated the further we progressed and soon all work on deck was rendered impossible. The men remained below in their bunks, venturing out only where necessary, as when climbing to the wheelhouse to do a trick on the wheel, or to fetch food from the galley, or, in the case of stokers, to dash aft to gain access via the after casing to the ladder descending to the engine-room and stokehold. "We're in for a rough ride," predicted a seasoned trawlerman. "See that little bastard out there?" indicating a small bird fluttering just above the waves, "Stormy Petrel, that's his name. You only see him in stormy weather."

The two little ships were under orders to round Cape Agulhas a hundred miles out to sea in order to avoid the minefield and as we approached that area we encountered the full fury of the tempest, which kept up a shrill, ululating wail in the rigging, driving mountainous waves measuring some 50 feet from trough to crest that battered the bows, sending shudders throughout the ship and torrents of spray flying aft, drenching the glass frontage of the wheelhouse. As far as one could see, which was not very far, the sea was a mass of frenzied foam under low scudding storm clouds. Normal activities were arduous in the extreme. Meals were possible only by holding plates, bowls and mugs in hand. Anything placed on the table would slide off in seconds. Washing was well-nigh impossible, using the toilet a messy nightmare, and sleeping no better than fitful dozing. One turned in still clad in overalls, seaboot stockings and oilskins.

The stokers shovelling coal into open furnaces to maintain steam had a particularly harrowing, even perilous yet utterly vital role to play. When they came off watch they were bone-tired and flopped, black and begrimed as they were, into their bunks. They conceded grudgingly that it was at least dry and warm in the stokehold.

Doing a trick on the helm was physically exhausting. Under less trying conditions the helmsman could use the small, steam-powered wheel but as every ounce of steam was needed just to maintain headway he had to resort to steering manually on the big wheel. As this connected directly by chain to the ship's rudder, which was gripped and buffeted by raging seas, the helmsman's task was backbreaking and frequently, when the might of nature threatened to swing the ship beam-on to the storm, the skipper or anyone else on hand would grab on the wheel and assist the helmsman to bring the prow roughly back on course. Our skipper, Lieut. Taylor, was a seasoned mariner and knew his way around but plainly even he felt the strain. His was the task and responsibility to navigate the ship and bring it safely to Cape Town, but how he accomplished this I could not imagine. How could he obtain a fix with his sextant when there was nothing in sight, nothing to aim at but foam, no landmarks, stars at night or sun by day, no radio beams? He had to guess the position of the sun, the lie of the horizon and distance covered. A logline with rotator had been streamed from the stern at the start of the voyage, as was normal procedure, but it would hardly be accurate in that weather and in any case struggling aft to read the register dial with waves breaking over the gunnels would have been foolhardy in the extreme. The ship had an antiquated echo-sounding machine for determining depth of water, but in that turbulence it would have been of little benefit. Taylor, I believe, plotted his course by instinct, a gut feeling garnered and cultivated from years of seafaring in small ships – a nautical sixth sense.

Then I awoke one morning from erratic slumber and slowly became aware that the ship, although still pitching and rolling appreciably, was no longer shuddering and taking the battering of the past few days, and sunlight was filtering through the skylight above the mess. As I climbed up the steps to the fo'c'sle I heard the call of a seagull and when I emerged onto the foredeck I was greeted, to starboard, by the glorious panorama of the Twelve Apostles, peaks of the Table Mountain peninsular range, with Hout Bay receding astern, Kloof Nek and the tip of Lions Head looming up ahead. Our sister ship, the *Bluff*, which had maintained contact throughout, was lying a mile or two away off the port quarter. The skipper had made landfall spot-on, and in another hour or so we would be entering Cape Town docks, albeit a day behind schedule. We had weathered the 'Cape of Storms'.

During the days following no time was lost in preparing the Mine Clearance Flotilla for an Agulhas expedition. The flotilla consisted of six ships: *Babiana*, which was designated leader, having the most senior commanding officer, *Bluff, Crassula, Aristea, Africana* and *Swartberg*, under overall command of Lieut. Commander F J ('Dizzie') Dean in the lead ship and so on 21 May, after weather conditions had abated sufficiently, we set sail. Early the following morning the flotilla was in position west of the Agulhas lighthouse to commence operations.

Sweeping was done by the standard oropesa method (see Diagram 1), four of the ships doing the actual sweeping while the other two operated as markers, whose function it was to demarcate the channel swept. The four sweepers, A, B, C and D, having taken up station along the line P S at the western edge of the bank about 8 miles from shore, set off on the first leg in an easterly direction, streaming their sweep wires in an arc to starboard, the end of each sweep wire indicated by the position of its oropesa float, or 'Donald Duck'. As explained earlier, the sweep wire would be kept submerged at the required depth by a frame of louvred steel slats called the 'kite', and be carried outwards in an arc by an "otter board" acting as a rudder

SWEEPING FOR MOORED CONTACT MINES BY OROPESA METHOD

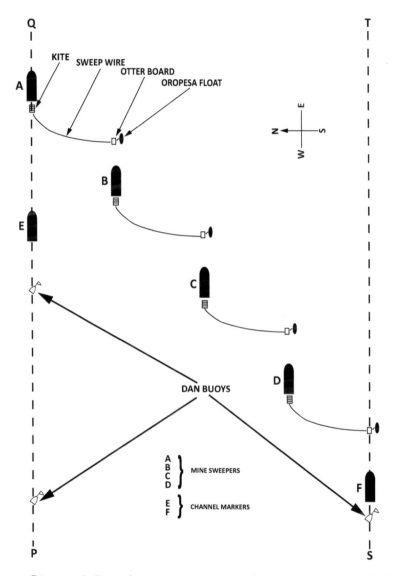

Diagram 1: Procedure in sweeping moored mines by oropesa method

below 'Donald Duck'. *Babiana, A,* led, steering a course along the line P Q, B following a line just inside that of A's Duck, with C and D, the third and fourth sweepers, doing the same relative to the ships ahead of them. Theoretically, B was protected by the sweep of A, C by the sweep of B, and D by the sweep of C. A, on the first leg, had no such comforting 'protection' and its crew had to trust in the Good Lord to take them safely through to the other end. The two marker ships, E and F, followed on behind, E astern of the leader, A and F astern and just inside the line of the hindmost sweeper D's Duck, dropping anchored Dan buoys at intervals as they went, thereby marking the width of the swept channel.

Having reached the eastern edge of the bank, the flotilla would execute a U-turn and, maintaining their prearranged stations, come back on a westward return leg, having first switched their sweep wires from starboard to port. The leader A would then steam flush along the line of Dan buoys that had been laid along the line S T by marker ship F, which buoys would then be lifted by marker ship E steaming behind the leader A on the return leg. The sweepers would now be clearing a channel on the south side of T S and the marker ship F, following the Duck of the hindmost sweeper D, would lay a fresh line of Dan buoys to mark the new southern extremity of the swept area. Continuing in this manner, sweeping alternately east-wards and westwards, the width of the swept channel would gradually be increased to the extent required.

When the mooring wire of a mine was snagged by a sweep the practised ear of a stern watchman would often detect it and alert the crew, but in any case all hands on board who were not engaged in other duties were posted as lookouts for floating mines which, if they had not exploded, would bob up to the surface, their mooring cables having been severed either by the sweep wires or by cutters affixed to the otter boards. The ship spotting a mine would blow her siren, the flotilla would heave to, taking care not to drift into unswept waters, and the vessels closest to the mine would despatch it by small arms fire. As mentioned, the mines laid on that occasion at Agulhas were of the internationally standard type that deactivated themselves when their mooring wires were severed and none that were swept there in that manner exploded but were sunk by holing their upper buoyancy compartments with rifle and machinegun fire. Some did, however, explode from other causes.

Minesweeping flotilla returning from Agulhas minefield - taken from stern of HMSAS Babiana. *Note twin roll-off depth charges*

After two days of sweeping under Lieut. Commander Dean the weather deteriorated and the flotilla returned to Cape Town, but on 4 June it was back, this time under command of Lieut. Commander L E Scott-Napier, a man of wide and distinguished service in the Royal Navy, and for three more days, until the Cape's capricious weather again intervened, the operations continued, another five mines being destroyed. To give my 19-year ego a boost, opportunity at last came my way to tackle one of the mines myself with the Lewis gun, a task which, from above the wheelhouse on a rolling trawler, firing at a range of about 100 yards, was tricky. I had to fire in bursts whenever I could, for a brief moment, align my sights on the target. Words of encouragement came from Scott-Napier standing behind me with binoculars: "Fine! You're hitting her. See how it rolled" – and presently the great black ball sank out of sight.

After that second expedition there was a brief lull in operations on the Agulhas bank, and *Babiana* and *Bluff* returned to East London. In subsequent missions spread over nine months, in which *Babiana* and *Bluff* did not participate, only four more mines were cleared while several others broke adrift, of which two were eventually washed ashore.

German mine washed ashore, Cape Agulhas

What happened to the approximately 70 to 80 remaining mines is a matter of some speculation, but no ships were sunk or damaged as a result of the raider *Atlantis'* nocturnal incursion on 10 May. It might, however, have had disastrous consequences and there is still conjecture as to what providentially caused a mine to explode three nights later and so give the game away. Nearly two years later, in March 1942, another German commerce raider, the *Doggerbank,* laid mines within eyeshot of Cape Town and again off Agulhas, resulting in three ships being mined.

But back in May 1940 the whole world knew that at last the war had begun in earnest. Past and done with was the 'phoney war', or as Neville Chamberlain coined it, 'the twilight war' – that odd, uncanny period that bemused many into thinking and hoping that hostilities were fading out, that Hitler, as stated by Chamberlain only a month previously, 'had missed the bus' and would soon embark on peace overtures. After the conquest of Poland both the Franco/British allies and the Germans had, as it seemed, hibernated for the European winter behind their frontier fortifications, contenting themselves with patrol and reconnaissance activities. Tentative probes had indeed been made towards the border town of Saarbrucken by units of the British Expeditionary Force and millions of leaflets had been dropped on towns and cities by the R A F with the only effect, according to a cynic in parliament, of supplying the German population with toilet paper for a year. The general complacency was manifested in popular patriotic music on radio and on stage with lyrics such as 'We're going to hang out the washing on the Siegfried Line. Have you any dirty washing, mother dear', and George Formby, the Lancastrian comedian and virtuoso on the ukulele, singing 'Sitting on a mine in the Maginot Line', or Vera Lynn's piquant rendering of 'Somewhere in France with You'. Even the catchy 'Run, Rabbit, Run' was converted to 'Run, Adolph, Run', and much more. But all that changed on May 10 with the full-throttle German invasion of the Low Countries, whereafter the Teutonic colossus swept aside everything before it.

The 'Blitzkrieg' surged across northern France to the English Channel, Allied anguish assuaged only by the "miracle" of Dunkirk where, by 4 June, 338,000 British and Allied troops were evacuated from the town and beaches by a motley armada of small seagoing craft – naval, commercial and civilian – and transported to England. A further 156,000 men were later extricated from French harbours in the Cherbourg/Brest/St Nazaire area but Paris fell on the 14th and France, under her new premier, Marshall Petain, capitulated three days later.

The Balkans were next to suffer the onslaught and, with Hungary, Rumania, Bulgaria and Albania willy-nilly collaborative, the German juggernaut overran Yugoslavia and Greece, with Crete, Rhodes and other Greek islands falling subsequently. By April 1941 the Axis powers stood astride the entire land mass of Europe apart from Soviet Russia and four neutrals: Sweden, Switzerland, Spain and Portugal. Britain, to all intents and purposes, then stood alone!

Yet, notwithstanding compelling concern in these developments, world attention was temporarily diverted in May 1940 to a comparatively minor but sensational incident which, while having no impact on the conflict situation, provoked dramatic headlines far and wide – Rudolf Hess, Deputy Fuhrer and third highest figure in the Nazi hierarchy, landed in Scotland by parachute!

Hess reportedly sought, through the medium of a Scottish dignitary of his acquaintanceship, to broker some sort of deal with the British Government, possibly as a precursor to Germany's impending invasion of the Soviet Union, but this is hardly within the bounds of credibility. That a man of his stature and intelligence could imagine Britain acceding to such a wish and abetment, and then seek to convey the proposition by commandeering a military aircraft, undertaking a hazardous solo flight to a rural drop area in Scotland, there to arrive by parachute, is bizarre in the extreme. (Hess was a qualified aviator, and on reaching the jump-off area he flew his aircraft upside down in order to fall out, having no ejector seat installed.) Presumably he anticipated being allowed to return jubilantly to Germany after successfully completing his mission. Instead his 'mission' evaporated and he spent the rest of the war 'in the bag' as a POW.

Zeesen radio downplayed the episode, claiming that Hess was mentally deranged. Ultimately, following the Nuremberg Trials after the war, he was sentenced to life imprisonment and he died in solitary confinement at an advanced age. But the full truth behind the Rudolf Hess saga, if known at all, has never been made public and probably never will be. Was he indeed an emissary from Hitler – or a fugitive?

The war at sea had been the exception during the 'phoney' period; no lull, no break in the conflict was felt there. The Battle of the River Plate, the sagas of HMS *Rawalpindi*, of HMS *Cossack* and the *Altmark*, had been noteworthy episodes of that time, while submarine warfare had continued relentlessly. For the *Babiana* crew the exhilaration of having been 'in action' soon subsided as she was not required to return to the minefield but reverted to doing routine A sweeps with *Bluff* and other vessels in the approaches to South African harbours. Obviously, it seemed, my ship was being sidelined when it came to the more important jobs, and the focus was shifting to the bigger and faster whale catchers, these being converted and commissioned in increasing numbers. They were equipped as antisubmarine (AS) hunters or as double L (LL) sweepers for dealing with magnetic and acoustic mines, and enjoyed the prospect of doing duty in other theatres, notably the Mediterranean. Understandably, I became restive for change but it was not these whalers that attracted me; my hankering was for the bigger and, to me, romantic, far ranging, 'see-the-world' ships of the Royal Navy that frequently put in at Simonstown and Durban – ships that often included in their complement South African friends I knew: those who had not, under the same misapprehension as I, volunteered for minesweeping at the outbreak of hostilities.

I felt that as an RNVR rating I was entitled to request transfer from the SDF back to the RN and accordingly started to make representations to that end. But the new skipper of *Babiana* had no inclination to assist me. I had signed on, he said, for service in the SDF for four years, thereby forfeiting any affiliation to the RN, and if I had not understood that at the time then that was 'too bad'. I disagreed that the connection had been broken and argued that my official number was still prefixed by the letters RNVR, but to no avail. I then directed my appeal to the base commander at East London, where we were operating at that time, but received no co-operation from that quarter either. In desperation I then wrote a personal letter to Commodore J Dalgleish in Cape Town who, after the death of Rear Admiral Halifax in an air crash, had been appointed director of the Seaward Defence Force, asking to be transferred to Royal Naval Command. However, I held out little hope of reaction, unless perhaps a rebuke via my commanding officer and a peremptory injunction never to address requests to high authority except through approved channels.

Shortly afterwards, to my astonishment I was summoned to the office at the base and told, "You are being transferred to the Royal Navy and will leave for Cape Town tomorrow night by train. En route you will act as escort to a prisoner: a rating who has been sentenced to detention barracks in Wynberg, but you will hand him over to naval police at Cape Town station. Make sure you receive from them a receipt for the prisoner. Transport will then be provided to take you to Seaward House down at the docks, where you will deliver the receipt and where your transfer to the RN will be finalised."

I was flabbergasted, sensing a strange mix of exhilaration and apprehension.

"Wow!" I exclaimed. "Do you know what ship I am going to?"

The officer scrutinised the papers before him and said after a pause, "You are being drafted to DEMS."

"DEMS," I stammered. "What is DEMS?"

A female voice close by murmured, "D-E-M-S – dirty evil-minded sailors."

FUNNELS THREE

We don't want to
March with the infantry
Ride with the cavalry
Shoot with artillery
We don't want to
Fly over Germany
We are the Royal Navy

1

R N AHOY

All right, if that's what you want

DEMS (officially) stood for Defensively Equipped Merchant Ships. By international convention a merchant ship was permitted, in a war situation, to mount a single gun on the stern, usually of 4.7 inch calibre or smaller, as a defence against hostile, usually submarine, attack. Any ordnance in excess of that would classify the vessel as a warship, thereby forfeiting any privileged treatment supposedly accorded non-combatant vessels but which, in practice, soon dematerialized towards total non-observance. Within a remarkably short period after the outbreak of hostilities all merchant ships operating under the authority of the British Ministry of War Transport were equipped with stern-mounted guns, much of the work entailed being assigned to South African ports. Understandably the guns so fitted were mostly of old World War I or earlier vintage and it was jocularly bandied around that if all the merchant ships in a convoy opened fire on a U-boat in their midst, the safest spot would be on the U-boat itself.

The Royal Navy drafted a gunlayer (that is the one who, as a rule, aimed and fired the gun, usually RNVR trained) to each merchant ship armed with a gun on the poop. The gunlayer's job, apart from captaining and maintaining the gun, was to train the other members of the gun's crew drawn from seamen serving aboard. South Africa was expected to provide about fifty gunlayers for this purpose and obviously, as I soon realised, I was now earmarked for inclusion in the project. To many, the job of the DEMS gunlayer was attractive and easy-going for the most part, with none of the usual naval routine and rigid discipline, no 'rig of the day' which stipulated what attire was to be worn, and being excused from most of the grimy chores that are a deckhand's daily lot. However, these advantages did little to stir my enthusiasm for DEMS. It was not what I had wanted and inevitably my imagination conjured up visions of helplessness against U-boats, pocket battleships and aerial bombers. Moreover, with my kind of luck I would, I was convinced, be drafted to a filthy, coal-burning, eight-knot, sitting-duck freighter or, worse still, to a tanker laden with high-octane aviation spirit: a gargantuan fireball in waiting. What had I let myself in for this time, I brooded apprehensively, while unwittingly my erstwhile decision hinging on poison gas again tormented me. Could I do anything about it now? Could I have my draft changed?

I duly departed for Cape Town by train in charge of my prisoner, whose name I cannot remember and the nature of whose misdemeanour for which he was sentenced I likewise cannot recall. However, he seemed a likeable young fellow and, feeling sorry for him, I offered, against orders, to discard my sentry-duty webbing and sidearms while on the train so as not to identify him before other passengers as a miscreant, provided of course that he remained in my company at all times and behaved himself – conditions which he readily accepted. Everything went smoothly until the next day when the train stopped for a minute or two at a tiny station in the middle of nowhere, when I suddenly realised that my captive was not with me in the compartment. He had not said that he needed to visit the toilet, both of which were empty anyway, and he was not standing in the corridor. I heard the steam locomotive whistle preparatory to departure and was gripped by panic, thoroughly alarmed. Already my charge could be out of reach, fleeing at full speed across the veld, and I had visions of facing a hostile court martial in Cape Town for gross dereliction of duty in allowing my prisoner to escape. Momentarily I considered halting the train by smashing the glass of the alarm box in the corridor (which probably wouldn't have worked) but instead thrust my head desperately out of the window again and, even as the train started to move, was horrified to see my prisoner stealing a hurried kiss from a girl serving at a platform kiosk! Thankfully he then ran and leapt aboard the moving train and, having contritely endured my frenzied tirade, gave me no further trouble.

I reported on schedule to Seaward House in Cape Town's dock area and eventually a duty officer diverted his attention to my case. "DEMS, I see," he said, studying my papers. "Well…"

"Please, Sir," I interrupted, "that is a mistake. I don't want DEMS; I asked for a warship."

He looked at me with slightly less indifference. "Well, that's what it says here. Why not DEMS? Some fellows prefer it – you don't get buggered around so much, you're mostly your own boss, sleep on a proper bunk in a cabin, and…" he added as an afterthought "in the tougher areas you get paid danger money. You don't get any of those things as a seaman on a warship."

"Please, Sir, I still don't want DEMS."

The officer eyed me wearily in silence for several seconds, then abruptly got up and strode out of the room, leaving me perspiring and shaking, feeling on a par with a criminal on death row agonisingly praying for a commutation of sentence.

After what seemed an age the officer returned. "All right," he said. "If that's what you want, there's a class of recruits at the Castle finishing a basic seamanship course before leaving for Simonstown tomorrow or the day after. You can join up with them."

And so, to my profound relief, off I went and in due course became part of a twenty-two man draft to Klawer Camp, Simonstown.

Every sailor who put in at Simonstown knew about the notorious Klawer Camp, whether or not he actually set foot in it. The camp was situated on top of Simonsberg, the mountain rising up from and over-looking Simonstown. Vehicular conveyances reached it via a steep, circuitous access road but a more direct route, for footsloggers only, presented itself in the form of concrete steps ascending and descending straight up and down between the town and the camp. Normally this was used not by choice but by ratings who had missed the last 'liberty boat' which, in this case, was a personnel truck. Reputedly there were 365 steps, one for each day of the year, and although I never counted them I would not dispute the figure. In fact, ascending them at night, clad in an 'oilskin' coat with the Cape winter rain pelting down, they seemed to me nearer the 1,000 mark.

The camp was encompassed by an 8-foot barbed-wire security fence, and it fell to the lot of the duty watch of the camp's temporary inmates to provide sentries at the gates and around the perimeter – not the most gratifying pursuit in the middle of the night in pouring rain. The sentries' discomfiture was not alleviated by the fact that the mountainous terrain in that part of the Cape Peninsula was, and still is, home to colonies of baboons, and members of that primate community regularly put in an appearance around the camp. At night, flitting agilely in and out of the shadows among rocks and abundant bush they frequently alarmed sentries into fearing that the camp was under threat from hostile elements, causing them to shout out the challenge, "Halt! Who goes there?" On occasion bolder specimens even gained entry into the camp by leaping over the security fence, resulting sometimes in the stillness of the night being shattered by the sharp report of a nervous sentry's rifle.

Liberty men, that is sailors on 'shore leave' from Klawer Camp, had the option of taking the local train into Cape Town or of seeking relaxation and entertainment in Simonstown. Beer and food were aplenty at the canteen and several times a week carloads of girls would arrive at the dance hall, where makeshift bands belted out 'Roll out the Barrel', Glen Miller's 'In the Mood', and other popular pieces of dance music of the period on a piano and any other instruments available on the night. I looked in at the dance hall one evening and watched the throng of gyrating and jiving sailors and partners performing with gusto, when I gradually became aware that the dancers appeared to avoid the centre of the floor. This, I discovered, was because a huge, tawny coloured dog, a Great Dane, lay stretched out on the spot, fast asleep. It was his undisputed right, if he so wished, to sleep in the middle of the floor. Indeed it was his right to do virtually anything he pleased, wherever in Simonstown, and whenever he pleased. He had the freedom of the town, had adopted the navy, and was affectionately known to every sailor who had set foot in Simonstown. He had his own, self-appropriated bed at Froggy's Pond, a naval barracks some five miles south of the dockyard, travelled unmolested on the local train in the company of sailors to Cape Town where, at the Union Jack Club he had likewise commandeered his own bed. He acquired an uncanny grasp of the ways and needs of sailors ashore, would associate only with those in sailor's uniform, and achieved fame for guiding overly inebriated sailors back to their ships or base. His name was Nuisance or, officially in Royal Naval records (he even earned inclusion therein) Able Seaman Just Nuisance. He was a legend in his own lifetime who loved the company of sailors, and walked, slept, ate and guzzled beer with them. When he died some years later, he was buried with full naval honours in a grave now marked with a memorial headstone.

We were not left long at Klawer Camp – a week perhaps – before two drafts were posted: one to HMS *Birmingham*, a modern cruiser of the 'City' class, main armament twelve 6-inch guns in four turrets, and the other to the much older HMS *Cornwall*, a heavy cruiser of the 'County' class, with main armament of eight 8-inch guns in four turrets. My name was included in the latter draft, the other members being Bill Flett, Jock Davidson, Eric Stephen, Peter Pare, Peter Versfeld, George Ferrier, Benny Vink and Trewick. We were to join the ship in Durban, where it was undergoing minor repairs to damage sustained during an engagement with a German commerce raider. Before leaving Simonstown we were issued with inflatable lifebelts which, worn across the breast, were commonly known as 'Mae Wests'; 'tin hats' unchanged since World War I, hammocks and gas masks. The efficacy of the masks issued had to be put to the test and for that purpose we repaired to the 'Snoekie gas chamber' – a single-roomed, windowless building with an airtight door. Once inside we all, including our instructor, donned our gas masks and adjusted the straps to ensure a snug, comfortable fit, whereupon the instructor closed the door and opened a can of tear-gas. Everything went off perfectly – no discomfort, no hint of smell.

"Right," said the instructor. "In case you think I've been having you on, I shall now stand at the door and give the order 'off masks', and as soon as I see that ALL of you have done so I shall throw open the door and you can rush outside. So be smart about pulling those masks off, by slipping your fingers in under your chins, so that none of you suffers too much waiting for the door to open."

And so it was done, everybody stampeding for the fresh air outside as soon as the door swung agape. None of us, noses burning and eyes streaming, was left in any doubt that the tear-gas was genuine.

Our draft duly entrained at Cape Town for the three-day journey by rail to Durban. Four of our group: Peter Versfeld, Peter Pare, Bennie Vink and Eric Stephen had originally signed on with a cavalry unit but had managed to transfer to the navy after learning that their equestrian transportation was soon to be replaced by motorised, armoured vehicles. The cavalry unit was garrisoned at that time at Ladysmith, Natal, and upon the train's arrival at that town at around 10.00 pm on the last night, the four were met at the station by many of their former cavalry comrades. The reunion was so lively and exhilarating that the four had difficulty in breaking away when the train started to move again, and at the very last they had to sprint frantically to jump back on board, the conductor's whistle blowing shrilly in protest. Alas, in the case of three of them it might have been better had they missed the train and been detained because ten months later they were dead.

*   *   *   *   *

2

ALL ABOARD

What's the latest buzz?

HMS *Cornwall*, when the truck deposited us alongside, was berthed at Maydon Wharf at the western extremity of Durban's Natal Bay. I had seen the ship in Cape waters from a distance on one or two occasions during my minesweeping days but now, from close up, I felt overawed by her size. From where I stood apprehensively on the wharf I could not, I remember, see her bows, obscured in the distance by cranes and the usual dockyard clutter. *Cornwall* was one of thirteen British-built heavy cruisers displacing in the region of 10,000 tons and loosely referred to as 'County' Class due to their territorial nomenclature. The largest cruisers in the Royal Navy, they had been built over a period from 1926 onwards and while they were markedly similar in their main features: exceptional length and high freeboard above the waterline, three tall distinctive funnels and heavy armament, they differed in minor details as, for example, *Cumberland* and others had a cutaway stern, *Norfolk* and others sported an admiral's stern walk like a small Spanish window box (on which no admiral was ever likely to set foot), while *Cornwall* and others were given a large, box-like aircraft hangar on the upper deck aft, just for'rard of the mainmast. Some, like *Dorsetshire*, were equipped with torpedo tubes while others, like *Cornwall*, were not.

These ships extended up to 633 feet from stem to stern – the longest of all British cruisers – and, in addition, had the highest hulls protruding above the water. Their width at the widest point, or beam, was 66 feet. Their bulk made them easier targets for an enemy to set their sights on, but on the other hand they provided a notable advantage in space, especially between decks, which in crowded warships was always at a premium. In that regard the "County" class were the most habitable ships in the Royal Navy. Furthermore, their operational range was exceptional: some 10,500 miles at 11 to 14 knots. It was indeed claimed that at a piddling speed of 5 or 6 knots they could circumnavigate the globe on one full load of fuel oil.

The Counties' main armament of eight 8-inch guns was formidable, capable at extreme range with barrels elevated approximately 42 degrees above horizontal 256 lb shells on targets 18 statute miles, or 16 nautical miles, distant. These guns, mounted in pairs in four turrets, could also attain an extraordinary maximum elevation of 70 degrees, enabling them to fire time-fused projectiles, set to explode among high-flying hostile aircraft. I know of no occasion where they were actually brought into action as anti-aircraft weapons. They would be slow and cumbersome fulfilling that role, but it was nevertheless a fascinating prospect because a projectile of that size, its high explosive content not restricted in volume by armour-piercing components, would, if exploding within a tight formation of aircraft, create a deluge of falling bits and pieces like withered leaves in an autumn gale.

When relatively new the Counties could exceed 30 knots, but fourteen or so years later during the Second World War it is doubtful whether any of them could still achieve that momentum and, in the case of *Cornwall*, additional wind resistance must have been caused by the bulky aircraft hangar on the upper deck.

These cruisers carried wartime complements of around 700 officers and men, and it was to fulfil that requirement that our draft of nine filed up *Cornwall's* gangway hefting kitbags, hammocks and other accoutrement. After reporting we were conducted to the Regulating Office, where a dapper, highly efficient Regulating Petty Officer – the ship's RPO with a South African accent – issued us individually with station cards which indicated, apart from name, rank and number, our 'part of ship', mess number, action and cruising stations and watch. My part of ship, I noted, was fo'c'sle and my mess number 5, which I thereupon set out to locate, not without difficulty.

The seamen's division was divided into three "parts of ship" – fo'c'sle, top and quarterdeck. Basically the fo'c'sle men were responsible for the forward section of the ship from prow to a point in line with the foremast; the quarterdeck men cared for the after section from the mainmast to the stern; while the top men were accountable for the area amidships between the two masts. Each part of ship for seamen had its own mess deck accommodating four or more messes – a mess consisting of a long wooden table top about 3 feet in width and varying in length from perhaps 18 to 24 feet, supported by iron trestle legs. Running the length of the table on either side was a padded bench about 8 inches wide while adjacent to the table was a metal cupboard for holding crockery, cutlery and the like. No 5 Mess, when I found it, was the foremost on the starboard side, with messes 7, 9 and 11 (the odd numbers) following on behind. The quarterdeck mess deck was similarly placed on the port side, its messes bearing even numbers. The top men's mess deck was situated one compartment, or 'flat', further aft, through a watertight (when closed) doorway in a steel wall, or bulkhead.

As in all RN ships, the 24-hour day was subdivided into seven watches, these being the morning from 04.00 to 08.00, the forenoon from 08.00 to 12.00, the afternoon from 12.00 to 16.00, the first dog from 16.00 to 18.00, the second or last dog from 18.00 to 20.00, the first (night) from 20.00 to 24.00 and the middle (night) from 24.00 to 04.00. There were therefore five watches of four hours each, and two of two hours. The lower deck complement were almost invariably disposed into two primary watches, port and starboard and, at least in the larger ships, each of these was again separated into first and second parts. I saw on my station card that I was in the second part of port watch. (In a few ships the men were sorted into three watches: red, white and blue.) This time-honoured arrangement ensured that watchkeeping would be done by the men in rotation. Under relatively tranquil circumstances the ship would probably operate in 'four (or cruising) watches', which meant that only one part of port or one part of starboard would be on watch at a time – in other words one watch in four. For example, if I in the second part of port had the morning watch ending at 08.00, I would not again do watchkeeping until the last dog, commencing at 18.00. On the other hand, under conditions of urgency the ship would in all likelihood switch to 'two (or defence) watches', which meant that the whole of port watch or the whole of starboard would be on watch at a time, in other words one watch in two. Alternately, assuming again that I in the port watch had the morning watch, I would then be required to do watchkeeping again at 12.00 for the afternoon. Obviously, operating in two watches was much more onerous and permitted much less sleep.

The availability of sleeping time was a crucial element in the life of a sailor at sea, precisely because watchkeeping imposed, as regards sleeping opportunities, a rate of occurrence both irritatingly irregular and woefully inadequate, especially so when the ship was operating in two watches. It was no joking matter, for example, having climbed into your hammock at around 04.15 after the middle to be roughly awakened again at 05.45 for dawn Action Stations. Apart from watchkeeping duties there were other factors that militated against reasonably sufficient slumber, and actual among these was dawn action stations, which was essential routine throughout the navy in the larger warships while at sea, the entire ship's company then participating. The main purpose was to ensure that at first light the ship would be fully prepared for instant action in any situation that might be revealed when the concealing veil of darkness lifted. It also served to keep everyone alert and efficient in fighting capability. Another hindrance in the way of sleeping was the obvious daily necessity of keeping the ship clean and tidy – sweeping, scrubbing, painting and a host of other chores which almost invariably had to be done during the forenoon watch between 08.00 and noon. All off-duty watchmen had to muster after breakfast and be detailed off to carry out these tasks, and they could therefore not 'get their heads down' during that period. Then again, emergencies were continually arising, as with the sighting of an unidentified vessel, which immediately set the Action Stations buzzer throbbing throughout the ship, the intercom crackling with orders from the bridge, and everybody up and running as fast as they could to their stations.

Watchkeeping was a lot easier when 'four watches' applied, especially when one had the last dog from 18.00 to 20.00 because, with one's watch occurring only once in four, one could then turn in and, save for unexpected interruptions, enjoy a relatively good night's sleep until Action Stations the following dawn. This happy occurrence was known on the lower deck as 'all night in'. The watch most detested was the middle, from midnight to 4.oo am because it plucked four hours from the heart of the night and left very little over for sleep. The middle watch was sardonically referred to as 'all night in with the guts kicked out'. In this respect *Cornwall's* ship's company were fortunate in that, due to the nature of her far-ranging relatively uneventful assignments, 'four watches' was for the most part the order of things and recourse to 'two watches' happened only in situations where danger or other emergency was perceived to be probable. At the outbreak of the Second World War *Cornwall* was operating on the China station and, admirably suited as her class was to extensive cruising and prolonged periods at sea, she was immediately put to patrolling far and wide in search of German shipping of whatever kind and to escort duties. These activities enabled her watch-keeping schedule to proceed largely on the basis of one in four.

No 5 Mess, to which I had been allocated, was the smallest on the fo'c'sle mess deck, the length of its mess table being restricted by the large, cylindrical column of A gun turret, which descended at that point from its gunhouse on the upper deck down to the shell handling room and magazines far below. I do not recall a No 3 Mess, the next lower odd number, but perhaps it did exist and was inconspicuously sited forward of A turret and utilised for special purposes, but No 1 Mess was positioned on its own, right for'rard near the bows. It was known as the CDA, or 'Caught Disease Ashore' Mess, where ratings, if any, who had contracted a sexually transmitted ailment, or venereal disease, were segregated at meal times. It must have been mortifying for anyone to be banished to No 1 but I do not remember any specifically in that quandary. However, there would certainly have been a number who, prone to reckless activity ashore, could count themselves lucky to have escaped doing a spell in that mess of unenviable repute.

Ratings were each allocated a numbered locker and mine, No 523, was on the Boy Seamen's mess deck, one deck below the fo'c'sle mess deck. Lockers were metal cupboards approximately two feet high by one and a half feet wide and two feet deep, and into that confined space one had to cram all one's possessions with the exception of one's hammock, which with related accessories would be rolled and trussed up in regulation manner like a giant polony and deposited with a hundred others in a small fenced-off pen (with the exception also of buckets, about which more later).

Cornwall, at the time of our joining her early in June 1941, had just had repairs to minor damage completed (this sustained during her engagement with the German commerce raider *Pinguin* on 8 May in the area of the Seychelle Islands) and was now again ready for sea. There was, therefore, a strong air of expectation on board and it marked my introduction to the dynamic 'grapevine' of the lower deck and its concomitant catchword 'buzz'. Any prediction or rumour, particularly regarding the ship's imminent movements, was called a buzz. "What's the latest buzz?" one would hear asked almost daily. Buzzes abounded on the mess deck, often several different ones circulating simultaneously. They might be prompted by the nature of stores brought on board, or the presence of other ships in harbour, or bar talk with merchant seamen ashore, but more often than not they turned out to be wrong. Buzzes that enjoyed more credibility than most emanated from officers' stewards who had reportedly overheard remarks made in the officers' wardroom, but truth was that the wearers of gold braid usually had no more inside information than had the ratings on the mess deck, where buzzes often excited the gambling spirit and led to betting. They were a lively feature aboard all naval vessels, particularly cruisers, which generally did more sea time and were given a greater variety of assignments. The men aboard HMS *Dorsetshire* and other ships whose home port was Devonport, nicknamed 'Guz', used to parody a well-known popular song by singing modified lyrics ending with, "You'll be hearing a buzz. We're heading for Guz, Side by Side."

But nobody besides the captain, and often not even he, and possibly one or two high ranking confidantes, knew for certain where the ship would next be heading, that is, not until the ship had left harbour and was well out to sea, when such information was announced over the loudspeaker system. While buzz swopping on board was mostly a matter of amusement, good-natured altercation and frequently wishful thinking, we were sternly forbidden to engage in it ashore, particularly in bars, where 'tongues are loosened and walls have ears'. Secrecy concerning ship movements was of the highest priority and advertised slogans such as 'Don't talk about ships and shipping' and 'Careless talk costs lives' were everywhere in evidence. Censorship of all outward mail was likewise strictly enforced. The chief censor aboard *Cornwall* was the navigating officer, or 'pilot', and I well remember being summoned to his cabin after writing my first letter home from the cruiser.

He held up the pages of my letter for me to see and I was horrified to find that his surgical scissors had excised probably a third of what I had written.

"You will have to get used to the necessity of not disclosing anything that could even hint at where the ship is operating or what it is doing," he said kindly. "You must not mention any geographical places, no ship's names or descriptions of them, not even weather conditions – nothing that could give a clue to the wrong people. Now perhaps you would like to rewrite your letter?"

"Actually, Sir," I said mortified, "I think it can go as it is. It will let my folks understand how important secrecy is. May I just add a line or two at the end to explain to them what has happened in this case?"

Enforcement of secrecy forbade the keeping of diaries which, it was averred could, if they somehow fell into the wrong hands, provide vital clues to the enemy. Some sailors ignored the directive and kept diaries clandestinely nevertheless. The demand for secrecy extended to the ribbons worn around sailors' caps, which in peacetime revealed the names of the wearers' ships, such as HMS *Ajax* or HMS *Norfolk*. These were replaced during the war by ribbons simply bearing the letters HMS. This frequently provoked among civilian acquaintances the jocular query, "HMS what? What ship, Jack?" to which the usual rejoinder was, "Hardship".

With *Cornwall* now preparing for sea the buzz merchants were increasingly voluble but for once there was a measure of unanimity and, as it later transpired, correctness in their predictions. The portents were compelling – far across the bay at the Point Docks near the harbour entrance were berthed three of the largest passenger liners afloat which had, it was surmised, been converted into troopships. Logically they would not languish in Durban for long and, having regard to the ominous situation unfolding in North Africa, where the arrival of Erwin Rommel and his Afrika Korps had already made their presence felt, and where the entire Middle East theatre was gravely imperilled following the fall of Greece and Crete, one could deduce that the troopships, when they sailed, would set course for the Red Sea and Egypt. They would need a powerful escort, and who but *Cornwall* could fulfil that role?

* * * * *

3

NORTHWARD HO

So much for secrecy!

Cornwall put to sea from Durban on 10 June 1941, a departure which for me was the most memorable ever. Having slipped her moorings at Maydon Wharf, the big cruiser glided slowly along the northern perimeter of the bay towards the protuberant promontory of the Bluff at the harbour exit, and her ship's company, excepting those otherwise engaged, stood to attention by 'part of ship' along the port side. To me, a raw newcomer to big-time navy, now paraded in line with other fo'c'sle men, the thrill was indescribable. The harbour seemed to come alive as we proceeded. People ashore, on foot and in cars, or aboard small craft, waved, hooted and called out. The clamour rose to a crescendo as we drew level with and passed the three great liners: the renowned *Mauritania, Ile de France* and *Nieuw Amsterdam,* now packed with khaki-clad troops, including the greater part of the 2nd South African Division. They crowded every vantage point aboard, even in the rigging, to cheer us on our way, knowing that we were to be their escort and protector during the voyage about to commence.

The vociferation did not arise from the troopships alone because the wharves beyond were a mass of humanity. Half the population of Durban, it seemed, come to bid Godspeed to the fighting men of their country or, in many cases no doubt, simply drawn to the scene out of curiosity. Unavoidably the uneasy thought must have troubled the minds of many: "So much for secrecy! Here in Durban three enormous troopships, each with an accommodation capacity of around 8,000 men, was leaving harbour bound for North Africa and everyone knows all about it, even to the time of departure!" Yet how could so massive an embarkation, spread over the preceding three days, proceeding from the Hay Paddock transit camp at Pietermaritzburg take place secretly, unnoticed?

As *Cornwall* swung to port to navigate the narrow outlet to the open sea large sections of the crowd ashore surged towards the end of the quayside area near the Point, still cheering and waving wildly. Standing a little apart from the throng, near the water's edge, was a woman dressed in white, singing through a hand-held megaphone – a personality whose fame and esteem was to spread far beyond the borders of South Africa. Widely known as the "Lady in White", Perla Siedle Gibson, an international concert soprano, had, in fair weather and foul, been singing to servicemen departing Durban Harbour from as early as 1940, vocalising popular songs befitting the emotive mood of the occasion, such as 'Wish Me Luck as You Wave Me Goodbye' – the ballad popularised by the celebrated 'Lassie from Lancashire', Gracie Fields. As Allied shipping was routed around the Cape due to the menacing situation in the Mediterranean, Perla's heartwarming songs reached out to servicemen and women of many nationalities, not only South Africans, and wrenched a reluctant tear from the eye of many a tough warrior. Later in the war she was still at her post with her megaphone, singing a welcome to the troops returning home. (Some twenty years later, in 1964, the Memorable Order of Tin Hats (MOTHS) organised a pilgrimage by ex-servicemen and women to war cemeteries in Europe and when they returned to Table Bay on the *Cape Town Castle*, there on the quayside was Perla, shining white in the morning sunlight, megaphone in hand, singing the boys home again, the exuberance in her voice undiminished since yesteryear.) WWII produced many very remarkable women, both in the forces and on the home front, and prominent amongst them was Perla Gibson. Today a memorial statue of Perla stands, deservedly, on Durban's dockside. It is recorded that she sang there one day just after receiving notification that her son had been killed in action. I cannot conceive of greater dedication and fortitude.

Training class, Cape Town Castle 1941 (Base Commander Copenhagen is standing right of centre. The author is standing at extreme right.)

Out on the open sea we were soon followed by the three majestic troopships which, with *Cornwall* in the van, took station in line ahead, increasing speed to approximately 24 knots, Durban's renowned beachfront receding in the distance off our port quarter. I thrilled anew at the powerful throbbing underfoot, the pulse of four turbine-driven propellers, the wind in my face, the surge of water down the length of the ship's sides and the white, foaming wake stretching far astern. Presently the loudspeakers crackled and the quartermaster's voice barked, as it always did preceding an announcement, "D'ya hear there? D'ya hear there?" Then, "Our ship will escort *Mauritania, Ile de France* and *Nieuw Amsterdam* into the Red Sea to within safe reach of Port Tewfig, then proceed to Aden, where we expect to arrive on June 19 for refuelling. Second Part of starboard watch to cruising stations. Special sea dutymen secure."

It was immediately important on joining a large warship to ascertain what one's cruising and Action Stations were and how to locate them, because failing to arrive punctually at these stations when required was sure to invite a 'bottle', or stern reprimand. Action Stations in particular brooked no indolence. When activated without warning over the loudspeaker system by bugle or buzzer, the entire ship's company transformed instantaneously into a frenzy of running, bustling, colliding, single-minded men intent on reaching their stations 'as soon as Gawd will let yer'. It could happen at any time of day or night, perhaps with you asleep in your hammock, or naked, sopping wet and covered in soapsuds in the washroom, or obeying the call of nature in the heads – all of which activities had then to be terminated in a flash.

My action station was the shell room of Y turret. *Cornwall's* main armament of eight 8-inch guns was divided among four turrets – two guns to each. A and B turrets were positioned for'rard of the superstructure towards the bows; X and Y turrets abaft the superstructure towards the stern. Turrets consisted basically of rotating gunhouses on the upper deck, each with its twin guns, the gunhouses being mounted on circular barbettes or platforms, which in turn were superimposed above cylindrical wells descending far below the waterline to shell handling rooms, and below that to shell rooms and cordite magazines from which, by a system of hydraulic hoists, shells and cordite propelling charges, were conveyed up through the wells to the guns at the top.

My first impression of Y shell room – my action station – was far from encouraging. One gained access to it through a manhole in a watertight hatch cover. Space in the shell room was taken up almost completely by racks about four feet high filled to capacity with 8-inch, 256 lb projectiles of different varieties, the great majority classified as semi-armour piercing, or SAP. Two senior ratings on either side operated the transverse and vertical movement of electrically driven clutches or grabs suspended from steel cables. My job was to start the chain of supply to one of the guns above by sitting or kneeling atop the projectiles in their racks, and as a grab was guided across and down to me I would snap its jaws around the middle of a projectile, the senior rating then raising the grab with its load out of the rack, moving it across and depositing the shell on a hydraulic conveyer belt which in turn would transport it up to the shell handling room immediately above for further transference to the gunhouse on deck.

Space in the shell room was extremely cramped, hardly designed for six-footers like me, and sitting on the shells in their racks left me scarcely any headroom. The shells were coated with grease and the rancid atmosphere was heavy with the cloying smell of oil, which dripped from the deckhead, or ceiling. Inevitably my mind was soon picturing the scene there under battle conditions. How would I perform in this claustrophobic dungeon in the midst of clamour and anxiety, deep down in the bowels of the ship? How to escape if the ship was sinking? It was hardly comforting to learn that in the event of uncontrollable fire nearby, the exit manhole could, as a last resort, be clamped shut from above and the shell room be flooded with its inmates still inside – this to prevent an explosion that would rip the ship asunder and annihilate its entire complement. For the umpteenth time I questioned my inceptive decision to opt for the navy. Would poison gas have presented a worse predicament? There at least my gas mask would help, but not so in this death trap. Furtively I glanced across at my opposite number, a diminutive British lad sitting on his own rack of shells for serving to the turret's other gun. He was a picture of idle contentment – calm, self-confident, chewing gum. I felt mortified.

On the other hand my cruising station, namely bridge lookout, was very gratifying. I was one of a squad of seamen in the second part of port watch who, under the direction of a Petty Officer, were posted on either wing of the bridge as lookouts. *Cornwall* had not yet been fitted with Radio Detection Finder, later universally known as 'Radar': the system of detecting the presence of aircraft, ships and other objects over great distances by emitting pulses of high frequency electromagnetic waves. This shortcoming made the efficacy of visual detection all the more important – something which was constantly impressed upon us – and any perfunctory performance by lookouts would bring down upon the culprits a tirade of invective, if not punishment. Lookouts on either wing had to man two large and powerful binoculars mounted on semi-rotatable platforms, each covering a 90 degree sector, from ahead to abeam and from abeam to astern. The port side sectors were designated 'red' and those on the starboard side 'green'. So if, for example, a port side lookout detected an object 40 degrees off the port bow he would cry out in a loud voice, "Port lookout to bridge. Object on the horizon bearing red four O," and would continue to keep the object under observation, repeating the cry if necessary, until the officer of the watch on the bridge acknowledged his sighting and bade him continue his 90 degree sweep.

Lookouts, particularly those not engaged on the binoculars, were expected also to scan the sky for aircraft and, if any were seen, their bearing and estimated degree of elevation had to be reported. Men on the binoculars had not only to survey the horizon and sky but also the surface of the sea for any floating material, or any oddity that could betray the presence of a submarine, for example a persistent white streak possibly caused by a moving periscope or, more ominously, the track of an approaching torpedo. This was no easy matter especially when the sea was choppy. *Cornwall* was not fitted with asdic or, as later termed sonar, systems for the detection of underwater objects by emitted or reflected sound. Men on the binoculars were changed at frequent intervals to relieve eye strain. This was especially suffered at night when, after peering for some while into the darkness it felt as if your eyes were being drawn from their sockets. We were shown that at night, ships, objects and the horizon appeared clearer if one's gaze was directed slightly above them.

The squad of bridge lookouts in each watch had, during daylight hours, also to detach men for lookout duty, one at a time, in the crow's nest. *Cornwall*, not having yet had the benefit of a modernisation refit, which would have provided her with tripod masts, still had the old single, very tall wooden foremast with the old-fashioned, drum-like crow's nest attached in front on its upper reaches and accessed via a Jacob's Ladder of wire with wooden bars affixed to the mast. Jock Davidson, who had joined the ship with me in the same draft, was one of those detailed to do duty in the nest but did not relish the thought of climbing up to it, and asked me to swop with him. Indeed, for anyone with a tendency towards vertigo the ascent up the ladder was daunting, especially as the mast tilted slightly sternwards, and for much of the way up one was leaning backwards. Before ascending the mast a lookout had to seek permission to go aloft from the officer of the watch on the bridge because wiring from the radio station to the aerials above ran up alongside the ladder, and contact therewith during a radio transmission would have been dangerous for the climber.

My stints in the crow's nest were some of my most enjoyable hours spent on *Cornwall*. I felt important in a unique way, high above the ship and everybody in it. It gave me a sense of superiority, even power, alone, away from crowded humanity and jostling working parties, not harassed by petty officers. Sublime stillness save for the murmur of wind through stays and shrouds. From that highest vantage point I would be the first (hopefully) to see and report anything. The safety of the ship, I fancied, depended on me.

The view was magnificent: the bridge and director tower immediately below me, then B and A gun turrets, and beyond them the for'rard upper deck extending and narrowing to the bows from which, on either side, the bow wave curled away and past, broadening to merge with the foamy wake astern. Just behind me I could look into the hazy maw of the three funnels, and then see our aircraft – one in readiness on the launching catapult, the other inside the hangar topped by the subsidiary after director tower. Still further aft the White Ensign flew stiffly from the mainmast while the muzzles of the four 8-inch guns of X and Y turrets protruded above the quarterdeck receding and narrowing towards the sternpost.

The three great troopships steaming astern of *Cornwall* in line ahead provided a superb spectacle although their position relative to ourselves changed from time to time as the cruiser manoeuvred this way and that, occasionally taking station abreast of her consorts. I delighted in studying these liners through the hand-held binoculars provided, their decks teeming with khaki-clad figures, many belonging to a regiment – the Kaffrarian Rifles – from my home town and alas destined to go 'into the bag' at Tobruk the following year, courtesy of Erwin Rommel, and to spend the remainder of their wartime service in prisoner of war camps.

Of course I could indulge in the joys of sightseeing, as described, only momentarily and intermittently as I dared not neglect the purpose and duty attaching to my occupancy of the nest. I was required to scan the horizon carefully through the full 360 degrees but to give priority to an arc extending 45 degrees on either side of the ship's bows, within which sector the probability of encountering other vessels was highest, as was also the rate of convergence. Any sighting was to be reported immediately by voice-pipe to the bridge, where appropriate action would then be put in train as deemed necessary. It behoved the lookout in the nest to be alert and vigilant at all times because it was expected of him to spot something on the horizon several minutes before it entered the line of vision of the lookouts on the bridge and if, as happened on occasion, the latter reported the object first then the man up aloft would inevitably be on the receiving end of, at the least, a vehemently sarcastic roasting.

The possibility of that embarrassment befalling me was forcibly brought home one forenoon a few days after leaving Durban. *Cornwall* and her consorts had entered the tropics and I was doing my allotted spell in the crow's nest, enjoying every minute, as usual. I was particularly intrigued with flying fish, which I had never seen before, and marvelled at the way they broke surface on either side of the bows, flying and gliding for twenty or thirty yards before splashing back into the water. The serenity of my moment was rudely shaken when presently I looked up and saw, to my alarm, with the naked eye, a clear spot on the horizon ahead. How long had it been visible? What if it had already been observed by the bridge? Frantically I blew into the voice-pipe, causing a whistle to blow at the other end, which alerted the officer of the watch.

"Yes?" enquired the voice-pipe.

"Masthead to bridge, Sir."

"Yes?"

"Object on the horizon bearing green five, Sir."

"Green O five," came the correction.

"Aye Aye, green O five. Sorry, Sir."

"Very good. Carry on."

Relieved, I watched from the nest as the officer walked down to speak with the lookouts on the starboard wing, and soon several pairs of binoculars were pointed in the reported direction. Before long I could tell from body language that the bridge had also sighted what was now to me clearly a ship, and *Cornwall* picked up speed to investigate. I felt chuffed – I, of all 700 men aboard, had seen it first! Lookouts received monetary rewards for worthy sightings, the amount varying according to the nature and circumstances in each case. I remember receiving one shilling on that occasion – enough to buy a couple of bars of 'nutty' (chocolate) at the canteen, or a packet of Players or Woodbine cigarettes.

My enjoyment of lookout duties in the crow's nest continued unabatedly. I recall in particular the Red Sea, which seemed to have an abundance of dolphins, many of which delighted in chaperoning the ship alongside her bows. They were particularly entertaining at night due to high phosphorescence in the water which accentuated their swirling, cavorting progress in streaks of green light. The sea was flat calm, and from the crow's nest in daylight my binoculars picked up the triangular dorsal fin of a shark quite frequently. When steaming in relatively shallow water paravanes – long torpedo-shaped devices that veered outwards from the ship's sides at a constant depth, designed to deflect moored mines and sever their anchor wires – were streamed on either side from the bows. At night the PVs added to the spectacular luminosity.

After escorting the troopships safely to within reach of their destination – although conquest of Italy's erstwhile East African empire adjoining the Red Sea: Abyssinia, Somaliland and Eritrea had by then almost been completed, there were still pockets of resistance and no chances could be taken with a convoy so valuable – *Cornwall* turned about and retraced her course southwards. I was in the nest as she exited the Red Sea through the strait of Bab el Mandeb, meaning 'Gate of Tears', and thrilled at beholding two of earth's continents simultaneously: Asia to port and Africa to starboard. Once through the strait and into the Indian Ocean we swung left along the southwest coast of Arabia, soon to enter the deep and commodious harbour of Aden, a seaport town which, with its accommodating territory, was then a possession of Great Britain and an important oiling and coaling station. Situated within the crater of an extinct volcano, Aden was my first port of call after joining *Cornwall* and my two abiding memories of our short stay on that occasion were, firstly, the grotesquely jagged mountain peaks on the northern horizon, reminiscent of illustrations in a children's Arabian Nights and, secondly, being one of a working party assigned to scraping off excess bitumen from between planking on the upper deck, in the baking sun, during the summer solstice, in one of the hottest spots on earth!

*   *   *   *   *

4

COMMERCE RAIDERS, ET CETERA

Formidable and dangerous adversaries

The tasks assigned to *Cornwall* at and about that time, as also with most other cruisers presumably, were largely twofold: escorting and searching. Both usually entailed protracted periods at sea, for which the 'County' class were eminently suited, combining as they did an exceptionally extensive cruising range (high speed when required) a powerful clout, reconnaissance aircraft and relative comfort. Escorting duties ranged from the slow, as when the escorted vessels participating were predominantly small freighters steaming at, perhaps eight to fourteen knots, to the fast, when our charges were able to maintain fifteen to twenty-five knots or more. The latter were of course much pleasanter in performance, especially in the tropics, the faster momentum producing a welcome, cooling breeze between decks. When not engaged in escorting we would usually be on patrol searching for enemy shipping, whether mercantile, passenger or naval.

Hostilities at sea in the Second World War commenced from the very outset, in contrast to the situation on land and in the air, excepting of course the German/Polish conflict. Germany had, in anticipation of a declaration of war by Britain and France, secretly deployed beforehand a number of naval units in pre-planned, strategic areas in the Atlantic, the pocket-battleships Deutschland in the north and Graf Spee in southern waters, submarines, or U-boats as the German equivalent was commonly known, in the North Sea and Western Approaches. Commerce raiders, which were converted, heavily armed merchant ships, followed soon after.

Exactly ten hours after the expiry of the British ultimatum to Germany on September 3 1939, the passenger liner *Athenia* was torpedoed by a U-boat, incurring heavy fatalities. Other maritime losses followed, including, two months later, that of the aircraft-carrier *Courageous*, and on October 14 came the shattering disclosure that a German submarine had penetrated the 'impregnable' defences at Scapa Flow, home base of the British Home Fleet in the Orkneys, and had torpedoed and sunk the battleship *Royal Oak,* made good its escape, and returned triumphantly to base at Wilhelmshaven.

Cornwall, when engaged in searching procedure, was mainly concerned with commerce raiders, or 'auxiliary cruisers', as the German *Kriegsmarine* preferred to call them. As already stated, these were merchant vessels, but specially selected for speed and endurance, converted into armed merchant cruisers intended for preying upon Allied shipping lanes near and far, sinking or capturing as circumstances dictated, and in some cases laying mines in strategic locations.

Commerce raiders could not be disregarded as minor irritants. Indeed they were formidable and dangerous adversaries which not only wreaked considerable loss and damage among unescorted Allied shipping but also caused large numbers of royal naval units to scour the seven seas in search of them, mostly without success. Their crews were handpicked for efficiency and temperament, and their commanding officers for daring and enterprise. The raiders' main and subsidiary armament was impressive, extending to torpedoes and mines. Ships' companies were well versed in international maritime situations and extremely adept at deception and disguise. In March 1942 one raider, the *Doggerbank,* was challenged twice within three days in waters off the South African coast: once by the light cruiser

Durban, and on the other occasion by the armed merchant cruiser *Cheshire*, but by cunning and improvisation she succeeded in allaying suspicion in both instances and, making good her escape, ended her parting signal to *Durban* with a cheery 'good night'.

Other raiders included the *Kormoran, Atlantis, Pinguin* and *Thor*. The British equivalent of commerce raiders were armed merchant cruisers, or AMCs, which made a valuable contribution overall but were allocated old, 'recalled from retirement' guns and were not, it seemed, equal to the combative standard of their German counterparts. *Thor* was brought to bay by AMCs *Carnarvon Castle* and *Alcantara* on separate occasions, and in each case escaped after inflicting casualties and appreciable damage on her attacker without, as subsequently emerged, sustaining a single hit in return.

On the other hand it was ordinarily accepted that the commerce raider was no match for a British warship of cruiser classification and if it came to a straight fight that supposition would, in theory at least, prove to be true. In the event, however, the situation was seldom that simple. The raider, when tracked down, would maintain a dogged, all-embracing charade to the last, claiming by signalling to be a specific Allied or neutral vessel, having already been disguised to resemble the same, citing name, nationality, port of registration, destination, cargo and other information as might be required. Often crates apparently of deck cargo were visible to support the facade while all weaponry and trappings of war were effectively concealed but ready for action at a moment's notice.

Also, to add to uncertainty in the mind of his antagonist, it was a common ploy for the German to radio a general raider alarm claiming to be harassed by an unidentified warship, and while there was an element of doubt on the part of the British captain he, the latter, was in an extremely invidious situation. Were he to open fire mistakenly and sink the other ship only to discover too late that it was not an enemy, there would be an outrage and a court of enquiry. If, in his effort to reach certainty, the British captain ventured too close he could court disaster because the raider, if it indeed was one, would certainly, when the 'chips were down', fight like a cornered wild cat. In the twinkling of an eye she would simultaneously strike her false national flag, hoist the Swastika, lift or drop the flaps concealing her weaponry, and let fly with everything she could bring to bear, including torpedoes, at close range. For several crucial seconds at least she would hold all the aces, actualising the old aphorism 'Twice armed is he whose cause is just but thrice armed is he who gets his blow in fust'. If on the other hand the cruiser kept a safer distance, possibly eight miles, identification would be more difficult and it would eliminate the possibility of sending over a boarding party. The problem of establishing the identity and bona fides of a merchantman was not infrequently aggravated by the doltish demeanour of some of their masters, especially those from neutral countries, who resented taking orders from warring naval authorities, regarding this as an affront to their independence and pride.

The fighting capability of German commerce raiders, even against warships, was graphically demonstrated in November 1941 when the *Kormoran* chanced upon the Australian light cruiser HMAS *Sydney* off the west coast of Australia. Astonishingly, *Sydney*'s captain, an experienced and highly rated officer, allowed his ship to be lured to within a mile of his quarry, which then opened up at point-blank range. The brief intensive encounter that ensued left both ships crippled, on fire and, as was soon apparent, doomed. But whereas 80 per cent of *Kormoran*'s crew were eventually rescued and survived, the only trace ever found of *Sydney* was a small damaged float. There was not a single survivor to reveal what finally happened. Presumably she blew up. Twenty-seven years earlier, almost to the day, her First World War predecessor of the same name had battered the German cruiser *Emden* to destruction not very far, in global perspective, from where she and *Kormoran* perished.

A similar situation developed with *Cornwall* on 7/8 May 1941, one month before my draft joined her, when the cruiser located and finally engaged the German commerce raider *Pinguin* in the Indian Ocean north of the Seychelles. The same tactics of deception were tried by the raider, posing on that occasion as a Norwegian, again succeeding in drawing the cruiser to within range of its own guns, although not as close as *Sydney* came to *Kormoran*. That notwithstanding, the opening salvoes from *Pinguin* were fast and accurate, soon scoring two hits which had *Cornwall* temporarily in serious difficulty: holing her on the waterline, disrupting ventilation fans, upsetting the main steering mechanism and severing electrical circuits governing gunnery control. Fortunately for the cruiser the circuits were soon restored. Her superior 8-inch batteries regained accuracy and started registering hits, one eventually exploding among *Pinguin's* cargo of mines, blowing the ship asunder. But fate could so easily have swung the other way. In the event, *Cornwall* suffered only one fatality – that of the engineer officer in charge of one of the engine-rooms which, when ventilation was disrupted, was transformed in seconds into an oven and had to be evacuated with utmost speed via a narrow, perpendicular ladder. The last but one to escape collapsed on reaching the deck above and had to be carried by comrades to the sick bay, but the last to come up – the engineer officer – overcome by the heat, could not be resuscitated and died. Apart from that, one rating was hit in the buttocks by shrapnel and two or three others received superficial lacerations. The German raider lost over 500 men, including their captain, and more than 200 of their Allied and neutral prisoners of war. Approximately 80 German survivors were picked up as well as a number of their erstwhile POWs.

As already noted, it is generally conceded that the British armed merchant cruisers, while probably faster, were inferior on balance to the German commerce raiders as fighting ships due to poorer ordnance and other equipment. Nonetheless it is fitting to record that two of the most gallant naval actions of the Second World War were fought by AMCs. Both, in defence of their convoys, unflinchingly assailed suicidal odds head-on, namely *Rawalpindi* versus *Scharnhorst* in November 1939 and *Jervis Bay* versus *Admiral Scheer* in November 1940. Both these British ships were horrendously battered and sunk, suffering extremely high fatalities, including their commanding officers, one of whom was posthumously awarded the Victoria Cross, though both officers deserved this honour.

It is also seemly and fair to acknowledge at this point that the commanding officers of German raiders, both of merchantmen and conventional warships, consistently displayed competence and valour of high order and in addition were scrupulous in observance of chivalry. These attributes were a heritage passed down by their counterparts in the First World War, among whom Captain Karl von Muller of the light cruiser *Emden* was renowned.

Cornwall had no definite functional schedule beyond the next port of call and sometimes not even as far as that. Her movements were dictated by the exigencies of war unfolding day by day, sometimes hour by hour, but beyond June 1941 her operational theatre was destined to be the Indian Ocean. In the longer perspective she was overdue for a major refit, probably in Simonstown or possibly even the United Kingdom, but for the time being she could not be spared from escort duties and, when these were not required, raider hunting. Escorting provided the advantage of knowing with reasonable certainty what port would be reached next, when that would be, and what prospects of shore leave and amenities could be expected. With the build-up of Allied forces in the Middle East and the virtual closure of the Mediterranean as passage for their transports and supplies, Aden and Durban, and to a lesser extent Mombasa, were much in the equation. Durban was understandably the favourite, with much to do and see, pubs galore, movie theatres and Services-friendly people. Usually all-night leave was allowed in Durban, and sailors could get a bed at the Victoria League club for a shilling, a wholesome grill with dessert for one and threepence (bob and a tickey) and free riding on public transport. *Cornwall's* complement included slightly more than a hundred South Africans, of whom a large contingent hailed from Durban, and these frequently invited friends to their homes. Some others struck up friendships with girls assisting at Services establishments and who extended similar hospitality.

Cornwall made several more escorting trips from Durban to the Red Sea, sometimes including one or more of the troopers that had sailed with us on my first voyage. Escorting in the opposite, south-bound direction happened less frequently but on one such occasion we were puzzled on entering Durban harbour to see the national blue and white striped flag of Greece run up to the yardarm, discovering shortly afterwards that King George II of the Hellenes, his family and other dignitaries had taken passage in a ship that we had brought back. The royal party had come from Egypt, where they had taken refuge when Greece and subsequently Crete had been invaded and overrun by Germany in April/May 1941.

When we returned to Durban on another occasion an incident of a different kind – the loss of one of our aircraft – occurred. *Cornwall* had, for reconnaissance purposes, two small Walrus flying boats which, when not airborne, were housed, one in the hangar and the other on its catapult, positioned athwartships. The Walrus was a biplane powered by a "pusher" type engine located behind the wings, the fuselage on its underside shaped like the hull of a boat to enable it to ride on water. The Walrus was launched, in fact shot off abeam, on the port side when at full throttle by an explosive propellant and then, on a full tank, it could fly for perhaps four hours. To recover the plane the ship, if underway, would slew hard aport at speed, which had the effect of creating a wide area of placid water along its port side on which the Walrus, timing and directing its approach skilfully, would alight and then steer to the ship's side to be hoisted inboard by crane. Under each of its lower wings the Walrus had a small float attached to prevent the wing dipping below the surface of the water, but on the occasion recounted here one of the floats of a returning aircraft snapped off on touchdown, the wing plunged into the sea, and the plane began to ship water and sink. The pilot and observer escaped in time and were rescued, but it was not possible to save the Walrus – a costly forfeiture.

Walrus reconnaissance plane immediately after launch

The port of Aden and its environs did not have much to offer a sailor on shore leave. Beer and other liquor could be bought in bazaars, but one lacked confidence in the quality and possible after-effects. Considerable business was done by taxi drivers, who offered trips in open tourer-model cars to adjacent areas at fares which, if four or five passengers went along, were not ruinous to a sailor's pocket. These were indeed interesting, including as they did Crater Town and the Queen of Sheba dams, so called, which were a series of huge reservoirs built one above the other across a deep, precipitous ravine, each with an overflow into the one immediately below. As I recall, they contained little or no water at the time of our visit, but if the catchment areas were blessed with a heavy and sustained downpour – a very rare phenomenon – one can imagine a vast storage of water for the benefit of the region, though how it would be channelled or piped and reticulated was not explained to us.

According to local lore the dams were built at the behest of the Queen of Sheba which, if true, would date them in the 5th or 6th century BC. But if that tale from the mists of ancient times were not enough to evoke emotions of mystery and romance then there was also the legend that Noah's Ark was built within the shelter of Aden Bay, from whence it sallied forth in due course with its animated and diversified cargo for Mount Ararat in Armenia. Unfortunately I cannot authenticate the veracity of either claim. I wasn't there at the time.

The taxi trip also took in the renowned salt pans, where brine was pumped out of the sand by ancient windmills of the type, one imagined, Don Quixote tilted at in the celebrated Cervantes novel. Radiating outward from the upper reaches of tall slim towers were long arms – poles fitted with cloth sails – spanned to catch any movement of air, thereby causing the arms to rotate on horizontal bars, which in turn activated the pumping mechanism inside the towers. The mills were also reputed to be very old, a theory strongly borne out by their unique, mechanical construction which was entirely fashioned out of hardened wood, including the gearing. Although hardly detectable, there was breeze enough to nudge the giant arms into ponderous, dawdling rotation, and Peter Versfeld, one of our party, who was standing close to one of the mills, decided to stop the revolving motion by grabbing hold of one of its sails as it passed by at the lowest point of its circumferential journey. Alas, like Don Quixote, he underestimated the potency of the breeze-driven arm which showed no inclination to stop but continued past and then upward, with Peter still attached to its extremity.

The incident could have had serious consequences had it not been that Peter's bodyweight at last overcame the force of breeze in the sails, just before he reached the apex, some thirty or more feet above the ground, where the arm to which he clung stopped momentarily and then reluctantly reversed and delivered Peter back to terra firma. Had the arm passed over the apex, his bodyweight, augmenting the wind-driven rotation and gravitational pull, would have made his descent rapid and hazardous and, moreover, he would have had to change his grip as he swung over the top. While this was happening I was holding a camera, the property of a consortium of six of us, and had the presence of mind to snap the scene. When the film was later developed and printed by the ship's photographer that photo showed Peter up in the sky hanging on for dear life, the taxi driver down below dancing in agitation, and a camel that had somehow material-ised on centre stage wearing that characteristic expression of bored indifference. The photo would have evoked wide interest in years to follow but sadly, along with more than three hundred others, it was destined for Davy Jones's locker.

On our way back to the harbour our taxi took us through Maalah, a place which appeared to consist of a street lined on either side by low buildings occupied by a motley community of ladies, mostly Arabian and African in appearance, who plied the oldest profession, vociferously exhorting passers-by to enter. Sailors would have con-stituted a large proportion of their clientele and not surprisingly the incumbents had acquired some grasp of naval colloquialism, which they put to use in the enticement of customers. 'Come in, Jack' they would call out, or 'In here, Lofty', or 'Come look, Shortarse. Very clean. Very cheap'.

It took no stretch of imagination to appreciate that anyone avail-ing himself of the amenities at Maalah (or its counterparts at other ports around the world) would be placing his health seriously at risk yet, despite that and on-board warnings given from time to time, some sailors could not, or chose not to, withstand the urge. Condoms, although not robustly promoted, were available from the sick bay on a one-per-man basis. These were of rugged manufacture and sardonically referred to on the lower deck as 'dreadnoughts', due to alleged toughness comparable with armour plating. I never saw one of these devices but one of the older seamen of profuse indulgence pleaded in vain with me and other non-subscribers to draw our ration, which he would then buy from us at a generous price. I recall another seasoned old salt who regularly patronised establishments of that sort but disdained the protective use of condoms. "I always wash meself good when I come back on board," he explained.

"But don't you think you should use a dreadnought just to be on the safe side?"

"Naw."

"Why not?"

"Naw. That's like paddlin' with yer boots on."

Two likely destinations during that period were Mombasa on the southern coast of Kenya; and Victoria, on the island of Mahe and capital of the Seychelles. The former was not very popular – hot and humid with few attractions ashore. Victoria, on the other hand, was on one of more than eighty picture-book tropical islands with verdant, lush foliage, white sandy beaches fringed with coconut palms, and crystal-clear coral lagoons, against a backdrop of mountains of volcanic origin. Unlike Mombasa, the equatorial heat among the Seychelles was usually tempered by a sea breeze and the atmosphere was friendly and peaceful with a tinge of religious fervour derived from the early French settlers. A wayside crucifix in the central area of Victoria frequently induced men passing by to doff their hats and women to incline their heads. Mombasa and especially Victoria were geographically well situated in the Royal Navy's strategic design for hunting commerce raiders – a constant threat at that time – that ventured into the Indian Ocean.

Shortly after joining *Cornwall* we newcomers were conducted by Petty Officer Donovan on an instructional tour of the cruiser's offensive and defensive weaponry, starting with the main 8-inch armament. Accordingly we clambered after the P O into the gunhouse of A turret, which housed the two foremost of the ship's eight guns of this calibre, and were shown how the turret operated, and how the shells and the cordite propellant charges in silken bags came up from the shell rooms, shell-handling rooms and magazines far below and were fed into the breeches. We saw how the great breechblocks opened and shut, how the gunhouse was trained around laterally and the two guns elevated and depressed in obedience to indicators activated and controlled from the director tower above and abaft the bridge, how the electrical firing mechanism functioned, and much more.

The 8-inch guns in cruisers of the 'County' class were prestigious weapons. The weight of their projectiles was two and a half times that of the 6-inch guns in other cruisers, and an eight-gun broadside of 8-inch projectiles was one and two thirds heavier than a twelve-gun broadside of 6-inch as fired by some of the then latest 'Colony' and 'City' class ships such as HMSs *Kenya* and *Belfast.* Moreover, the 8-inch gun could outrange anything of smaller calibre and, in fact, could in that respect contend with any larger gun. The weakness or Achilles' heel of 8-inch guns, indeed of guns of greater calibre as well, was their dependence upon primary and auxiliary electric circuits and if these were disrupted, as by enemy engagement, then the guns would not function. They were fired in unison from the main director tower or, in need, from the after secondary director, and if these were both knocked out the turrets would switch to 'quarters' or local independent control. But if electric power was completely eliminated then the guns could not fire at all. Their 256 lb projectiles were too heavy to manhandle, besides which the cordite propellants in the breech could be fired only by an electrically impelled flash – no flash no shoot. These guns could not, as with those of lesser calibre, be fired by percussion, as with a striker mechanism.

We were given a brief run-around on the secondary armament, the 4-inch, high-angle guns, of which there were eight in four twin-gun mountings protected by steel gunshields. While their primary function was to engage hostile aircraft with nose-fused projectiles set to detonate after a predetermined time lapse, thus at an estimated height and distance, these guns could also be brought to bear on surface targets. Fixed cartridge and shell ammunition was rammed into the open breeches by hand, and the block sliding closed automatically. Unlike their larger accomplices, the 4-inch could, in need, be fired by percussion, the strikers in the breechblocks being sprung manually by lanyard.

Our orientation tour took us aloft to the main director tower – the highest manned position on the ship apart from the crow's nest – from where the cruiser's guns were fired and controlled, unless prevented by damage. The director was in direct communication with, among others, the bridge and by electrical transmission with the guns and the transmitting station, or TS, deep down below the waterline.

The fighting nerve centre of the warship was the TS – a small room dominated in the centre by a large box-like contrivance called the 'table' – a forerunner, it could be said, of today's sophisticated computers. The table was fed an astounding assortment of information, which it collated, amalgamated and reduced to but two essentials – bearing and elevation – which it passed on to the guns, via the director, in continuous transmission denoted by pointers moving on screens. The gunlayers and trainers in the gunhouses, by lining up their own pointers with those transmitted, effected vertical or lateral adjustment to the guns which, when fired, would despatch their shells intended to fall in a group on and around the calculated position of their target. The TS absorbed, in a constant stream, the estimated distance, or range, from six independent rangefinders; enemy's course and speed; own course and speed; wind direction and velocity; air temperature; 'spread', being the linear differential between the turrets according to their disposition along the length of the ship; 'dip', being the height of each gunhouse above the waterline; 'drift', being the natural sideward veer of a shell from spin imparted by rifling in the bore of the gun; and even, amazingly, estimated rotation of the earth during flight of shell. During battle, adjustments would be made from observation of fall of shot.

Donovan acquainted us briefly with the ship's anti-aircraft defences which, apart from the 4-inch high-angle guns already described, consisted primarily of two mountings of multiple pom-poms, eight barrels to each mounting. They were positioned two levels above the main upper deck, one to port and the other to starboard, close behind the bridge superstructure and for'rard of the foremost funnel. More detail will be given about this weapon, its potency and limitations, later in this narrative.

Atop the hangar were two mountings each of four .5-inch machineguns arranged one above the other perpendicularly, firing non-explosive, belt-fed rounds. Both the pom-poms and the .5s were manufactured by Vickers on the principle of their famous World War 1 water-cooled machinegun. Two pan-fed, air-cooled Lewis guns of .303-inch calibre, positioned on the wings of the bridge, completed *Cornwall's* anti-aircraft defence arsenal.

Courses in gunnery were conducted on a regular basis to train and capacitate new entrants for replacement of those redeployed and it was during our orientation tour that I resolved mentally to apply for inclusion in the next AA class, with a view to having my action station changed from Y shellroom to one of the anti-aircraft posts. If I was to be killed in this war, I reasoned, let me die in the open air on deck and not in a rat trap down near the bilges.

* * * * *

5

ALL IN A DAY'S WORK

Cut towards your pal

When at sea, everybody's day started with Action Stations. It had the whole ship's company tumbling out of hammocks or other places of slumber, scrambling, running and cursing in the pre-dawn darkness to report to their appointed posts and there to remain in readiness until the clear light of day revealed no sign of anything untoward, when the order to secure would be given. Thereafter all seamen not on watch duty fell in on the upper deck by 'part of ship', fo'c'slemen, topmen and quarterdeckmen to be assigned pre-breakfast chores. Commander Fair, *Cornwall's* second-in-command, presided, attended by the chief bosun's mate, known throughout the navy as the 'buffer', who would apprise the commander of the morning's special requirements: frequently the procurement of alimentary stores from the nether regions of the ship. So typically, the commander would mutter something to the buffer, who would then bellow out something like 'Two hands from each part for flour party'. Thereupon the Chief Petty Officer of each part would detail off two unfortunates to fall in at the double amidships, then to be marched off by a leading seaman down, down and down to the flour store. Other ratings would similarly be detailed off for different chores, whereafter those remaining would be marched off to their respective parts of ship to wash down and scrub decks.

Reg Peard, from my home town, and I in the second part of port watch had good reason to dread the mornings when stores parties were required because CPO Standing, port watch chief, took, we were convinced, malicious delight in ferreting out the pair of us for the tough jobs. We were the tallest in our group – a head above the rest – and Standing apparently equated height with strength. "Right," he would smirk, "we'll need big strong lads for this one – you, Lofty, and you, wotsyername, yes, you, off yer go and look smart about it." So off Reg and I would trot unwillingly with the other unfortunate ratings down to the flour store. The job required bags of flour weighing anything from 100 to 150 lb to be dumped unceremoniously on your upper back and neck, for you then to transfer the load to the ship's bakery on the upper deck, ascending en route three or four companions, or stairways. As both your hands were committed to holding grimly onto the ears at the upper end of the bag above your head you had nothing left, in the absence of a third hand, to assist you in maintaining equilibrium, your faculty for which, under the strain, teetered on a knife edge. The cruiser's propensity for rolling was not put on hold during the operation and it was not uncommon for a rating, labouring up iron steps, to lose balance and control and drop his bag of flour onto the deck below where, apart from endangering the lives and limbs of others, it would burst open and discharge its contents far and wide.

When the job was finally done the working party, covered from head to foot with flour, and sweaty, would head post-haste for the washroom to clean up before breakfast. There were of course other provisions besides flour that working parties had to bring up from the depths as and when required, like sacks of potatoes (or 'spuds' in mess deck parlance), dried peas, dehydrated vegetables, frozen meat, crates of tinned bully-beef, et cetera for the galley, all of which likewise entailed backbreaking exertion. This frequently provoked among the disgruntled labourers impassioned queries, liberally garnished with obscenities, as to why the designers of warships, or their lordships of the Admiralty, apparently never thought of disposing flour stores alongside bakeries, and stores of other edibles alongside galleys.

In the normal way forenoons were for working and afternoons were free, except of course for those on watch duty. After breakfast, which consisted largely of bread and jam swilled down with mugs of tea, hands not on watch fell in by part of ship, and the forenoon's work commenced. 'Rig of the day' would have been piped over the loud-speakers during breakfast indicating which clothing was to be worn, for example, overalls, tropical gear or number 3s. The CPO would check to see there were no unauthorised absentees, to which band of dodgers I was not a total stranger, and then bark, 'Carry on, sweepers', and a number of men would trot off. Sweepers were designated cleaners, responsible for the cleanliness, tidiness and functionality of their respective areas. There were, for example, gun sweepers, who cared for specific guns and their surrounds, greasing, lubricating and polishing, flat sweepers, who had to sweep and frequently scrub the thick, corticine deck covering, wash down paintwork, and dust off overhead pipes and ventilation ducts. There were numerous com-partmented areas in the ship, usually accessed at either end through watertight doors in bulkheads, which were called 'flats'. Then there were mess deck sweepers, or 'cooks', two to each mess, who did duty in rotation, scrubbing the mess tables, swabbing the benches, washing crockery and utensils after meals, drawing provisions from a storeman who, throughout the Navy, rejoiced in the title 'Tanky', preparing food, like peeling spuds, for delivery to the galley staff for cooking. Bathroom sweepers had a sodden, sloshy, steamy job, dousing away old soapy water from the tiled floor and tip-up basins. The bathrooms had to be available for odd users throughout the day but 'peak hour' was during the dog watches after 16.00. The 'bum' sweeping job was in the heads (toilets), which, understandably, had to be open and hygienically clean 24 hours a day. The seamen's division had two sets of heads – one on the starboard side and the other on port. One was always open, the other usually closed for cleaning. The senior hand in this sweeping party endured the sardonic appellation of 'Captain of the Heads' or, less politely, 'Skipper of the Shits'. But sweepers generally were happy with their lot, and were allowed to get on with their job without being 'buggered around'.

Then, with duty watchmen and sweepers out of the way, the CPOs of the three parts of ship would set the remaining men to work on whatever they felt, or had been told, needed to be done. Frequently that had to do with paintwork. Apart from the decks, virtually the entire visible exterior of the ship was clothed in a coat of paint or, more accurately, in numerous coats of paint. I wondered on occasion how much of the cruiser's displacement tonnage could be attributed to the weight of paint on its sides and superstructure because normally fresh paint was simply slapped on top of the old, over and over again, the old being scraped off only where, in places, rust was in evidence. The colour of the paint was almost entirely 'battleship grey' with some oblique panels of black by way of camouflage, which I doubt would have deceived an enemy.

The CPO might decide that the paintwork in a certain area needed merely to be washed down to remove an encrustment of salt from spray blown over the fo'c'sle or discolouration caused by oil or other substances. So buckets, cloths and soft soap would be drawn from a 'caboose' – a small storage apartment on deck – and the work would get underway. If evidence of rust was anywhere apparent a detail would be assigned to remove it. If the rust was a deep infestation the detail attacked the area with chipping hammers, then with scrapers, and finally with steel wire brushes until not a trace of rust remained and the metal underneath shone like burnished silver. Then a coat of red lead primer would be applied and when that had dried, probably the next day, a fresh coat of grey completed the job.

Some painting tasks were quite hazardous, as for instance painting the tall foremast, when the painter would be seated in a bosun's chair – a short plank secured at both ends with ropes, which could be raised and lowered by block and tackle. This was fortunately not a job frequently undertaken, and then only by a competent and responsible sailor who could be relied upon not to allow blobs of paint to fall as, with the connivance of wind, these could alight on the bridge – the holy of holies and sanctum of gold-braid. The lyrics of a popular song of the day were parodied thus:

> When painting up – the old masthead
> The pot fell on – the skipper's head
> I'm so – sorry for myself.

The tough one was painting the ship's side, that is the hull above the waterline, which operation was, for obvious reasons, tackled best when in harbour, moored or anchored away from wharves and jetties. Stages – planks two to three yards long with a rope secured to each end – were lowered over the side from the upper deck, each stage usually manned by two ratings armed with paintbrushes. Pots of paint were lowered on the ends of yarn to the men on the stages and the painting proceeded, starting at the top. The ropes holding the stages would, after two or three turns had been taken around a stanchion, be tied to any convenient fixture on deck. As the work progressed, Leading Seamen, nicknamed 'killicks' in reference to the small anchor insignia of rank worn on the upper arm, would lower the stages by carefully paying out the ropes holding them and simultaneously lowering the pots of paint to enable the work to continue at the lower level. This procedure was followed until the painters were able to reach the waterline. That was fine in theory but not always in practice. When a stage had to be lowered, two killicks, or men under their supervision, had to pay out the ropes – one at the fore end of the stage and the other at the after end, in unison. The result was, at best, a jerky uneven descent with the men on the stages clinging on for dear life. At less than best a stage might in a split second find itself closer to perpendicular than horizontal, its occupants dangling and kicking, turning the sea air blasphemously blue.

Painting ship's side (not HMS Cornwall *in this photograph)*

In such circumstances the odd painter on occasion landed in the drink and had to be fished out by the crew of a duty boat that had been tethered nearby. Unofficially it was policy not to put men on the stages who could not swim. I found it strange how many sailors serving in the vast seafaring force suffered this disability, and how remarkably their numbers swelled in the run-up to painting the ship's side. I tried it on once, light-heartedly with CPO Standing.

"I can't swim, Chief."

"Well now, this is a good time to learn how, innit? Go grab a brush and get over the side and look smart about it… and you lot over there, what are you gawking at? Get on them stages and start painting, and

I want a good job done. If I find any holidays I'll have the lot of you over the side in the first dog."

A common expression in the navy for 'missed out spots' was 'holidays'. In the rough and tumble of painting over the side it was to be expected that brushes were frequently dropped and surrendered to the depths, resulting in regular requisitions for new ones, so adding to the war's financial burden.

The pride and joy of RN ships were their gleaming white wooden decks. They had to be spotless, especially on the quarterdeck aft, which was officers' domain, and on the fo'c'sle for'rard as far as the breakwater, and on B gun deck, which areas were unavoidably always under scrutiny from the bridge. The CPOs affected were therefore highly sensitive about the appearance of their decks and while these were routinely hosed down and scrubbed before breakfast they frequently received specialist attention during the forenoon, removing a grease mark here and a smudge there. Now and then holystoning was applied whereby rectangular blocks of sandstone encased in metal frames and fitted with broom handles were vigorously rubbed back and forth across the wooden surfaces.

There was an endless variety of odd jobs, general tidying up, greasing shackles, wire ropes, swivels, replacing worn cordage in boats and on Carley floats, et cetera.

"'Ere, Lofty, cut off four lengths about this long from this 'ere coil of rope and... What's that? What to cut it with? With yer knife, of course! Where's the knife you was issued with? What? In yer bleedin' locker? What use is it there? A sailor must 'ave 'is knife on 'im at all times, like tied on the end of a lanyard around 'is middle. You might need to use it at any time; could save yer life – not wot YORE life is worth saving. Now see that you 'ave yer knife on you in future. 'Ere, use this knife for now and cut them lengths off. NO, not like that, you numbskull; if it slips you could slice yer thumb off... or somethin' else off. NEVER cut towards yerself. Golden rule – cut towards yer, pal."

At 11.00 came the pipe 'Stand easy', and everyone disappeared with new-found alacrity to the mess deck for a mug of tea. Fifteen minutes later the bosun's pipe shrilled again, "Out pipes, hands carry on with your work." The bosun's mate, or 'buffer', was responsible for all broadcasts over the loudspeaker system, whether done by himself or by delegation. It would start with a long, shrill blast on the bosun's pipe, followed by an order or an announcement. If the message was of special interest or importance the buffer would commence his act with the exclamation, "D'ya hear there!" and the whole ship's company would freeze in anticipation. He was a typical, dyed-in-the wool RN man.

"That buffer must have been born with a bosun's pipe in his mouth," muttered one sailor.

"'E wasn't born; 'e was issued," opined another.

"But what about that officer looking down on us from X gun deck – he hasn't said a word?"

"That's because 'e knows nuthing'. 'E thinks Haul Taut Singly is an Indian cricketer."

At 11.30 the pipe was, 'Afternoon watchmen to dinner', and about half an hour later, 'Cooks to the galley' and 'Up spirits', at which latter pipe some irreverent wag was likely to be heard uttering a blasphemous allusion to the Third Person in the Blessed Trinity. 'Up spirits' was the order to leading hands in each mess to muster at a location amidships to receive the quota of rum for their respective messes – more about that procedure anon. The next pipe shortly afterwards would be, 'Hands to dinner'.

Dinner was, on the basis of plateload, by far the biggest meal of the day and the 'cooks', under scrutiny by the leading hands in each mess, saw to it that every man received a fair share. Diversity of fare depended to a large extent on how long the ship had been at sea since the last port of call and what stores had been taken on board there. When the latter were exhausted after three weeks or so it was back to basics, and exclamations such as the following, with lewd trimmings, would be heard at the dinner table: 'Wot, dehydrated spuds again?' or 'Hell! Back to corned dog' (bully-beef) or 'Dammit, more herrings in' (canned herrings in tomato sauce). Nevertheless, these unexciting dishes were, in retrospect, quite tasty. Dinner also became progressively rowdier as the stimulus bestowed by Jamaican rum took effect. Thereafter, an abundance of calories demolished, the men not on watch were, in the absence of anything untoward, at leisure for the afternoon, which in most cases commenced with a nap, commonly referred to as 'getting your head down' or 'crashing your blinking suede', the origin of which latter expression is obscure to me. Frequently this was indulged on the upper deck in a spot sheltered from wind and spray. Traditionally it was a period of 'make and mend' (clothing) although the term was seldom heard by the time World War II arrived.

Hands were piped to tea at 16.00 at the start of the first of two dog watches – each of two hours. During the dogs one did, if not on watch, very much one's own thing, and high on the list of probabilities would be the bathroom. That was no trivial matter due, it seemed, to another mental lapse on the part of the designers of naval vessels, who took pleasure in the belief that an ablution chamber measuring some 15 by 10 yards provided ample space for, as I recall, the greater part of a heavy cruiser's complement below the rank of Petty Officer and, further, that tip-up cold water basins lining one length and one breadth of the chamber, plus a single hot water tap, adequately fulfilled the bathing and laundering aspirations of the crowds who assembled there. The bathroom scene, therefore, particularly during the dogs, was of masses of steaming, naked men soaping themselves, sluicing off with water, shaving and dhobying. The word 'dhoby' derived from Hindi, meaning laundry, had in course of time attained universal usage throughout the navy. Buckets, featured earlier, were much in evidence. Indeed, one could hardly do without one. Relatively few men managed to capture a tip-up basin, which in any case could not contain hot water without it being conveyed thither from the only hot water tap in some receptacle like a bucket. The canteen did a steady trade in buckets which, once acquired, were speedily inscribed in paint with the names or initials of their owners. Sometimes buckets had more than one owner sharing. Others were borrowed.

A visit to the bathroom was unavoidably an aqueous experience with sailors, for the most part using buckets, taking up every available floor space, and sloshing water over themselves and anyone else within range. Inevitably on occasion something would block the outlet scupper and the tiled floor would then soon acquire a covering of frothy water an inch or two deep which, with the roll and pitch of the ship, would surge from side to side and fore to aft like a miniature tidal wave. Despite these discomforts the mood in the bathroom was generally light-hearted, with laughter and wisecracks abounding. Invariably it encouraged those who imagined themselves as Bing Crosby soundalikes to render their interpretations of 'Sweet Lelanie' and 'Home on the Range'.

Just above and abaft the bathroom was the drying room – a heated chamber open during the dogs, where men could hang up their dhobied clothing to dry. Usually a sentry was posted at the exit, to which dignitary men retrieving dried clothing had to show the imprint of their names on each article to ensure that they did not walk out with someone else's kit 'by mistake'. It was, to say the least, a dubious precaution because the sentry could hardly have known more than a quarter of the men by name who removed dried laundry. Dhobying was not the most appealing means of spending one's free time, the reality of which was exploited by certain enterprising individuals who teamed together to establish 'dhoby firms'. They equipped themselves with, among other things, electric irons which could be plugged into a power socket, and offered laundering and ironing services subject to graded tariffs according to the size and type of each item. This was a boon for those sailors who, lethargic when confronted with do-it-yourself laundry, still prided themselves on looking smart, or 'tiddily'. I was never a customer, being classified, no doubt, as 'scruffy'. My shirts, or 'dickies', after I had washed them, were smoothed against my chest to remove creases and then hung up to dry.

Two of the three Rs of primary education, namely Reading and Rite-ing, were copiously indulged in on the mess deck during the dogs, the third, Rithmetic, being the odd one out. For men, after weeks, even months at sea and long away from home, reading matter was a precious commodity. Memorable were the days when the mailbags caught up with the ship and were brought aboard, usually at the start of the dog watches. Men leaned over the guardrail to watch the duty boat approach the gangway, and guess the number of bags. These were speedily emp-tied in the sorting office and the mail thereafter conveyed to the respec-tive messes, where it was welcomed with cheering and banter.

"Your Judy dumped you, Townie?"

"Not a chance, mate – here's three letters from her... and the local rag."

"She must be hard up."

And

"Your Liverpool lassie still love you, Scouse?"

"Nah, she's still chokka[1] with me."

"Why so?"

"Last time I saw her I said her hair smelled like new-mown hay. "

"But that should please her."

"Yes, but you see I added on: 'after it's been through the horse'."

Joe Geisler, the ship's irrepressible Jew and as such, in the view of some, lucky charm, would hear someone shout, "Four bags from

---

[1] Chokka: A common lower-deck expression meaning 'extreme annoyance', derived from 'choc-a-block', a naval term indicating 'full up' in relation to block-and-tackle usage.

Palestine, Joe." The chatter and laughter would subside a little as men eagerly tore open envelopes and devoured their contents, often weeks old but no less appreciated. Overall the mood was happy and animated but for a few, sometimes, tidings from home would not be good. For some others nothing arrived.

Newspapers were always much in demand and their recipients would usually leave them in the mess after perusal for the benefit of shipmates. Most popular were the *Daily Mirror* and the bulky *News of the World* with their wide coverage and spicy bits. On one such mailbags' day my messmate, Hedley Beswetherick, also from East London, was grinning from ear to ear, his eyes full of joy albeit a little moist. "I've got a baby daughter," he exulted. "Our first child." He was warmly and jocularly congratulated. "Let's hope she looks like her mom, Bes!" and at grog time he was plied with "sippers" of rum all round and rendered happily tipsy. But sadly Hedley did not live to see his little girl.

The dogs were convenient also for writing letters home, to relatives and friends and, by no means least, to girlfriends. The mess tables were the main writing desks as soon as the afternoon tea paraphernalia were cleared away. This activity was understandably at its peak immediately and shortly after the arrival of mailbags but continued intermittently thereafter. At least one sailor wrote to his wife every day, which could result in her receiving up to thirty letters from him at a time; some others were apathetically remiss. I recall another, a Liverpudlian, setting pen to writing pad with a flourish, saying as he wrote, "My dearest, darling," then to me, leering wickedly, "Got to flannel the missus a bit like that to make up for all the weeks I haven't written."

"You should write more often, Scouse," I said. "Must be lonely for her."

"Oh, she thinks it's because I'm in action – the bleedin' hero fighting the enemy all the time. But she's all right. Meets up with the girls regular like at the local and enjoys herself, and spends my allotment."

Many, probably most of the married men, arranged for a portion of their pay to be deducted and allotted to their wives.

During the dogs the canteen, staffed by NAAFI personnel (Navy, Army and Air Force Institute – an organisation established for that purpose) was, in the absence of emergencies, open for business selling cigarettes, chocolate bars (or 'nutty'), chewing gum, soap, toothpaste and a host of other imperatives, duty free, while in the recreation space, located off the upper deck amidships, one could, for one penny, purchase a cold 'goffer', or lime juice. On certain days the clothing store, nicknamed the 'slops', would also be open, and naval attire and accessories ranging from overcoats to cap ribbons could be bought at very affordable prices. I clearly recall acquiring a quality Burberry raincoat, the largest in stock (on another ship subsequently), for two pounds one shilling and seven pence which served me admirably in good condition until stolen twenty-two years later.

At sunset the loudspeakers would blare 'Darken ship', requiring total prevention of light emission, including the lowering and clamping shut of heavy porthole covers, or 'deadlights', although in hot and relatively safe areas the concession: 'Light-excluding scuttles may be used on mess decks' was made. This allowed a light metal scoop to be inserted into the porthole which, while effectively maintaining an exterior blackout, provided an inflow of fresh sea air. The off-watch activities commonly pursued during the dog watches frequently continued after supper, taken at around 18.00, and during the first watch, commencing at 20.00, until 'lights out' two hours later.

And so, hopefully, to sleep. The standard and traditional equipment to accommodate the sleeper was the hammock, its components being a heavy-duty sheet of canvas measuring approximately 6 feet long by 3 feet wide, hemmed and eyeleted at its farthest extremities; a 'bed', or thin coir mattress; a bed cover or jacket; and a blanket. Along the width of the canvas at both ends were attached 'clews',

or sets of 16 cords called 'nettles', which converged from the eye-
lets on, and were spliced to, a metal ring to which also was spliced
a 'lanyard', or length of rope. For sleeping purposes the hammock
was 'slung' by its lanyards at either end between steel hooks welded
onto beams riveted to the deck-head, the canvas, by adjustment of
the lengths of the nettles, forming a trough along and within which
would lie the bed in its cover and upon which the owner would
stretch out to sleep, having heaved himself up and into the trough
from the deck below. He would provide his own pillow, usually in
the form of a rolled-up garment. A thin plank or pole, notched at the
ends and called a 'stretcher', was inserted at the head end of the slung
hammock to prevent the sides folding inward over the sleeper's face.
Another length of rope, or 'lashing', was supplied for the purpose of
lashing up the hammock with its contents in the morning into a long
polony-like shape, the lanyards and clews having been folded back
in. The lashing had to seal and secure the ends of the polony tightly
and truss up the area in between with seven turns spread along its
length, each secured with a marling hitch.

A hammock was comfortable and warm in cold conditions but in
the tropics many sailors preferred simply to lay out the bedding on
any convenient flat surface and doss down there. Some were content to sleep on the narrow benches on either side of the mess tables,
lying on their sides facing the tables and stabilising themselves with
a forearm and lower leg resting on their table surface. One way or
another, at appropriate times and the exigencies of warfare permitting, Jack managed to drop off into the 'Land of Nod'.

* * * * *

6

EASTWARD HO

Someone cut the end off

Ever eager to see new places, I was pleasantly excited when the loudspeakers announced that the ship was heading for Colombo, the capital and main port of Ceylon, and I looked forward to our arrival there. Ceylon is a beautiful tropical island, having deservedly earned the sobriquet 'Pearl of the Orient', separated from India by a strait 50 miles wide. It has a spectacularly mountainous interior, alluring luxuriant lowlands and white, palm-fringed beaches. Colombo on the south-western seaboard, the island's commercial hub, had a spacious man-made harbour with buoy-mooring facilities, encompassed by extensively constructed moles. I do not recall any quayside wharves where passengers and crews could disembark and embark directly, on and from land but a long passenger jetty protruding from the southern perimeter was busily utilised by boats plying to and from ships moored within the enclosure. More importantly, however, the harbour boasted a capacious graving dock, from a naval perspective a valuable resource.

The topography of the city and its surrounds was largely flat with little structurally that might be considered 'high rise' except that to the north of the harbour a large dome was prominent which, I was told, belonged to the Catholic cathedral, while in the same area a giant signboard rising skywards proclaimed: CEYLON FOR GOOD

TEA, acclaiming the product for which the island, then still a British crown colony, was world-renowned. Another commodity under full production and, pertinent to the war situation probably more important, was rubber.

First impressions on going ashore were an intriguing kaleidoscope of streets teeming with pedestrians; unending shops displaying silks and other fabrics, jewellery, copper and bronze wares, tea, coffee and liquor dispensaries, vegetables and tropical fruit, griddle cakes and spices; and an abundance of scavenging black crows. Above all one was conscious of a friendly, smiling population, the majority on the island being Singhalese, and the largest minority being Tamils.

The ship's company was happy to learn on arrival that our stay in Colombo would be of about two weeks' duration as certain urgent repairs had to be done in dry dock, where the opportunity would also be taken to rid the ship's bottom of the usual accretion of crustaceans and seaweed and, as a corollary, starboard and port watches would in succession each be granted four days' leave as guests on the estates of tea and rubber planters. Jock Davidson, Peter Pare, Peter Versfeld and I were part of a large group who travelled to our destinations by train, which set off from Colombo Railway Station in a south-easterly direction on what I noted was a track of exceptionally wide gauge. Batches of sailors were put off at stops along the route in accord with the organised arrangements and eventually the four of us, along with others, alighted at a station in the vicinity of Ratnapura. Planters or their representatives were waiting to welcome us and, when a lady among them announced to the travelling official that she could take four, the two Peters, Jock and I grabbed the opportunity.

We soon found ourselves at the homestead of Mr and Mrs May, manager and mistress of a rubber plantation, to commence a most memorable and enjoyable sojourn in what, to us, was the lap of luxury. Our hosts' hospitality and kindness knew no bounds; the food was sumptuous, with waiters in attendance clad in white and gold livery and turbans; while to sleep again in comfortable beds with clean linen was a delight, yet a little strange on that occasion because the beds were, of necessity, under mosquito netting. We were soon taken on a tour of the estate and shown the whole process of primary rubber production, from 'milking' the trees by means of highly technical, slanting incisions made to the inner layer of bark to induce the latex sap to run down and be collected in small receptacles such as halved coconut shells, through to the factory on site where, after progressive treatment the finished product emerged as thick sheets of yellow crepe rubber for shipment overseas in due course, there to be metamorphosed in a hundred ways to serve the Allied cause. We were each given a souvenir sheet of crepe about a foot long.

On another day we were taken to a tea plantation some distance away and again conducted on a tour covering the evolution of tea from the picking of select leaves from small evergreen bushes through to the airy sorting and drying sheds, arriving eventually at the packaging of the final commodity. The workforce consisted overwhelmingly of women, those in the sheds mostly young girls whose slender, lithe figures and striking facial beauty could hardly escape admiration. The finest variety of black tea, we were told, was Broken Orange Pekoe produced from the leaves around the buds and the planters themselves, it seemed, drank no other. We were each given a sizeable quantity of BOP tea, wrapped in tinfoil, to take back with us. Upon return to *Cornwall* I carefully stowed my samples of tea and crepe rubber at the back of my locker in anticipation of taking them home one happy day but, alas, they were destined never to be taken out again.

Evenings spent relaxing in the spacious living room of the homestead were specially enjoyable, sipping cold beer and chatting to our hosts, who had a wealth of interesting information and experience to relate. To offset heat and humidity, punkahs – large frames of cloth – swung to and fro above our heads, fanning the air, operated by a cord passed through to an adjoining chamber, where a punkah wallah applied himself to the other end much as he would a bell-rope. The Mays told us that their son was a junior officer aboard HM Submarine *Parthian*, thought to be operating then in the Mediterranean. Later in the war I noted in an official bulletin that the *Parthian* had been lost and fervently hoped then, as I still do, that the younger May was no longer a crew member at the time of the loss.

Ceylon in 1941 had one other harbour of importance, namely Trincomalee on the opposite, north-eastern coast, although there was also a third, smaller and of little strategic consequence, at Galle near the southern tip of the island. It was for Trincomalee, colloquially nicknamed 'Trinco', that we next set course. It was a vast, natural deepwater sanctuary spacious enough to accommodate the largest fleets. Accessed from the sea through a narrow entrance, it contained numerous bays and inlets, the land in places rising steeply out of the water, making it possible to drop anchor a stone's throw from shore. Apart from having essential war-related establishments including a Royal Air Force station at nearby China Bay, fuel storage tanks, army barracks, a landing jetty, among others, the region had not yet succumbed to the destructive invasion of progress and development, so much of the surrounding, wooded countryside was still in verdant, pristine condition.

It was at Trinco in September 1941 that we first made the acquaintance of the two 'queens' – two of the world's three super-heavyweight ocean liners. The largest, at 83,675 tons, was the two-funnelled *Queen Elizabeth*. It was also the newest, having secretly made its maiden voyage to New York in March of the previous year, painted a drab grey. The other giant was the three-funnelled *Queen Mary*, the third-largest at 81,235 tons. Both had been converted to troop carriers and could together transport 30,000 troops at a time, at speeds approaching 30 knots. The second-largest at the time was the French liner *Normandie* at 83,423 tons, then holder of the 'Blue

Riband', or record for the fastest Atlantic crossing by a passenger vessel, which she had achieved in 4 days, 3 hours and 5 minutes. *Normandie* was impounded in New York after the fall of France and was likewise intended for conversion to a troop carrier renamed USS *La Fayette* but in February 1942 a fire broke out aboard, causing her to capsize and sink at her berth – a disastrous, entirely avoidable loss to the Allied war effort and ultimately to France.

The queens, when we joined them, were packed with Australian troops bound for Egypt, and *Cornwall's* assignment was to escort them thither. There followed a memorable voyage across the Arabian Sea and Gulf of Aden into the Red Sea, very fast at approximately 25 knots. Everybody aboard *Cornwall,* I believe, felt the undercurrent of excitement and animation, the sense of wonder, honour and pride at having been entrusted with the conduct, and protection of those magnificent monarchs of the ocean and their priceless human cargo. As seldom before, men off watch (and more than a few on watch) crowded *Cornwall*'s guardrails to gaze at the two stately queens following astern, seemingly motionless as if captured in oils by some consummate artist on a vast expanse of canvas – a moment and spectacle long to savour down memory lane.

It should be appreciated, by the way, that escort duty, quite apart from providing defence against enemy attack, comprised more than simply sailing along in company with other vessels. It demanded constant vigilance, quick response, and seamanship of the highest order. This was especially so in fast convoy, as with the queens, steaming at up to 30 knots and zigzagging every five to fifteen minutes to offset the aim of hostile submarines. The danger of collision was ever present, particularly under impaired visibility, as at night. On one occasion *Cornwall* provoked a strident blast on the siren from one of the queens for seemingly crossing 'Her Majesty's' bows too closely. The reality of this hazard was never more dramatically demonstrated than when, in late 1942, the *Queen Mary,* laden with American troops in the North Atlantic, sliced through the light cruiser *Curacoa*, sinking her and more than half of her crew – a catastrophe that was hushed up until after the war.

But, reverting back, *Cornwall*'s acquaintanceship with the queens was repeated two months later when we rendezvoused with the two behemoths in the vicinity of the Cocos Islands, north-west of Australia, and again escorted them into the Red Sea. That was a period when fighting for supremacy in North Africa was critical and the movement of Anzac forces was westward from the Antipodes to that theatre. In a matter of months, however, that movement, in part at least, was reversed when war clouds gathered on Australia's northern horizon. On one of *Cornwall*'s fast runs with the queens we had an unusual visitor in the shape of a wandering albatross that swooped down and settled on the top of the mainmast to rest. The bird aroused considerable interest among the ship's company, reviving in some a sailor's ancestral superstition regarding that species as featured in Coleridge's poem *The Ancient Mariner*. Was this one an omen of things to come? The wandering albatross inhabits mostly the southern oceans but is known to wander far from home waters at times and, with the longest wingspan known to ornithology – 12 to 15 feet – it has prodigious gliding and endurance capacity. Our visitor remained perched on the mainmast for hours, surveying the world around and beneath, unperturbed by funnel fumes and other disagreeable attributes of 'County' class cruisers, occasionally spreading its great, elongated wings as if to cool its armpits in the wind. Eventually, almost imperceptibly, it again became airborne, and then soared away in a whirling arc towards the horizon astern. It was suppertime, no doubt.

There were not many sights at sea that would induce an 'old salt', set in his ways, to abandon his habitual, off-duty pursuits during the dogs to go up on deck to see. It would have to be something special, like, for instance, the two queens steaming in company close by, or perhaps a wandering albatross cadging a lift, or a school of whales frolicking and blowing on the surface. But just to look at the sea? "Not bloody likely, mate!" unless there was something really extraordinary about it – incredible tranquillity possibly. Of the five oceans, which, I was told at school, cover nearly three fourths of our planet, I would surmise that the Indian is, by and large, the least turbulent; there, calm seas are commonplace and unremarkable. However, on rare occasions, for oceanographic reasons beyond my ken the sea acquired the ultimate: a surface as flat as a sheet of glass, stretching 360 degrees around to the horizon. The world around seemed to recede into unnatural quietude – an eerie stillness coinciding with shimmering, visual distortions, mirage-like, in the far distance. When the sun set radiant beams lit up the western sky in flamboyant glory, mirrored in every detail on the glazed surface of the water. That was indeed something to behold and I recall *Cornwall*'s fo'c'sle crammed with sailors, 'old salts' included, their other activities temporarily forgotten, gazing at the firmamental phenomenon in wonder.

Water spouts, another rare occurrence in our experience, also evoked interest. These we encountered south of the Persian Gulf, sometimes four or five at a time at a distance of probably four or five miles, and it was fascinating to watch their formation – a spirally cone of water rising out of the sea towards, and then fusing with an inverted cone of watery vapour descending from a cloud to become a maritime 'twister'. We never came close to a spout but there was some light-hearted speculation among sailors as to what would happen if the ship were hit by one – not much, apparently, according to an opinion said to have emanated from the navigating officer. Water spouts as generated under the prevailing meteorological conditions were not strong enough to constitute a serious hazard to ship or crew although they might inflict damage to wireless aerials and carry away lightweight articles; careless sailors might soon find themselves bereft of their caps. From the sea itself small marine life on or near the surface

would no doubt be taken up in the vortex and flying fish might experience aeronautical accomplishments far beyond their wing capacity.

The daily ration of rum, or 'Nelson's blood', was a deep-rooted
tradition in the Royal Navy and was consumed at dinner – the midday
meal. The dispensing of the liquor, initiated by the pipe "Up spirits",
was a solemn ritual overseen by an officer, at least one Petty Officer
and an armed marine, and ladled out of a polished ceremonial barrel flaunting in bold, copper lettering the words: THE KING, GOD
BLESS HIM. The leading hand of each mess would be present with
a 'fanny', or saucepan, into which was carefully measured the exact
quantity of rum for decanting into cups of such of their messmates
who 'drew'. Into the fanny iced water was added in the ratio of two
parts water to one part rum. Every man 20 years of age or older was
eligible to 'draw'. Those who elected not to were paid threepence per
day extra on pay day, but they were few and far between and likely to
be regarded by their messmates with the same degree of compassion
as they would an inmate of a padded cell. Each man's standing relative to the rum ration was recorded on his station card – G for grog,
T for temperance and UA for under age.

The ritual was continued in the messes, where cups were laid out,
one for each grog rating and, under aquiline scrutiny to ensure scrupulous equality, the thick dark liquid was apportioned. The shares of
ratings on watch at the time, or otherwise absent, were withheld at the
barrel in 'neat' form, to be dispensed later. It was common practice
to reward favours or convey congratulations by offering 'sippers', or
a sip of one's tot. For a very big favour, like standing in as substitute
for a four-hour watch, the reward might be 'gulpers', or a mouthful
of the tot. In lower deck theory there were also 'grounders', whereby
the whole tot would be given, but I never encountered a case of such
colossal magnanimity and cannot contemplate a favour so enormous
as to merit it. Celebrating a birthday, or announcing the birth of an
offspring was an audacious undertaking because your messmates,

all plying you with congratulatory sippers and gulpers, dangerously impacted upon your level of sobriety. It was not uncommon to see the recipient of such largesse pass out at table, and then be carried away lifeless by messmates to some inconspicuous corner to sleep it off.

Gambling, I believe, is a failing prevalent to a greater or lesser degree among most adult members of the human family, and when circumstances conspire to bring them together in appreciable numbers this deleterious trait is bound to assert itself. Sailors huddled together on a warship are no exception. Several clandestine poker pools operated on *Cornwall*, and doubtless on other large ships as well, care being taken to ensure ample warning of the approach of anyone of menacing rank and to keep all money well concealed. The only approved form of gambling in the Navy was tombola. At tea during the first dog watch, weather and other considerations permitting, the pipe might announce that 'tombola will be played in the port waist at 16.30', whereupon a large crowd of off-watch men of all categories below commissioned rank, would forgather by the appointed time at that partly sheltered location to participate in the popular flutter. Tombola, much like the bingo played at church recreational functions, comprised the purchase of tickets with three rows of numbers on them. The 'master of ceremonies', a Petty Officer comprehensively conversant with the job, would draw out numbered tokens from a bag, and sing out the numbers as they emerged, whereupon the players would, if the numbers called appeared on their tickets, cross them off. The first player to cross off all the numbers in a row would shout out, "Here you are," and the MC would respond "And a line called." The player would have his ticket confirmed and then be paid a given small percentage of the takings. Thereafter the MC would order, "Eyes down for the house," and the game would continue until someone again shouted, "Here you are," having crossed off all the numbers on his ticket which, when verified, would yield the 'house' prize, being a substantial percentage of the takings. Then when things had settled down, the next round would commence.

Tombola was an excellent catharsis amid the humdrum, tedium, pressures and tensions of living and working under crowded, confined conditions. It was characterised by light-hearted badinage, fun and laughter, and one felt refreshed after participation, or even after only looking on.

Proficiency in fighting capability, in the expert utilization of available weaponry was, it goes without saying, the first priority in the cruiser's daily preparedness programme but there were other contingencies that also required foresight and expertise – operations that, if an emergency other than fighting arose suddenly, could be carried out quickly and effectively. Practice was therefore needed and from time to time this was arranged by means of what was termed 'evolutions'. These were imposed at the whim of Commander Fair, the ship's second-in-command, at any time of the day but usually, for reasons of convenience if not popularity, they took place during the first dog watch. Examples of evolutions were 'tow for'rard', 'tow aft' and 'collision starboard amidships'.

'Tow for'rard' envisaged our being towed by another vessel ahead of us, while 'Tow aft' visualised our towing another vessel astern of us. In both cases the evolution required, *inter alia*, the procurement and laying out on the deck, for'rard or aft as the case might be, everything needed from line-firing rifles, heaving lines, fenders, grass rope which would float on water, heavy manila rope and, most arduous of all to manhandle, steel wire hawsers up to 6½ inches in circumference. In the event this resulted in droves of men running and stumbling, panting and sweating, urged on by verbal whiplashing from POs, CPOs and divisional officers. Ropes had frequently to be hauled up manually from storage compartments below deck, provoking grumbling and wide-ranging profanity. "How much longer is this bloody rope?" "Where's the bloody end of it?" "Perhaps someone cut the end off."

When the commander was satisfied – 'You must know exactly what has to be done; where to find what you need. You may one day have to do it for real, in heavy seas and in the dark" – everything had to be retrieved, coiled up and stowed away. 'Collision and other damage control' usually involved fewer but more specialised men, bringing into play shipwrights, electricians and other artificers, the hauling into position of heavy collision mats, and assembling fire-fighting equipment. 'Use anything handy to block a hole temporarily – hammocks can be very useful'.

Another infliction, at least to many rated as such, was physical training, or PT, conducted on the quarterdeck at irregular intervals during the first dog, and also deriving from an impulsive notion on the part of the commander. Again all off-watch unfortunates, attired in shorts and plimsolls, were mustered aft and put through a vigorous routine of calisthenics by a Chief Petty Officer qualified as a PT instructor. The session ended with a fast run in single file over five or six laps around the perimeter of the quarterdeck, circumnavigating Y gun turret in the process, to the lively strains of the marine band. But not everybody regarded PT with jaundiced displeasure; Reg Peard, a friend from my home town where, as a scholar at Selborne College, he had won *Victor Ludorum*, and I were both 'keep fit' addicts and relished corporal exertion of this nature, in addition regularly repairing to the seclusion of B gun deck after dark to work out our own regimen of exercises with the aid of broomsticks and other available and adaptable paraphernalia.

Less of an infliction took place when, in mess deck parlance, 'the ghost walked' or, more properly, when pay day dawned once a month. The 'pay bob' or paymaster, a lieutenant-commander whose gold stripes on sleeve or epaulette had white strips between them to denote his function aboard, would be seated at the middle of a long table placed usually on the upper deck when in harbour, or in a windless space if at sea, assisted by officers of lower rank and 'writers'.

Hands would muster and queue in single file close by. Their names were called one at a time, whereupon each rating in turn doubled smartly to the table, halted in front of the paymaster, and removed his cap in regulation manner, placing it on the table in front of him. The rating's eligibility and amount of entitlement was established and the money due to him was placed on his cap. "Thank you, Sir," said the rating, taking up his cap and pay, then doubling away. My pay as an able seaman amounted to five pounds five shillings approximately per month, which at that stage was dispensed in South African currency, the equivalent in those bygone days of the same amount in British Sterling. Occasionally some unfortunate arriving before the paymaster would be dismissed with a 'north-easter', the letters NE, for 'not entitled', appearing opposite his name on the pay list. This might be the case for a newcomer aboard whose personal records had not yet caught up with him, or a defaulter whose pay had suffered forfeiture as punishment. For the newcomer it was a temporary, if onerous hardship; for the defaulter, 'toughies'.

> Happy is the day when a sailor gets his pay
> Rolling, rolling, rolling, rolling home.

Colombo was a pleasant and interesting port of call for sailors on shore leave, or 'liberty men' in naval terminology. For those seeking recreational activity, soccer and cricket matches were organised, while sea-bathing at palm-fringed Mount Levinia beach a few kilometres south of the city was delectable. For those interested in buying gifts and souvenirs there were shops aplenty offering ornaments, elephants carved from indigenous ebony and coconut palm, silks, trinkets of gold, silver, copper and bronze, and abundantly more but, most importantly, jewellery. Ceylon was bounteously blessed with an astonishing variety of gemstone deposits ranging from the precious ruby, sapphire and emerald to the semi-precious amethyst, tourmaline, topaz, garnet, zircon and aquamarine, among others. Pearls were fewer and for the most part were brought in from far-flung islets in the greater region, but the unofficial national gem, the moonstone, a pearly, iridescent feldspar readily converted into polished cabochons, was in great abundance.

We were warned against vendors of fake jewellery to whom guileless Jack, probably accommodating below the breastline a surfeit of beer, would be easy prey, and we were advised to make our purchases at the Navy's Fleet Club, where genuine articles were assured. "Ceylon has everything in the jewellery line," the attendant in the club's gift shop told me, "except opals, which Australia monopolises and, of course, the greatest of them all, which your country, South Africa, has so much of, the diamond." The Fleet Club was an excellently run Services institution offering leisure facilities, hot showers, good food and, for those on all-night leave, a clean bed. Another commendable establishment for the forces, run entirely by women, where non-alcoholic beverages and light repasts were served, was the SWOC Club. I don't know what the letters stood for but my wild guess would be Services Women of Ceylon (or Colombo).

Interspersed among the ordinary run of shops in the city were barbers who cut hair, trimmed beards and shaved throats, flourishing 'cut-throat' razors with reckless abandon, dental mechanics who repaired dentures 'while you wait', sidewalk tea and coffee houses, squalid drinking dens specialising in arak – a fiery spirit distilled from coco sap – and pimps on the prey to promote unsavoury diversions. There were also fortune-tellers who, for a rupee or two, unravelled the hidden secrets in one's future with the complicity of crystal balls, palmistry, cards and other mysterious devices. Most customers, I should think, sought the soothsayers' prognosis out of amused curiosity, just for the fun of it, few giving it a second thought. I certainly had never attached any credence to their divinations, but one incident of which I learned later gave me pause to ponder. During one of *Cornwall*'s several visits to Colombo four or five sailors, among them Peter Pare and Peter Versfeld, who had both joined the ship in the same draft with me, were strolling through the congested streets when, on the spur of the moment they jokingly decided to have their fortunes told by one of these pavement practitioners. They sat side by side facing the fortune-teller, who dealt with them one by one using one of the procedures described. In cheerful vein the seer prophesied all manner of good tidings – long life, abundant wealth, marital bliss, children galore and more of the same, until he came to Peter Versfeld, who was last in line. According to Pare, who related the story to me, the fortune-teller's disposition then changed abruptly to one of unease and foreboding. "No," he said sombrely. "I can't tell you your fortune," and turned away. Astonished, the sailors all pressed him insistently to explain but he simply shook his head sadly and said no more. A few months later Peter Versfeld was dead.

HMS Cornwall, *1942*

* * * * *

7

MESS DECK MISCELLANY

What shall we do with the drunken sailor?

You soon learned to know, on board ship, without being told, from roughly where the next man hailed because your ear quickly acquired the knack of recognising and associating accents. You detected the Londoner, particularly the irrepressible Cockney, who reputedly was born within hearing of Bow Bells; the Scouses from Liverpool; Geordies from Tyneside; Lankies from Lancashire; Taffies from Wales; Jocks from Scotland (the closer to John O'Groats the less intelligible to me); Paddies from Northern Ireland (and the odd one from Eire); Newfies from Newfoundland; and then of course the South Africans and Rhodesians, and so on. This wide diversity of tongue and ethnicity gave rise to frequent good-natured ribbing and argument, although at times quite heated. On one or two occasions the altercations became so inimical that the adversaries would invite one another to "step up on deck" where hostilities were renewed in a flurry of fisticuffs, though seldom enduring beyond half a minute or so before intervention by their messmates for fear of discovery by an officer, which would result in serious charges being brought. With certain 'short-fused' individuals one sensed what not to say, or when and how not to say it. It was not a good idea, especially after several beers in a canteen or after a tot of rum in the mess, and more especially for a Southern Irishman to taunt an Ulsterman with the gibe that he came from 'occupied Ireland'. That would be tempting dire fate. However, under different circumstances, in an atmosphere of equanimity, similar exchanges took place in good spirit.

"What's up Paddy? Why so glum? Don't tell me you're homesick for Ireland of all places."

"Begorra, Limey, let me recite you a rhyme."

"What?"

"Ireland was Ireland when England was a pup. Ireland will be Ireland when England's buggered up."

Fighting on board was prohibited unless conducted under proper supervision in an improvised boxing ring and with gloves. But friendly sparring was in order and Jock Davidson, who had distinguished himself as an amateur boxer in pre-war days, enticed me to ascend to the flat top of the hangar whenever opportunity arose and there, with gloves borrowed from the gymnasium, proceeded to teach me some painful rudiments of the 'noble art'.

Two British seamen who had also gained valid reputations in the boxing arena (bogus 'ex-champions' were plentiful in the Navy) were Slinger Wood in my mess and Bungey Williams, an older and most likeable man who was ever ready to show ignorant newcomers like myself how things ought to be done. Throughout the Navy certain nicknames attached automatically to particular surnames, every man with the name of Wood or Woods being unfailingly 'Slinger', and every Williams dubbed 'Bungey'. Other examples were Pincher Martin, Tug Wilson, Whacker Payne, Knocker White, Shiner Wright, Dusty Miller, Jack Frost, Spider Webb and Nobby Clark. No doubt there were more that have slipped my memory.

Mealtimes were especially conducive to argumentative banter.

"Feed the slide," called young Armitage, meaning 'Pass the butter'.

"Speak English."

"Whadder you South Africans know about English?"

"Well, South Africans speak better English than the English."

"Ach man, sis man, tickey man, bioscope man," mocked Armitage, mimicking South African expressions.

Others joined in:

"You colonials should come to Blighty to get civilised – see the green fields of Old England."

"Better still the braes o' Bonnie Scotland," interjected a man from beyond the Cheviot Hills.

"See what? You can't see bugger all; it's always pissing down with rain."

"Rain is good for you, mate. Good for things that grow, like wheat, roses and daffodils; good for birds and animals in the wild."

"What animals? All you've got in the UK are field mice and hedgehogs. South Africa has the largest variety of wild animals in the world."

"Och, aye. Some o' them joined the Navy."

"Rhodesia beats them all," piped up Davies, a hefty sailor who hailed from north of the Limpopo. "It's God's own country."

"Aye but ye ken why, don't ye?"

"Why?"

"Because the devil winna hae it."

At such times Vere Parkins from Cape Town would affect the superior air of a university don. "Is this a dagger which I see before me?" he would muse, holding up his table knife.

"What sort of a question is that?"

"Question? To be or not to be, THAT is the question."

"There goes Mr bloody Shakespeare again, wafflin' his high falutin' arse off."

"I'm quoting from Macbeth and Hamlet, my dear man," derided Parkins, drawing himself erect and peering disdainfully down his nose, "something you sods should know more about – you should take great pride and joy reading your famous compatriot, William Shakespeare."

"Rubbish! Most of the time you can't understand what the bastard is trying to say."

"That's because Shakespeare used picturesque speech, telling things in a roundabout way."

"How do you mean, roundabout way?"

"Well, let's say you meet up with a bow-legged chap in the street. You would just say, 'Here comes a bandy-legged man'."

"And Shakespeare?"

"Shakespeare would say, 'Lo, what manner of man is this who carries his balls in parentheses?'"

The broadcasting system was an important factor in mess deck life, particularly during the 'off-duty' dogs. Apart from announcements made from time to time, as for instance, 'Clocks will be put forward one hour at 24.00' if the ship was steaming an easterly course (and 'put back' if proceeding westwards), recorded music was played from a sizeable stockpile aboard, interspersed with relayed radio programmes from the BBC. The pervading buzz of conversation would be stilled abruptly when the 6.00 pm news from London was broadcast, preceded at that stage of the war by the stirring strains of 'Hearts of Oak'. Later, after the tide of hostilities had turned in favour of the Allies, the theme melody heralding the news changed to Purcell's 'Lillibullero'. The men listened attentively to the polished rendering of bulletins by the newsreaders, including Richard Dimbleby, a relative of our shipmate Ken Dimbleby from Port Elizabeth, of whom mention is made in the preface and elsewhere in this book. Events around the world covered in the newscasts were followed intently with the aid of a wall map noting place names, many familiar, others never heard before, like Kiev, Kharkov and Smolensk. The seemingly unstoppable German juggernaut was rumbling relentlessly onward towards Moscow, the fall of which, it was feared, might signal the end of Soviet resistance.

The overall bleak outlook was brightened in November by General

Auchinleck's early successes with 'Operation Crusader' in Cyrenaica but that too met with reverses, and ground to a halt. Despite wartime constraints sporting events in Britain were by no means totally abandoned, and discussions of these were frequently broadcast from London. British sailors in particular listened eagerly to accounts featuring their sporting heroes, like boxers Jack London, Eric Boon and the up-and-coming sensation Freddie Mills; and also from other sports: Stanley Matthews, Fred Perry, Denis Compton, Len Hutton and Sidney Wooderson, thus setting off spirited confabulation and argument at the mess table. Then there were the entertainment celebrities of stage and film: Tommy Trinder, Stanley Holloway, George Formby, Gracie Fields, Vera Lynn, Anne Shelton and many others.

When the radio was silent conversation in the mess turned to other interests: girlfriends, or 'parties', as the British matelot tended to call them, pre-war jobs and, of course, wartime experience prior to joining *Cornwall*. The latter, as becomes youthful exuberance, was frequently exaggerated and, in not a few cases, undoubtedly fabrication. I recall one occasion when a stroppy youngster, after lavishly recounting expletive-laden tales of his exploits to his messmates, turned to an older man, a three-badge AB with more than twelve years' service who had been regarding him silently and analytically.

"How about you, Stripey," asked the loudmouthed lad. "Why so quiet? Haven't you been no place in this war? Spent your time just swingin' round a buoy, have you?"

"Sonny," replied the older man with ill-disguised disdain, "I was in Baghdad when you were in dad's bag."

The use of foul and blasphemous language among the rank and file was fairly general and in some cases it seemed every sixth or seventh word spoken had a copulative or genital connotation. Verbal exchanges were particularly lewd and polluted when over-inebriated liberty men returned from shore leave. There were, of course, some 'naval gentlemen' on the mess deck, albeit a small minority – sailors like Reg Peard, Peter Pare, Monty Kirsten and Ivor Midlane, to name a few – who never uttered a coarse or blasphemous word, never drank to excess and were always congenial and obliging, which was why I managed to get on so well with them: it's called the 'attraction of opposites'.

Boozing was a sailor's likeliest hazard ashore. As often as not his first stop on terra firma was a canteen or bar, where he commenced the business of 'oilin' the engine-room'. If he was able, as in most cases, to moderate his intake (by sailor standards) and then proceed to find something to eat, ending up an hour or so later lustily singing 'Down at the Hole in the Wall' on the liberty boat returning to his ship, then all was well. If, on the other hand, he over-imbibed and, say, became a rowdy nuisance, became involved in a fight, passed out in a toilet, was picked up by a naval or military patrol or, worse still, by the local police, then he faced a range of serious repercussions such as confinement in cells, detention barracks, drastic curtailment of leave, docking of pay and demotion.

Liberty men proceeded ashore in 'boats' even when the ship was tied up at a wharf and no boat in the normal meaning of the word was involved. Depending upon circumstances there could on the day be two or even three 'boats', identified as 'first boat' at, perhaps, 1300 hours, 'second boat' at 1500, and 'last boat' at 1700. Before being allowed ashore, liberty men were mustered on deck in ranks near the gangway, their station cards were surrendered to the duty Petty Officer, and they themselves were meticulously inspected by the officer of the watch or his deputy. Any component of uniform not spotlessly clean, any cap not on straight, shoes not bright and shiny, any unshaven chin, would incur disqualification and its hapless owner would miss the boat. The officer of the watch would be in the offing when the men returned from shore leave, but then sensibly assumed a more detached and tolerant attitude. Jack would be allowed to proceed provided he saluted the quarterdeck as he stepped aboard, did not appear too dishevelled, kept a still tongue and seemed, without subjection to close scrutiny, capable of walking a reasonably straight line, albeit perhaps with a mate close in on either side. The words of the song 'What shall We Do with the Drunken Sailor' must frequently have crossed the officers' minds on these occasions but even overly-inebriated men instinctively pulled themselves somewhat together in order to pass muster when returning aboard. But now and then a hardcase individual had to be dealt with, drunk and disorderly, recalcitrant and swearing, possibly bloodied, cap missing and vowing 'fill you in' retribution to all and sundry. He would have to be manhandled below and locked in a cell for the night pending rueful arraignment next day.

After such an occurrence one morning at early deck-scrubbing time a mate of mine asked the Chief Petty Officer who had been on gangway duty the night before:

"Chief, I hear your lads had to put Big Bob in cells last night."

"That's right."

"What was the trouble?"

"'E was creatin' a riot, as usual."

"Was he sober?"

"Don't make me laugh. 'Im, sober? 'E was so pissed 'e'd 'ave took out 'is prick to 'ave a shit."

The day I had hoped for dawned at last – applicants being invited to undertake an AA3 gunnery course, that is, to qualify as an anti-aircraft gunner, third class – and I submitted my name with alacrity. If successful, my action station would be changed from Y shellroom deep down aft near the keel, which I regarded with claustrophobic disquiet, to one of the anti-aircraft mountings on the upper decks, in the open air, which I reasoned was far preferable as a venue for departing this life. My application was accepted along with about ten others to make up a class for daily forenoon instruction and drill. The practical side of the course concentrated on the eight 4-inch, high-angle guns mounted in pairs on four emplacements, and on the two revolving platforms, each with a mounting of eight pom-pom machineguns amidships, one bearing to port and the other to starboard. Both weapons have been described in some detail earlier in this narrative.

The course was overseen by the gunnery officer, the dapper and extremely competent Lieut. Streatfield, and on successful completion I was allocated to pom-poms under command of CPO Standing, who posted me to the port mounting as a feeder of belted ammunition to gun barrels on the fore end, a position where, I surmise, he deemed I would cause least trouble.

The Navy took considerable pride in their magnum mountings of eight-barrelled pom-poms, and indeed they were potentially formidable instruments of destruction. Each of the eight guns fired 2 lb explosive shells of 1.5-inch calibre, graze-fused in the nose for instantaneous detonation after leaving the muzzle upon contact with any object, even fabric, the eight collectively delivering 720 rounds per minute, spreading to form a lethal pattern through which, it was believed, no approaching aircraft could fly unscathed. Awesome indeed, but the sad truth was that they also had significant limitations. Firstly, on *Cornwall*, the port and starboard pom-poms were sited too deeply inboard between the bridge superstructure and the aircraft hangar, which restricted their firing arcs to little more than 100 degrees on either side. They were completely 'blind' for approximately 40 degrees to either side of the ship's prow, thus a crucial 80 degrees, head-on impotency. A similar, if less pronounced shortcoming obtained astern.

Secondly, and most importantly, aiming and maintaining the guns accurately on target demanded great skill and co-ordination on the part of both the layer, who controlled elevation and depression, or the vertical movement of the guns, and the trainer, who regulated their lateral or horizontal motion. The aiming device used by both the layer and the trainer, the latter also firing the guns, was the then standard, though somewhat antiquated cartwheel sight consisting of concentric rings with radiating spokes, and the endeavour of the two men, operating in close collaboration, was to keep the nose of an attacking aircraft on the outer ring and pointing directly towards the centre spot of the cartwheel. While this was not too difficult when practising on a drogue towed behind one of our own slow aeroplanes on a steady, roughly parallel course, it was an entirely different matter when encountering fast, highly manoeuvrable aircraft, and if several of these were flying within the approach sector simultaneously, the layer or trainer might well be unsure as to which enemy plane the other sought to engage. Thus single-minded, effective action was compromised. The pom-poms were best suited to defence against torpedo-bombers, which needed a few seconds of straight, steady flying, low above the water in their beam-on approach towards the ship before releasing their 'tin fish'. During those few seconds they were at their most vulnerable and relatively easy to be hit, but against fighters and dive-bombers, whirling in from different, high angles, it could be pandemonium.

Thirdly, although the pom-pom mountings, bulky as they were, operated smoothly and nimbly under power, their efficiency was abruptly and seriously impaired when, as was apt to happen in action, electric circuits were damaged and controls had to be switched from power to manual, causing performance to be slow and cumbersome as well as tiresome for the gun crew. Fourthly, clear and sustained visibility was a problem during operations because with eight compactly grouped cannon firing incessantly the target tended to become extensively if not totally obscured by flash and smoke notwithstanding conical muzzle-fitted flash suppressors. Later anti-aircraft installations in this category were inclined to be single or twin gun mountings, much lighter and with both lateral and elevation movement in the hands of one man, to markedly greater advantage. To a large extent aiming techniques also changed in favour of visually directing the stream of shells at the target by what was termed 'hosepipe firing'. This was accomplished by ensuring that every fourth round in the feeder ammunition belt was a 'tracer', which left a trail of smoke in its wake.

Pom-poms were an invaluable defence against surface craft at short range, such as motor torpedo boats of the German E Boat type. However, as the war progressed new weapons were increasingly introduced on naval ships, notably the Swedish-developed Bofors and the German-invented, Swiss-patented Oerlikon guns, with improved results. What mattered to me was that my action station now provided me with an open-air position, 'with a view', although without much protection against the elements in times of inclemency.

At action stations one was expected to don anti-flash gear, balaclava type helmets and long-sleeved gloves, to wear the inflatable Mae West lifebelt and, in exposed positions, the regulation 'tin hat' which had undergone no change since the First World War, the gas mask in its canvas satchel being either slung over the shoulder or placed close at hand. At 'cruising stations' none of these items had to be worn but needed nevertheless to be easily accessible. However, the regulation concerning gas masks tended to be more disregarded than observed, it being a bothersome encumbrance most of the time.

The big comfort at night cruising stations, and also at night action stations if nothing untoward was happening, when conditions were generally cheerless and cold, was 'kye' (my spelling, pronounced as in 'sky'). Kye was regarded with appreciative esteem throughout the Navy. From every group during night watches a rating would be despatched to the galley from whence he presently reappeared with a 'fanny', or saucepan, full of steaming hot kye and two or three enamel mugs, he having borrowed these utensils from his mess. Kye, or in layman's terms simply cocoa, was prepared nightly by the galley staff in a large vat by grating huge slabs of dark brown, bitter-to-the-taste chocolate into boiling water and kept simmering throughout the dark hours and ready for ladling out. A mug of piping hot kye, with one's fingers wrapped around it for warmth at around 02.00 during the middle watch was really something to be savoured – like manna from heaven.

* * * * *

8

ROBINSON CRUSOE REVISITED

("Hope they're not planning to have us for lunch")

Cornwall was given an unusual assignment towards the end of September 1941: escorting supply ships to the Maldive islands, of whose existence the lower deck had, up to that point, been almost totally oblivious. "Where the hell is that?" was the general query heard when our destination was piped over the broadcast system, and men set about trying to locate the islands on the wall map, not with immediate success. "What the hell for?" was the next cry.

The Maldives are a chain of about 2,000 small coral islands stretching north to south, varying 400 to 600 miles south-west of Ceylon, mostly comprising atolls, or coral reefs roughly circular in shape, having risen from the solid foundation of extinct volcanic vents protruding from the seabed. The coral perimeters of the atolls are usually broken on the windward side, forming an opening or passage to and from the lagoon within, through which its waters are refreshed and nourished by oceanic tidal flow. (What a boon encyclopaedias are!)

Most of the islands are too small for permanent habitation and even the largest are barely a couple of miles along and across. Our specific destination was in due course announced as Addu Atoll, one of the biggest in the chain at its southern extremity, situated just below the equator at approximately 1 degree south 73 degrees east, its special attraction from the Navy's perspective being its vast interior lagoon of acceptably navigable depth, accessed through an equally traversable entrance channel. Indeed it was spacious enough to provide uncongested anchorage for a large fleet of warships. First impressions were of an enormous expanse of emerald-green water, crystal clear to astonishing depths and illusory to the extent that ships or boats at a distance appeared at times to be levitated above the surface as in a mirage, and of gleaming white sandy beaches fringed with palm trees and scrub foliage.

We learned presently that a naval and airbase was being established at Addu and at Gan, an adjoining island, and that the ships we had escorted thither contained material and supplies for that purpose. They were in fact the forerunners of others to come, including tankers and depot repair ships for replenishment and maintenance of naval vessels expected to put in at the anchorage from time to time. The base, we were informed, was officially codenamed Port T and was meant to be top secret, and we were enjoined strictly to avoid mention of it when on shore leave at other ports of call, particularly in bars and canteens, where liquor indulgence tended to loosen tongues.

Cornwall would during her week-long stay render assistance in whatever ways possible including the detachment of working parties on shore every day, to whose ranks I found myself assigned. Shipwrights and others with technical skills were organised to help in their specialist manner but in my case, my useful attributes and talents having been accurately identified and evaluated, the task designated was portage or, to be specific, the hefting and carrying of ponderous stores of all kinds from where they were deposited on the beach, through the jungle to whatever point on the island where they might be needed. It was hot, humid and arduous labour, with sweat running off our bodies in torrents, but at least it was a break from normal shipboard routine, something completely different, even interesting, and generally the mood was jocular. Dressed in any old makeshift rags and tatters, winding our way through the undergrowth in single file carrying boxes, bags and articles of all sorts on our backs, shoulders and heads, dirty and unkempt, we certainly looked a curious, comical bunch.

"What would your missus think if she saw you now, Shiner?"

"... And smellin' like a Sumo wrestler's jockstrap!"

In the oppressive heat even scant clothing tended to be stripped to the minimum. One rating, I seem to recall, was eventually clad only in the ID disc compulsorily strung around his neck.

"Robinson Crusoe returned to his island," observed one.

"Well, I wish his Man Friday would return too and take this bloody crate off me."

"Say not the struggle naught availeth," quoth Parkins.

"Hope the cannibals don't return."

"No such luck, mate; there the cannibals are, over there" – and a short distance away a row of black islanders stood looking at us inquisitively and somewhat warily. This particular group were clad in little more than loincloths and one might imagine that Daniel Defoe's 18th-century novel could well have been influenced by people such as these. We waved to them and they grinned back broadly.

"Hope they're not planning to have us for lunch!"

The native population of the Maldive archipelago numbered in all about 90,000, and were mostly of Muslim persuasion and of mixed Arab and Singhalese stock. Their lifestyle was primitive, living in huts constructed from indigenous saplings and palm leaves; their food edible roots, millet, coconuts and fish, which were in abundance. Those with whom we came in contact displayed friendly yet distant interest in the rowdy, fair-skinned strangers who had invaded and disturbed the tranquillity of their tropical habitat, but they were not intrusive. A few among them had obviously had, somewhere, a measure of education and one individual that I remember did approach us as we stretched out under palm trees during a 'dinner' break. He had with him an old school type exercise book and a pencil and, squatting down on his haunches in the manner at which Indians are adept (but which if emulated by a European would soon threaten ligamental dislocation and skeletal deformity), he indicated that he sought some enlightenment. He knew no English but, smiling amicably, pointed enquiringly at a stone on the ground. When someone ventured to say 'stone' he repeated the word once or twice, then wrote it into his exercise book, translated by sound into what appeared to be Arabic characters. He then did the same with 'sand' and a number of other things conveniently at hand, such as 'tree', 'water', 'leg', 'arm', 'nose', 'shirt' and 'shoe', and in that manner compiled a mini, acoustic-related English vocabulary.

Among our immediate observations upon coming into contact with the islanders was that many of them suffered from grossly swollen legs, particularly below their knees, the skin appearing discoloured and leathery. This, we learned from the ship's medics, was a disease called 'elephantiasis', the name obviously deriving from a resemblance of the diseased limbs to the legs of an elephant. The condition (my encyclopaedia again to the rescue) is caused by lymphatic obstruction by a tropical nematode parasite, whatever that means.

One of the more specialised tasks undertaken by *Cornwall* at Port T was surveying the great lagoon for underwater obstructions. In particular the entrance channel to the anchorage was inspected to ensure that there were no hidden hazards and to that end the ship's diving team was called into operation. This was conducted from one of the ship's cutters, an oar-propelled boat, into which was loaded a bulky pressure pump and related appurtenances. A leading seaman holding a diving certificate donned a cumbrous, watertight suit, the headpiece of which was a large copper detachable spherical helmet with a glass visor in front to see through. Two rubber tubes protruded from the helmet to allow the transmission of fresh air to the diver within and for the expulsion of exhaled breath which, when the diver was submerged, rose to the surface in a stream of bubbles. The inflow tube extended into the pump in the cutter, which was activated by two large rotator handles, one on either side, operated by two seamen continually while the diving suit, with helmet screwed on had a diver in occupation. Manning the pump handles, rotating non-stop during the unrelenting heat of an equatorial day, was one of the least sought-after jobs at Port T, and I, true to my brand of luck, was roped in for that as well before our sojourn at the atoll came to an end.

Relaxation was provided for the working parties at cessation of a day's labour – particularly gratifying for those who enjoyed swimming in the superbly clear waters along the coral reefs inshore, where the array of colour and grotesque shapes under water was a wonderland to experience. Strong swimmers like Ken Collier and Ian Keith from Port Elizabeth excelled in diving down and pulling themselves along from one coral configuration to the next, eventually to resurface sixty or more yards away.

When *Cornwall* eventually weighed anchor and steamed slowly towards the atoll's exit, sailors standing at the rail regarded the receding white beaches fringed with green foliage with mixed feelings. After the breathless humidity ashore it was pleasing to savour the refreshing breeze caused by the ship's movement, but the week's interlude had been a pleasant change nevertheless.

"How many years," questioned one, "did Robinson Crusoe spend on an island like that?"

"He was on a different kind of island, with mountains and valleys and things, not flat like this one."

"Come on, you twerps. Robinson Crusoe is just a character in a story. He wasn't real."

"Yes, but I think the story was based on some other bugger who really did get marooned on an island somewhere."

Speculation by a leading seaman close by was more pragmatic. "Whose bright idea was it anyway to build a naval base in this isolated god-forsaken place?"

The Maldives today have been developed into a tourist paradise, if one believes the travel brochures, and I presume Addu Atoll has been made part of it. Perhaps a casino, with neon lights glittering, gambling facilities abuzz and neoteric music blaring, now marks the spot where we sweated and toiled like pack donkeys sixty-odd years ago. 'Progress', they call it. Neither do I know whose 'bright idea' it was to establish a naval base there sixty-odd years ago, but I firmly believe that, whoever he was, a monument on the island today proclaiming in his honour would be incalculably well deserved. Such a memorial could then be viewed by our present-day tourist, attired in wide-brimmed panama, floral flapover shirt, Bermuda shorts and sandals, festooned with dark Polaroids, binoculars and zoom-lensed camera while sipping iced pineapple juice through a straw. He might pause momentarily before it, absently read the inscription, perhaps by force of habit, even photograph it – and then move idly on without the foggiest comprehension of its significance.

* * * * *

9

NIPPONESE DIMENSION

But what about Jappy Jap Jappy,
Smiling so happy hap happy,
The jolly Jack Tar
From the islands afar
In the East on the mappy map mappy
                    Adapted from a music hall ditty

Armed conflict during the first two years of World War II was waged predominantly across continental Europe, supplemented by significant engagements in the Mediterranean, North Africa, on the Atlantic and in the air. *Cornwall's* lower deck followed these events as broadcast daily in BBC news bulletins and portrayed in newspapers, as and when mailbags caught up with the ship, with keen interest and lively discussions ensuing. But generally, in our Indian Ocean backwater, a sense of detachment pervaded, of distance, of apparent restriction to minor roles peripheral to the centre stage, 'far from the sound of shot and shell', except for one notable contingency which, if it materialized, could change the nature of events in our part of the world abruptly and dramatically, one factor which dangled above our heads like Damocles' sword – entrance on stage by the Land of the Rising Sun. Would Japan enter the fray and, if she ranged up on the side of the German–Italian Axis, how formidable an adversary would she be, what strategy would she espouse, what objectives pursue? Certainly the Indian Ocean theatre and its maritime community would be drawn inexorably closer to the reality of war and the Royal Navy would most decidedly not, as in the words of the old patriotic song, be "lacking foes to scorn".

It is a maxim of international diplomatic philosophy that enemies of today might well be needed tomorrow as friends and allies but, alas, the reverse is also true and today's comrades-in-arms could, in this uncertain world, be baying for our blood tomorrow. Japan entered the First World War on the side of Britain and her allies almost from day one and within two months had laid siege to the German naval base and fortress at Tsingtao in northern China, forcing its capitulation. After the war, however, the pendulum of allegiance began to swing the other way, with relationships cooling increasingly between Japan and her former wartime allies, in particular the United States, eventually to the point of hostility. The main bone of contention then was China.

Japan, comprising four main islands and numerous smaller ones in a long chain off the eastern coast of continental Asia, and wanting in natural resources and space for expansion, had in 1931 embarked upon establishing interests in Manchuria, the vast, northern mainland territory rich in coal and iron which Japan desperately needed for her burgeoning industries. Taking advantage of local political turmoil she rapidly gained control in the region, sending in army units to protect her rail, shipping and mining investments there, eventually installing a puppet government in 1932 which proclaimed independence from China. These developments caused hackles to rise in the West but under the constraints of the Great Depression worldwide no countermeasures were taken at that stage.

July 1937 saw the start of the 'Chinese Incident', sparked by a skirmish between Japanese and Nationalist Chinese troops, which rapidly escalated into a full-scale offensive and invasion of China. Two years later the situation deteriorated further when the United

States, upon whom Japan was heavily dependent for steel and other strategic materials, took steps to abrogate their mutual commercial treaty with the ominous prospect of launching an embargo. The outbreak of World War II in Europe at that time had the effect of distracting western attention from the Far East, thus providing impetus to the Japanese drive southward along China's seaboard, and the spectacular successes of the German armed forces in 1940 encouraged Tokyo to seek and exploit new opportunities.

After the surrender of France in June of that year, the Low Countries having succumbed earlier, Britain stood alone against the might of the Third Reich, and was severely weakened following the evacuation of her Expeditionary Force from Dunkirk and forfeiture of all military equipment she had had on French soil. In the bleak days, weeks and months that followed many around the world, not least the Japanese (but excepting the British themselves), believed that Britain faced inevitable defeat before long. In the Far East and Indian Ocean neither France nor the Netherlands were in any position to defend their possessions in the region, and it was left to the Royal Navy to keep a protective surveillance over them while supporting, somewhat tenuously, her own sparse garrisons and air force squadrons. In her parlous situation Britain acceded to Japan's demand that she close the Burma Road – China's supply artery from the sea – and the Vichy government of vanquished France allowed Japan, under duress, to occupy the northern area of French Indo-China for inclusion in what Japan called the 'Greater East Asia Co-prosperity Sphere'. Reacting to these moves, the United States stopped the sale of aircraft and aviation spirit to Japan who, doggedly undeterred, then entered into a pact with the German–Italian Axis, then bringing into being the ominous Tripartite Alliance hoping, apparently, that this would deter the USA from further antagonistic measures.

In July 1941 Japan heightened the tension by assuming full control of Indo-China, nominally in partnership with the Vichy, thus acquiring a strategic base from which to launch incursions westward into Thailand, Malaya and Burma if circumstances called for such. At this the United States, alarmed at the threat posed, finally 'shut the door', freezing all Japanese assets in the US and implementing a lethal embargo on vital oil supplies. This led to the fall of the Japanese government and its replacement by another headed by the erstwhile war minister, the belligerent and intractable General Hideki Tojo. Then only a miracle of diplomacy and mutual accommodation could avert a cataclysm.

Cognisance and comprehension of the implications of these developments largely eluded us on *Cornwall's* lower deck, despite our lively interest in the war's unfolding progression as radioed news bulletins at the time focussed predominantly on the European theatre and in particular the Soviet Union, against whom Hitler on 22 June had unleashed Operation Barbarossa with the full might of his armed forces along a vast front – the greatest invasion in history up to that point. The weeks and months that followed brought sensational German victories and territorial gains but by November the dreaded Russian winter, aided by stiffening resistance before and behind the invader, brought forward mobility, temporarily at least, to a halt. Nevertheless Russia was in dire straits, with Leningrad isolated and under siege, and Moscow threatened along its distant approaches on three sides. The fall of Moscow, the capital and nerve centre of the nation, would, it was widely believed, have spelt defeat for the Soviet Union. Indeed this might have happened had commencement of Barbarossa not providentially been delayed by six weeks due to insurrection in the German-controlled Balkans.

The possibility of Japan taking up arms on the side of Germany and Italy did not alarm us sailors unduly. She probably wouldn't go that far anyway, we thought, because the United States and the British Empire were too powerful to tangle with and were known to have already taken countermeasures in this regard. President Roosevelt had in 1940 ordered the main base of the American Pacific fleet to be transferred from San Diego on the west coast to Pearl Harbor, west of Honolulu on the Island of Oahu in the Hawaiian Archipelago, a move he hoped would discourage any Japanese adventurism southwards, and in the following year the dynamic Douglas MacArthur was given command of all US Army forces in the Far East, with the special assignment to strengthen defences in the Philippines. Churchill, for his part, resolved, against the advice of the Admiralty, to send a strong naval detachment to Singapore as a further deterrent, the core components being the battle-cruiser *Repulse*, at that time already in the Indian Ocean; the newest battleship *Prince of Wales*; and the modern aircraft-carrier *Indomitable*. The last-named had, however, to be held back to undergo unforeseen repairs. In stark contrast to the rigidly promulgated 'Don't talk about ships or shipping' directive the despatch of *Prince of Wales* enjoyed ample publicity, apparently to leave Tokyo in no doubt about the build-up of strength on its western flank and British determination to utilise it if deemed necessary. En route the battleship docked at Cape Town, where the local population were soon abuzz with curiosity. Admiral Tom Phillips, commander of the British force, took the opportunity of flying to Pretoria to confer with General Smuts who, with characteristic astuteness and foresight, warned the admiral against imprudent enterprise, pointing to the virtual absence of protective air cover in the Malaysian region where the assumed enemy, Japan, apart from his ample naval resources, was already strongly established in Indo-China and on Hainan Island.

In the forecabin flat amidships – a large open space available for church services and other gatherings when the weather was unkind, or for recreation – photographs, sketches and 'silhouette' reproductions of enemy ships, aircraft, uniforms and weaponry, including Japanese, were drawing-pinned on noticeboards for study and general information. Everybody who manned anti-aircraft guns was expected to familiarise himself with the appearance and features of hostile aircraft, and in this way we became acquainted in rudimentary fashion with some of Japan's warplanes. For ease of pronunciation these were usually known by elementary nicknames such as, for example, 'Dave', a reconnaissance seaplane; 'Kate', a naval torpedo-bomber; 'Betty', a high-level bomber distinguished by its large tail-fin; and 'Val', their redoubtable naval dive-bomber with fixed undercarriage similar to the German Stuka. Most famous of them all was the 'Zero' ubiquitous high-performance fighter, later dubbed 'Zeke' by the Americans.

Comments expressed round and about the noticeboards were generally not very complimentary. "Forget it, mate. The Japs are just copyists; can't make the real thing", and "How good are these aeroplanes really, made of bamboo and rice paper", and "Look at them battlewagons, top-heavy like that bastard there, whatsisname, 'Ise', its control tower like a bleedin' skyscraper. One hit and I reckon she'll keel over, bottoms up" and so on. A rather different picture was portrayed by an officer, a former naval attaché, who had had as close an insight into the Japanese navy as was possible for a westerner up to that time. He had been invited aboard *Cornwall* to give a talk on the subject based on his own experience. Much of what existed and was happening, he told those of us assembled, was concealed behind a curtain of secrecy, and those Japanese in the know about anything outside the obvious were disingenuously tight-lipped while in the company of westerners. That Japan had a large and powerful navy was common knowledge, and also that much had been done to improve and modernise her older fighting ships. Less was known about newer additions to her fleet but patently much attention was being given to developing their naval air arm. Their gunnery capability was of a high order and their equipment dependable, in some respects superior to our own. The quality of their fighting men was thought to be good, their training commendable, their officers competent and upper-echelon staff work "excellent, as good probably as the German, which was considered of the best".

It would soon be realised that the Japanese antagonists were indeed outstanding, often fanatically so, making up in toughness, resourcefulness and endurance for what they might have lacked in stature. It would also emerge that, copyists or not, their naval air capability at that point in time was the best in the world, their naval aircraft superior, their aviators fearless and better trained, and their techniques in aerial assault and in night fighting unsurpassed. In addition, some of their equipment could not be matched, for example optical instruments, while their 'Long Lance' torpedo outshone all others, both in running performance and explosive power. But these were lessons that, at that time, were still to be learnt 'the hard way' by Britain and her allies.

So it was that as December dawned, heralding yuletide, the season of goodwill, the last two major antagonists of the Second World War confronted each other from across the ring, waiting for the gong to sound and reverberate around the global arena. It had taken Uncle Sam a long time to reach that degree of commitment. The nation had historically been strongly isolationist dating back virtually to Independence and the subsequent Monroe Doctrine – America for the Americans, no toleration of outside interference and, conversely, no American participation in foreign conflicts. Sympathy among the great majority of Americans lay strongly with Britain and her allies, coupled with an aversion to Nazi Germany but, short of the United States herself being attacked, the abiding policy of non-involvement prevailed. Accordingly, though deeply troubled, she did not actively intervene when Germany overran Denmark, Norway, the Low Countries and France, nor when the Soviets assailed Finland. Indeed, in preceding years she had not actively intervened in the Spanish Civil War, or when Italy subjugated Abyssinia or when Germany annexed Czechoslovakia, and had not in fact been a member of the League of Nations.

Both Renaud, prime minister of France, and Churchill had urged Roosevelt, who was fiercely pro-Allies, to declare war on Germany, for which plausible justification would not have been difficult to conceive, but he was effectively stymied by an isolationist-dominated Congress and, in the case of France, a declaration would have come too late to save her anyway. The American president determined nonetheless to give Britain every assistance possible short of war, realising along with his countrymen that if the island kingdom fell, the outlook on the farther side of the Atlantic would be bleak indeed, possibly irreversibly so. He therefore walked a tightrope of providing Britain with critically needed materials while maintaining the rudiments of neutrality. A policy of 'cash and carry' had already been adopted by America, followed later when Britain's dwindling financial resources became precarious, by the 'lend-lease' bill which enabled Britain, in effect, to receive vital supplies without immediately paying therefor, eliciting the accusation, though never challenged in a court of law, that it was an evasion of the Neutrality Act of 1835 as amended.

Another brush with legality was the swapping of fifty antiquated US destroyers for a number of British bases in the western Atlantic, which as the U-boat menace spread, had been proclaimed by the United States a 'neutrality zone', extended later to include Greenland. The compelling need to bolster Britain's capacity to withstand the German menace of invasion induced Roosevelt to seek, and attain, an unprecedented third term as president although still baulked by a doggedly isolationist American public, 67 per cent of whom favoured all aid to Britain, though only 27 per cent were prepared to send their sons to fight at her side. A startling manifestation of the nation's determination to avoid putting American lives on the line occurred in August 1941 when its domestic conscription period expired and the bill authorising its extension was passed in the House of Representatives by a majority of just one vote. In other words, less than four months before the Pearl Harbor onslaught the greater part of America's armed forces was saved from abolition by a solitary vote!

In the first week of December, however, it seemed inevitable that the entire perspective of American neutrality was set to crack. All indications increasingly pointed to war with Japan, which logically would extend to war with Germany and Italy, the other members of the Tripartite Alliance. Nevertheless the United States was careful to the last to observe neutrality at least to the point of non-belligerence, and would not be the first to cross the line, and not shoot until she herself was shot at. She was in that regard in the relatively comfortable position of being able to sit back and await developments, but not so Japan, who was then in the grip of a strangulating embargo, most crucially that on oil, without which her immense industrial machinery would, within a foreseeably short period, grind to a halt. Both countries, at the eleventh hour, served ultimatums on the other, somewhat hypocritically because the terms stipulated in each patently left no room for compromise or manoeuvre, no provision for preserving national pride, for saving face, therefore neither ultimatum was fruitful.

The 'twelfth hour' struck on the morning of December 7 1941.

* * * * *

10

HAWAIIAN HAVOC

("Don't worry about it")

I have always had high admiration for America, specifically the United States, a great and immensely powerful nation, a great 'do and die' land of bounteous resources, phenomenal industrial capacity (what other country could produce 'liberty ships' at a rate of one every four days?) and spectacular achievements generally. But, by way of modification, she was, in relation to the war situation in 1941, a dozing giant, superficially in readiness yet in some vital aspects gravely unprepared, deficient in her overview of possibilities, complacently sitting back and waiting for something to happen. It did – where least expected, and it took a severe mugging to awaken the leviathan, wounded and bleeding, to the light of reality. Much the same penchant for untimely slumber is endemic in Great Britain, who historically suffers a bloody nose before galvanising into action.

Washington had no illusions – neither had Whitehall – war clouds were gathering. Imperial Japan was in the grip of an American embargo, backed by Britain and the Netherlands, which, if not removed, would within a relatively short period bring her as an industrial and military power to her knees. Failing an acceptable negotiated solution, her alternative to war, whether on a total or limited scale, was abject submission and humiliation, including the withdrawal of Japanese troops from China and other mainland territories

– impossible to contemplate. Armed conflict was therefore no longer a question of 'if', but of 'when and where'.

Augmenting this prediction American Naval Intelligence, which had broken the Japanese diplomatic code, was deciphering wireless communication between Tokyo and her embassies abroad, most importantly that in Washington, from which it could be deduced with certainty that something momentous was in the offing, even revealing the deadline date for decision taking, namely 29 November. The US War Department accordingly despatched an urgent warning to Hawaii and other Pacific commands to expect hostile action at any moment, and urged appropriate precautionary measures. The Navy Department backed this up with its own strong directive in similar vein to all its commanders in the region. At the highest level Roosevelt cabled Churchill.

Yet American prognostication among their top brass was, as regards the likely Japanese focus point in opening their offensive, astonishingly lacking in vision and imagination. Of all the locations considered probable targets, the least feasible in their estimation should in fact have topped their priority list, namely Hawaii, specifically Pearl Harbor and environs, the source and concentration of American power in the Pacific and, conversely, where the most strategically devastating blow could be struck. But this apparently did not seriously impinge on their calculations. On the one hand underestimation of Japanese capability probably still influenced their thinking at that stage – disbelief that Japan would, or could, mount an offensive on massive scale 3,400 miles from home. Surely, it was assumed, she would strive at the outset to seize and secure areas nearer at hand – the Dutch East Indies, Malaya, Thailand, the Philippines – which in any case were the repositories of the raw materials she so desperately needed. Backing that assumption, the defensive capacity of the Philippines under MacArthur was being steadily strengthened by a build-up of military equipment, notably aircraft, and by recruitment and training of Filipino forces on the ground. This, it was optimistically believed, would provide a bulwark against Japanese aggression southwards while the British for their part were doing what they could, with resources they could ill afford to spare, to counter advances westwards. At the eleventh hour the new battle-ship *Prince of Wales* and battle-cruiser *Repulse* arrived at Singapore.

These precautionary measures, as we have seen, did not directly include Pearl Harbor, the supreme stronghold and nerve centre of the entire Pacific theatre, due to its remote position, yet the simple truth, which America should have identified and anticipated months earlier, is that an adversary, particularly one smaller and less powerful than his opponent, will, once committed to mortal combat, swiftly and without warning, 'go for the jugular'.

The incalculable advantage held by the United States in its abil-ity to decipher Japanese coded communication was, unbelievably, not thoroughly exploited due to the large volumes encountered and, as a result, some messages of vital importance were missed. One in particular, requesting their Hawaiian consulate to report the exact location of ships berthed in Pearl Harbor would, had it not escaped notice, surely have electrified Washington, forcing it to switch antici-patory focus immediately to that locality. Most remarkably, Pearl Harbor, the hub of operations, had not up to then been given direct access to information gleaned from deciphered Japanese coded sig-nals although this privilege had been accorded to the Philippine com-mand and to the British.

In the circumstances, precautions taken in Hawaii were not to any great extent focussed on repelling an enemy attack but were mostly relevant to the prevention of sabotage by local residents of Japanese affiliation. By contrast a significant weight of US War Department opinion expected the first offensive to be launched against the Soviet Union's eastern frontiers, the time being opportune as the Soviets were then desperately embroiled in a life and death struggle with the German invaders 5,000 miles to the west. In fact, considering the urgency explicit in the final signal from Washington – "Expect hostile action at any moment" – the degree of complacency at Pearl Harbor is astounding. Heightened radio traffic among Japanese naval units had been noted and analysed, indicating build-up towards a major operation, but when this subsided markedly from around the middle of November it was assumed that their fleet had resumed a state of relative immobility for the time being in the Inland Sea. The stark reality, however, was that from that moment a Japanese task force of 31 warships under command of Vice-Admiral Chuichi Nagumo, including six fleet carriers, two fast battleships and three cruisers, had commenced moving secretly to their starting line far to the north among the Kurile islands, observing strict radio silence; all but one of the carriers was capable of speed in excess of 30 knots and between them could despatch 423 aircraft. On 26 November the force set sail thence for Oahu along a predetermined unfrequented North Pacific course, subject to receiving en route the ultimate order whether to proceed with the Pearl Harbor attack or not, war or submission. The armada that US naval headquarters in Hawaii imagined tranquilly 'swinging round the buoy' in home waters was in fact silently approaching launching position to the north, bearing with it some 400 of the world's best naval aircraft, manned by the world's then most capable naval aviators.

With little change in routine activity deemed necessary in Hawaii, naval ships putting to sea ordinarily returned to harbour at weekends to facilitate rest and relaxation. The attitude seemed to suggest that nothing defensive needed to be done before the other side showed its hand. A reassuring factor, if one were required, was evidence of a large Japanese amphibious build-up in the Gulf of Siam, indicating that, if hostilities commenced, the obvious target area would be Thailand and Malaya. To a degree that proved to be true but there was, unfortunately, another area afar that took precedence.

Vice-Admiral Chuichi Nagumo, Imperial Japanese Navy

On Saturday 6 December, as on any Saturday, the beaches, bars, restaurants and other popular venues were crowded with servicemen happily indulging in the amenities of shore leave, or the army equivalent, and in the evening a number of social functions claimed the presence of many officers, some of highest rank. In the meantime, the fateful decision by the Japanese Imperial High Command had been taken – war! Last-minute negotiations and diplomacy had failed, and the die had been cast.

Nagumo's carriers were set to launch their air strike at 06.00 on Sunday morning, 7 December from 200 miles due north of Pearl Harbor in Oahu, reaching that objective, according to plan, at 08.00.

To comply, technically at least, with International Law demanding due notice before commencing hostilities, Japan's note to the United States breaking off diplomatic relations – in effect a declaration of war – was ordered to be delivered by their ambassador in Washington at 1.00 pm local time – half an hour before the first bomb was due to fall. But Murphy's Law, which persistently harassed America that day, decrees that 'if anything can go wrong it will'. Logistical quirks delayed delivery of the note but American cryptographic experts had already decoded the message, which was rushed to the office of the chief of staff, General George Marshall. He, however, was out riding and could not be contacted for some time. When Marshall eventually had sight of the message he deemed it important enough to despatch, via the War Department, a last warning of imminent attack to key executive centres, but the copy for Pearl Harbor, due to atmospheric turbulence, had to be sent by commercial wireless via Honolulu, whence it proceeded no further because at the critical moment no motorcycle courier was available to deliver it to Pearl.

Another clear indication of things to come happened during the night when a periscope was sighted some way off the harbour entrance. This belonged to one of several midget submarines on a mission to penetrate the harbour and, in unison with the aerial onslaught next morning, to unleash their torpedoes upon shipping within. The midgets were spawned by five 'I-boat' submarines – giant submersibles designed to accommodate and launch a midget submarine or an aircraft. An American destroyer raced to the scene and eventually, at 06.45, with the aid of a seaplane, sank the midget. The destroyer's commanding officer immediately reported the incident to naval headquarters, but to no avail. In those days in Hawaii, early on a Sunday morning, the buck clearly found nowhere to stop and, in this case, was still being passed around when the bombs began falling. Another midget submarine actually gained entry into the harbour, the world's strongest naval base, passing unmolested through the gate in the boom defences, which had neglectfully been left open. Fortunately for the US, that particular midget encountered instrumental malfunction. Both her torpedoes missed at point-blank range and she herself had to be beached, contributing nothing to the destruction that was soon to follow.

The first wave of 183 Japanese warplanes, under overall command of Commander Mitsuo Fuchida, had been launched on schedule and was winging its way southwards towards Oahu, their progress benefiting from the frugality of the island authorities who had recently, to save fuel and expense, cancelled weekend reconnaissance flights and so no long-range aerial searches were operating. That could wait till Monday. Some mobile radar units had shortly before been acquired and introduced rather experimentally at suitable points on the island. They were not of very high standard and not continually manned, their function being mainly for training purposes. At about 7.00 am on the Sunday morning two trainees operating a unit at Opana on Oahu's northernmost coast were about to shut down for the day when they observed a large blip on their screen indicating, they thought, a goodly number of aircraft – more than 50 – about 140 miles distant and approaching from due north. On reporting this to their commanding officer they were told, "Don't worry about it," the latter surmising the arrival of B17 bomber reinforcements from California.

Captain Mitsuo Fuchida, Imperial Japanese Navy

Fuchida's assault force made landfall at about 07.30 and proceeded down the west coast until Pearl Harbor at the mid-southern end of Oahu came into view in the hazy distance. At that moment the chiefs of the Hawaiian army and navy, both stationed at Pearl, were preparing to do battle of a different description, against each other on the golf course. To Fuchida's disappointment there was no sign of the US aircraft-carriers, which were away delivering airplanes to the outposts on Wake and Midway islands, but all eight envisaged battleships were there – seven moored off Ford Island in 'Battleship Row', and the eighth in dry dock – as well as numerous naval ships of smaller dimension. He gave the prearranged signal 'To-To-To' for 'attack', whereupon his force split up: 49 level bombers, 40 torpedo-bombers, 51 dive-bombers and 43 Zero fighters, each group intent upon its own objectives, each aircrew knowing precisely what it had to do. Then, observing no sign from ground level that their approach had caused alarm, Fuchida radioed 'Tora (tiger) Tora Tora' to the Naguma task force, indicating 'surprise attack successful'.

Surprise was indeed complete. The Honolulu broadcasting station was playing cheery music, the ships in harbour were in tranquil Sunday morning mode, sun-excluding canvas awnings were rigged over the quarterdecks of larger vessels in preparation for the Sabbath's religious services, their crews at breakfast or otherwise relaxingly occupied, some making ready for 'hoisting the colours' at 08.00. A few sparsely spread anti-aircraft guns were routinely manned, which under the prevailing mood meant that guns' crews lolled about in overalls in the vicinity of the mountings, chatting, reading magazines and dozing. People elsewhere at ground level who had noticed the Japanese planes during their run-in down the coast had idly assumed that they were American engaged in a training flight, and paid them no further attention.

The attack opened shortly before 08.00 by dive-bombers and Zeros on Wheeler and Hickam airfields, followed minutes later on the airbase at Kaneoke. Immediately thereafter the 40 type Nakazime ('Kate') torpedo-bombers swooped down abeam of 'Battleship Row', releasing at point-blank range their 24-inch, lethal 'Long Lance' torpedoes specially fitted with wooden fins to allow for a drop into shallow water from a greater height than normally, while men aboard the targeted vessels gaped in shocked disbelief. Within seconds peaceful serenity gave way to a hell of clamour, flames and smoke. Adding to the devastation, dive-bombers type Aichi 99 ('Val') screamed down steeply, each unburdening a 550 lb bomb with deadly precision, followed by type 97 level bombers making their runs at approximately 10,000 feet, each armed with a 1,760 lb, armour-piercing, time-fused bomb improvised from battleship shells, designed to penetrate deck armour and explode deep down within the ship.

A little before 09.00 the second wave of Japanese planes arrived, comprising 54 high-level bombers, 80 dive-bombers and 38 fighters. They flew in across the island's eastern coastline and continued the pounding of shipping, airfields, hangars, barracks and other installations, enjoying virtually complete dominion of the sky although, following the initial shock, anti-aircraft fire from ship and shore gradually stiffened.

By 10.00 the attack was over. Another day pre-eminent in the annals of warfare had been born and the United States had suffered its most crushing defeat of all time. In the space of two hours 18 warships, including all 8 battleships, had been sunk or badly damaged, 347 warplanes, virtually all, destroyed, 2,433 personnel killed and 1,178 wounded. The heaviest casualties were suffered in the battleship *Arizona,* hit by armour-piercing bombs causing her forward magazine and boilers to explode in a vast pyrotechnic display of flame and smoke, the ship sinking immediately to the bottom, taking with her 1,102 permanently entombed men. By contrast, their assailants had lost only 29 warplanes of all types and 64 lives, including 9 from midget submarines. The crucial two hours had witnessed the broad perspective of power and influence in the region turned upside down, leaving the Japanese navy to reign supreme in the Pacific for months to come.

Fuchida's aviators, understandably cock-a-hoop on returning to their task force, strongly recommended a further strike, hoping thereby to locate the US carriers which by good fortune had escaped discovery and certain annihilation. In addition, destructive attention could be paid to certain targets on land that had surprisingly been overlooked during the raid just completed. Nagumo, however, felt that the main objectives had been achieved and for several other reasons deemed it imprudent to 'stretch his luck' by launching a follow-up assault. His decision to terminate the operations and return to home waters evoked strong criticism in other quarters, including Admiral Yamamoto, commander-in-chief of the Japanese Combined Fleet, and in hindsight it seems that had the task force returned to the attack, at least one US carrier would have been ensnared and eliminated. Furthermore, targets on land neglected in the earlier raid lay prostrate and defenceless, including the gigantic fuel storage farm adjacent to the harbour containing 4,500,000 barrels of oil, as well as extensive machine shops for repairs and maintenance, all of which were soon to make a major contribution towards the American recovery.

Cornwall was at breakfast and entering the Mozambique Channel on a southerly course (I am indebted to Ken Dimbleby's *Turns of Fate* for this information – I would not have recalled the locations mentioned) when the drama of Pearl Harbor was announced on board, over the broadcasting system. Details were not immediately available – these would filter through during the course of that 7th day of December 1941 – but we were informed that we were, from that point on, effectively at war with Japan. Ironically Britain's declaration of war actually preceded that of the United States, whose territory had been ravaged because Roosevelt, still constrained by isolationist tradition, could not decide whether Germany and Italy, the two other members of the Tripartite Alliance, should be included and in the event and for the time being at least, asked Congress on the following day for a declaration of war on Japan only. However, his quandary was overcome shortly afterwards when Hitler, followed by Mussolini, realising no doubt the inevitable, declared war on the United States. Neither dictator had been accorded any prior knowledge of their Nipponese ally's Hawaiian intentions, and one can imagine their consternation when the news reached them.

Part of Roosevelt's speech to Congress was relayed to us on the mess deck – an impassioned oration recounting the events of the past two days. I recall how the President, for dramatic effect, repeated several times the accusatory words "without warning", to the extent that sailors forgathered there and sensing the right moments in his delivery, would gleefully and with gusto chorus "without warning" in accompaniment. The catchphrase, 'Day of Infamy', was spawned on that occasion, not without reason, although cynics, having regard to American lack of co-ordination and negligence in the run-up might, also not without reason, have labelled it 'Day of Indolence'. There was, one might suggest, a touch of naivety in Roosevelt's condemnation of Japan's deceptive abrogation of rules governing the declaration of war, bearing in mind America's strangulating embargo against that country in respect of oil and other essential materials. After all, if you are choking a man to death you can hardly expect him in retaliation to abide by the Marquis of Queensberry rules.

Japan too, despite her meticulous and skilful planning, her spectacular success at Pearl Harbor and victories elsewhere thereafter, had been prey to serious errors of commission and omission. To start off she had dismissed any thought that her secret codes might have been broken by her main adversary, the United States, despite having been warned of that possibility by Germany. By good luck and American remissions she 'got away with it' at Pearl Harbor but, with this obstinacy persisting, was destined to pay dearly therefor later. In addition, she did not sufficiently exploit her initial triumph and concomitant US bewilderment by striking without delay at other vitally strategic targets, commencing with thus-far undamaged installations on Oahu, simultaneously seeking and destroying her enemy's elusive carriers and, further afield, bombarding and rendering non-functional such key establishments as the Panama Canal. The time to do these things was unquestionably while her naval air fleet held dominance in the Pacific and her opponent was reeling off balance, because the dozing giant, having been roughly awakened, would soon shake off its torpidity, become fully roused and start growling. Pearl Harbor was

America's metamorphosis, her moment of truth, stimulus to national unity and patriotism, to decision and action, spurred on far and wide by the impassioned slogan: 'Remember Pearl Harbor'.

American resilience, inspiration and gallantry was spectacularly manifest barely four months later in probably the most daring and ingenious raid of World War II. Sixteen Army B25 (Mitchell) bombers led by Colonel James Doolittle were launched on April 18 from the aircraft-carrier USS *Hornet,* a feat never before attempted with planes so large, in rough seas 650 miles east of their targets and, flying in low above the waves, achieved the 'impossible' by bombing four major Japanese cities, including the capital Tokyo, thereafter continuing their flight eastwards to land or crash-land on the coast of China. Of the 80 airmen who took part 71, including Doolittle, survived.

Colonel James Doolittle and his bomber crew (Doolittle is second from left).

* * * * *

11

ORIENT EXPRESS

(Another 'Germany')

Any belief, notion or hope permeating minds in the 'free world' in 1941 that the martial capability of Japan was not really of much consequence and did not impose a serious threat, were, at Pearl Harbor and increasingly during the days, weeks and months that followed, proven patently delusional. The Japanese onslaught, once unleashed, was staggering in potency, ruthless efficiency and sheer speed of execution, shocking not only the Allies arrayed against them, as well as the Soviet Union, but alarming also Germany and Italy, their Tripartite Alliance partners who had been given no forewarning. Indeed even the Japanese High Command felt some disconcertment, mixed with exultation, when they realised towards the end of March 1942 that their armies had outstripped hierarchical planning to the extent that, temporarily, they did not quite know what to do next. After a mere three and a half months since Pearl Harbor their western flank forces had swept away all opposition, and were advancing up through Burma with the Indian frontier beckoning, while their spearheads to the south had almost reached a point in New Guinea where only a narrow stretch of sea separated them from continental Australia – in much the same manner as German panzers ensconced twenty-one months earlier on the French coast had found only the narrow Straits of Dover between them and England. In fact a BBC commentator had observed that when Japan entered the fray many on the Allied side had anticipated having to deal with another 'Italy' but had soon come to the realisation that they were confronted by another 'Germany'.

Several widely-spread strikes were planned to synchronise with the Pearl Harbor attack, and troop transports for the invasion of Thailand and Malaya were already underway on the South China Sea days beforehand. Troops had embarked from southern Indo-China and Hainan Island, heading for peninsular landings at Singora, Patani and Kota Bharu straddling the Thai–Malayan border. The first Japanese troops, under command of General Yamashita, waded ashore even before the bombardment at Pearl Harbor had opened, their objective the conquest of the Malayan peninsula and Singapore at its southern extremity. Further north Japanese divisions from Indo-China poured into Thailand (the name having changed from 'Siam' two years earlier) completely overrunning that country and occupying the capital, Bangkok by the second day, thereafter commencing a rapid advance southwards in support of the amphibious landings.

Elsewhere furious aerial attacks were inflicted on Guam, Wake Island, Hong Kong and Manila. Strangely, Douglas MacArthur, commander-in-chief of the Philippines, a soldier who had proven his mettle in the First World War and was to do so again illustriously in the Second, displayed uncharacteristic inertia during the first hours of hostilities, with the result that when 200 Japanese bombers appeared over Clark and Iba airfields near Manila they found more than 130 US warplanes – the largest Allied fleet in the western Pacific – parked invitingly in neat rows to be virtually wiped out in a devastation of bombs and aerial cannon fire. The Japanese returning later therefore, and encountering no opposition in the air, were able to pulverise Cavite naval base and adjacent airfields with impunity.

One may speculate that MacArthur, highly decorated and later recipient of America's highest award for valour, the Congressional

Medal of Honor, might, were it not for his reputation and for practical reasons at the time, have been relieved of his command due to inadequacy, as had happened to army and navy commanders at Pearl Harbor.

The British battleship *Prince of Wales* and battle-cruiser *Repulse* had, as related earlier, arrived at Singapore on December 2. Clearly Churchill's optimistic expectation that these formidable warships would present a deterrent against Japanese aggression had been grievously misplaced. Indeed, it would seem that their presence in the area provided the enemy with further incentive to strike. The tables had in fact been turned. Yesterday's steel bastion defying hostile threats was today itself mortally imperilled – a situation that needed to be remedied with alacrity by the Admiralty who, regrettably, had no preconceived 'Plan B' in place for immediate implementation. Even so, Churchill was considering the possibility of despatching the ships posthaste across the Pacific to join up with the battered United States fleet at Hawaii, a move that would have been warmly welcomed by the Americans but, alas, dramatic events were happening too fast, effectively negating any such initiative.

Admiral Tom Phillips, in command of all naval units at Singapore, was in no mood to lie idle in the face of the deteriorating situation and, in the absence of counter-instructions from London and despite warnings that he could expect no land-based aerial protection, he sortied with the *Prince of Wales* and *Repulse*, escorted by four destroyers. This strike force, codenamed Force Z, headed up the east coast of the Malayan peninsula in the hope of surprising and destroying the Japanese invasion transports in the Kota Bharu area. Phillips, a flag-officer of the old school, was still a firm believer in the concept that battleships had more than enough firepower to deal with any airborne assault. His force arrived off the reported landing too late on 7 December and, noting that his ships had been observed by enemy reconnaissance planes and that the element of surprise had been forfeited, he reversed course to return to Singapore. However, he lost critical time en route investigating another reported landing which proved to be erroneous, leaving his ships by the following morning still within range of land-based aircraft from Indo-China, whence 85 Japanese high-level and torpedo-bombers had taken off at first light.

The attack started shortly before noon and was resolutely and expertly pressed home, and 90 minutes later both *Prince of Wales* and *Repulse* were at the bottom of the South China Sea, taking with them 840 men including Admiral Phillips and the commanding officer of the *Prince*, Captain Leach. Captain Tennant of *Repulse* would also have succumbed had members of his crew not forcibly wrestled him off the stricken battle-cruiser. The Japanese aviators had visited destruction only upon the capital ships and departed the scene once these had foundered. The three accompanying destroyers (one having left the group earlier) were left astonishingly unmolested and, surely by providential largesse, on hand to rescue more than 2,000 survivors bobbing around in the oily water. Why? one wonders. One can hardly conceive of the Japanese airmen (or any other airmen in a similar war situation) leaving the destroyers alone out of humanitarian sentiment. More likely it was that, caught up in the exhilaration of the moment, they all wanted 'to have a bash at the jackpot' – the much-vaunted 'battlewagons' – and contribute to their destruction. Then, having done so, their bombs and torpedoes expended, they had nothing left over with which to assail the 'small fry'. Had some of their number been tactically directed to attack the destroyers and had succeeded in sinking them, it is certain that virtually all hands, both of the capital ships and the destroyers, would have been lost. Instead the great majority lived to fight another day, some on board *Cornwall*.

The sinkings of *Prince of Wales* and *Repulse* sent shockwaves around the world, especially in the wake of publicity, so recently promoted, exalting the deterrent effect of their presence at Singapore. Loss of the *Prince* in particular dealt a stunning blow to British pride, it being regarded at the time as the Royal Navy's newest battleship (her younger sister, the *Duke of York,* had been completed one month earlier but had not yet been commissioned), and technologically advanced with a main armament of ten 14-inch guns and waterline defensive armour 16 inches thick. Churchill recorded that in all the war he never received a more direct shock, realising among much else that this disaster bestowed upon Japan, for the time being, virtual mastery of the whole expanse of waters between the east coast of Africa and the west coast of the Americas.

We on *Cornwall* followed these events, as broadcast daily in BBC bulletins, with some concern and more than casual interest in the wall maps provided. But the underlying feeling of detachment still persisted. These things were happening far away, to other ships and other people and, more importantly, "Tombola will be played during the first dog watch in the port waist."

Christmas 1941 found us in Aden following another escort voyage to the Red Sea, and it proved to be a memorable occasion. The ship's company, from Captain Mainwaring down, were in a festive mood. Routine chores were, as far as practicable, relaxed. The masthead and other lofty perches were festooned with palm leaves purloined from somewhere in Arabia, and coloured bunting was in abundance. After church service conducted on the quarterdeck by the ship's padre, Lieut. Reverend Bird, the marine brass band struck up loudly with happy celebratory melodies, the strains of which wafted across the waters of the extensive anchorage and must have caused the Arabian seagulls dominating airspace above to take fright momentarily and raise disapproving ornithological eyebrows.

Earlier, the senior naval officer ashore had fanned out a signal to all ships present, which read something like "Everybody wishes everybody a Merry Christmas and Happy New Year. Spare a thought for the signalman and the paper shortage." The galley and bakery staff excelled themselves in presenting some 700 ravenous seafarers with a great Christmas dinner which included what was claimed to be roast turkey together with stuffing, fresh vegetables and all the trimmings, followed later by icing-covered cake. Every man, whether 'grog', 'temperate' or 'underage', even the boy seamen, received a bottle of beer, which contributed appreciably to the spirit of merriment on the mess deck. The war of the past two and a quarter years, and even the disasters suffered during that ill-fated month of December, receded for the time being beyond the horizon, out of sight and mind.

An invitation had been extended on the previous day to Catholic sailors to attend traditional Midnight Mass ashore. I was 'duty watch' aboard and unable to go, but some others did, among them George Ferrier who found the experience, on the verge of the Arabian desert, along with a motley congregation of servicemen and civilians, spiritually stirring. They even managed to sing, fervently if not altogether harmoniously, universally loved 'Silent Night', the simple but superbly beautiful hymn that epitomises the feast of Christ's birth. I pondered for a while the disturbing paradox and pathos arising from the knowledge that, in a world aflame with war, killing and destruction, the same hymn which originated via Austria, the land of Hitler's birth, was being sung at the same hour, in a multitude of different tongues, around the world – in London, Paris, Berlin, Rome, Johannesburg, New York, Buenos Aires and Sydney, possibly even in Moscow and Tokyo, and most importantly in the Judaean town of Bethlehem – bidding peace and goodwill to all mankind.

'Sleep in heavenly peace' ('Schlafe in himmliche Ruh')

Our next call, following further escort assignment, was the port city of Bombay, capital of the Indian province of the same name, positioned halfway up the west coast of the subcontinent. Bombay city was of great interest, throbbing and teeming with multinational humanity, built for the most part on an island connected to the mainland by causeways. It was a prodigious industrial and commercial centre, rivalling Calcutta on the opposite side of the vast peninsula, with extensive docks and shipyards and many fine public buildings. Moving beyond the confines of urban sophistication, however, one found by contrast, as I suppose is common to most megacities around the world, large areas of slums, degradation and extreme poverty.

Cornwall moored in the roadstead adjacent to the Ballard Pier, familiar to ocean liner passengers and dominated by the magnificent 'Gateway to India', an arch comparable to the world's largest triumphal arch, the Arc de Triomphe in Paris. It was in that vicinity that our liberty men disembarked from the ship's pinnace and later re-embarked when returning. A United States cruiser was also in Bombay at the time, moored a short distance from *Cornwall,* and our liberty men soon came into contact with theirs. Immediately noticeable was that most of the American sailors sported service medal ribbons on their breasts, which evoked loud derogatory comment by our men, who had nothing of the sort: "Just like them big-mouthed Yankees. Been in the war for a dog watch, one bloody month, and already they're showin' off chests full of ribbons." Inevitably this was the precursor of occasional inter-navy jeers and altercations on the landing pier, culminating presently in a minor show of fisticuffs. Mindful of risks inherent in such circumstances, with RN and US sailors converging on the landing after leave ashore, imbued with liquor-boosted national pride, allowing verbal confrontation to deteriorate into a free-for-all with the incidental possibility of one or more of the feuding mariners being propelled over the edge into the waters of the roadstead where strong tidal currents were not conducive to healthy aquatics, the authorities aboard both cruisers agreed mutually that segregation was the answer. Consequently it was arranged for American liberty men to disembark and re-embark at a point a hundred or more yards distant from where we did the same, and that seemed to dispose of the problem.

The Gateway to India precinct was, as one might expect, home base for every soul who had something to sell, hawkers and vendors of every description, from merchandise to sightseeing guides, and eating and drinking houses to brothel pimps. One enterprising Indian lad of twelve or so years, selling local newspapers, would cannily exploit the separation imposed upon the American and British liberty men at the quayside. Aware of the strained relationship existing between them, he would stride jauntily over to us with his papers and placards calling out lustily, in probably the only English words he knew, "Read all about it; read all about it. Yankee bullshit!" thus causing much amusement and laughter, and, no doubt, boosting his sales. Then, when he gauged he had done as much business with us as he could, he would trot off down the quayside to the Americans assembling at their appointed re-embarkation spot to ply his marketing efforts at that point. When presently we heard distant laughter from that direction we knew that our newsboy friend was applying the same strategy among our allies there, taking care of course, when making his stentorian appeal, to substitute 'Limey' for 'Yankee' in relation to the bovine product specified.

On our first 'run' ashore Jock Davidson and I hired a gharry, or small horse-drawn carriage, on a sightseeing tour of the great city – a contrast of architectural splendour and depressant slums, of fabulous wealth and squalid poverty, of silks and satins amongst the tattered rags of street dwellers. Our gharry drive took in public buildings, a Hindu temple where we removed our shoes before entering, and the most impressive Government House on Malabar Hill. Of special interest was the Tower of Silence, a 20- to 30-foot high circular high wall within which the Parsees, in accordance with their creed, deposit their dead to be devoured by vultures, crows and other birds of similar disposition. Of unlovely memory was a drive down Grant Road, the notorious red light district of Bombay.

The provocative issue of American medal ribbons continued to crop up from time to time, particularly on the mess deck at dinner when the brown Jamaican spirit started to take effect. However, the matter was to some extent laid to rest by a 3-badge AB. There would usually be three or four of that select body on board a large RN ship – older men, probably thirty or more years of age, of which at least twelve had been spent on HM ships. These were men who knew their jobs (and the jobs of others) inside out and executed them expertly and meticulously. They had little ambition for promotion beyond their present, and to them comfortable, status, but they wore their three stripes on their left upper arms with pride, earning them the nickname of 'Stripey'. The 3-badger was probably the most respected figure on the lower deck, even among the commissioned ranks, and one never saw him being reprimanded by an officer or Petty Officer. He was regarded by the rank and file as something of a father figure, a source of sound judgement and guidance, even at times a 'sea lawyer'.

"Look," said Stripey indulgently, "leave the Yankees alone. This is the way of life. Wherever you go you'll find some as are better'n off than others. It's not the Yank's fault; 'E didn't lay down the rules. All right, 'e is a big-mouthed bastard some of the time – we got a few of them too – but 'e's doing a job just like you and me, and getting 'is arse blown to bits just like you and me. The difference is that 'is government appreciates what 'e is doing for 'is country and treats 'im according, like 'ow 'e deserves. So 'e gets 'is service medals quicker, don't 'ave to wait till 'e's dead. 'E is better paid, much better paid, better kitted out and better fed. Right now 'e is 'avin' 'is dinner downstream, just like you and me, but it's not this 'ere corned dog, or 'errings in'[2], 'e's 'avin' roast chicken, or duck, or mutton stew with icecream for afters, not this 'ard-baked duff what you can use for cannon balls.

"When 'e dosses down for the night 'e does it decent like in a

---

[2] 'Corned dog' and 'herrings in' were common messdeck expressions for Bully Beef and Herrings in Tomato Sauce respectively, both regarded as stand-by servings when other provisions were in short supply.

bunk, not a bleedin' 'ammick like you an' me 'as to sling from them 'ooks in the deckhead, but our government says, 'What was good for Nelson is still good enough today.' It says so because the Admiralty what sits in parliament says so, and the Admiralty is a civil ministry 'eaded by a First Lord, who probably never set foot on a ship. 'E'd be seasick before 'e got up the gangplank. It's the politicians what decides what is good for stroppy Jack. In the American navy the complaints of the ordinary seaman is listened to; there's ways and means of gettin' 'is views put across. Not so with stroppy Jack; 'e can put in a complaint, through all the right channels and all, but if them at the top don't like it 'e can find 'isself in the rattle for 'avin' the cheek to complain. Way back in '31 we 'ad a mutiny in the navy – you lot are too young to know about it. I was only 25 – on the old *Rodney* with other ships at Invergordon – because the old fogeys in government wanted to cut navy pay. The families of 'arf our junior ratings would've starved. But that didn't bother the fat politicians in the 'ouse of Commons. 'Stuff you, Jack; I'm all right!'

"Anyway, the mutiny jerked them and the whole nation awake, even went all the way to 'is Majesty the King, and the pay cuts was cancelled, but the leaders of the mutiny, the blokes who had the guts to stand up for the rest of us, they got dismissed from the service because they'd upset the gold braid – that's justice! But that wouldn't 'ave 'appened in the American navy; their folks in civvy street would've backed them up. Class distinction, that's what we're up against, and the likes of you and me can't do nuthin' about it. We don't count for nuthin' in, in…"

"This royal throne of kings; this sceptred isle," interjected Parkins of Shakespearean wisdom .

"Whatever you want to call it. In America the bloke what sweeps the dockyard gets as good a fair deal as the bloke what owns the shipyard. But not us. No fair deal for us. For us it's what Nelson said at Trafalgar: 'England expects every bastard to do 'is duty'.

"Me brother writes from North Africa – 'e's in the new Eighth Army there – three members of a tank crew escaped from the Jerries and set off on foot across the Libyan desert to rejoin their own forces a hundred and something miles away, with scarce nuthin' to eat nor drink on the way. One was a lieutenant, another a sergeant and the third a corporal. After more'n a week they staggered back to their own lines, exhausted, and a big fuss was made of them, in the papers back 'ome an' all. So the loot gets the DSO, the sergeant gets mentioned in despatches, and the corporal, who 'ad to carry the loot for the last twenty or so miles – the corporal, 'e gets Fanny Adams! Now you blokes moan because the Yankee sailors are issued service ribbons. I say, good luck to them."

Shortly afterwards we escorted another convoy to Colombo, the voyage memorable to me because somewhere south of the Persian Gulf I celebrated my coming of age – my twenty-first birthday. I was careful to divulge the singularity of the day to only one or two trusted friends for fear of mess deck involvement. It was customary on a man's birthday, as previously described in this narrative, for his messmates, as well as pals from other messes, to ply him at dinner with 'sippers' and 'gulpers' of rum, the effect of which, in addition to his own tot, usually led to the celebrating unfortunate passing out before finishing his meal and being hefted away like a sack of potatoes far for'rard in the region of the paint locker, a relatively remote and deserted area, to sleep the afternoon away. If he was due to go on watch one or two of his messmates would stand in for him. I did not relish receiving the sack of potatoes treatment, probably regaining consciousness an hour or two later with a hammering headache, so I kept mum about my birthday.

Thus my attainment of majority had no effect on 9 Mess, Fo'c'sle Division, to which I belonged. It had likewise no noticeable effect on the 'Orient Express' – the swift, relentless and innovatively brilliant surge of the Japanese war machine, which by that time, some seven weeks since the outbreak of hostilities, had overrun Thailand, percolated through the 'impenetrable' jungle of the Malayan peninsula, skilfully infiltrated and bypassed defences, and employed unconventional expedients such as bicycle transportation. They were already nearing Singapore, had taken Hong Kong and the American outposts of Guam and Wake Island, had occupied all key areas in the Philippines with the exception of Bataan and the island fortress of Corregidor, and invaded the coastal areas of Borneo with its vast oil resources, using the strategy of successive amphibious landings and establishing advance airfields as they progressed while enjoying overwhelming local superiority on land, sea and in the air.

These successes had generally been achieved with surprising ease and at low cost, but with one heroic exception: that at Wake Island on 11 December 1941 where the defending marines, having at their disposal only a few old 5-inch guns and a dozen Wildcat fighters, repelled an invasion, sinking in the process two Japanese destroyers and damaging four other warships – the only case during the war of an invasion fleet being repulsed (if one disregards the withdrawal, after the Battle of the Coral Sea, of Japanese troopships intended for invasion of New Guinea). In the euphoria of the moment the marines coined the slogan "Bring us more Japs", but twelve days later the Japanese returned in overwhelming strength, supported by two fleet carriers, and the gallant defenders were crushed.

Assisting in resisting the invaders were a fair number of construction workers who, being civilians, exposed themselves if captured to treatment unprotected by protocol relative to prisoners of war. Recognising this, the US Navy thereafter converted the work force into construction battalions, and gave them rudimentary military training, rank and attire, thus spawning the legendary 'Seebees' who were to provide invaluable support during the ongoing maritime operations in the Pacific theatre, constructing airfields, bridges, access roads and much else, often under fire and, when circumstances demanded, participating in combat.

The swiftly deteriorating situation in the Far East was understandably of deep concern in London where, at a distance of some
7,000 miles, the difficult task of counteracting Japanese expansion
was seemingly insurmountable. Not surprisingly, therefore, some
of the decisions and measures taken in Whitehall and Westminster
evoked a suspicion of indiscretion, even desperation about them,
albeit laudable for the trying. So it was that *Cornwall* found herself
early in February 1942 in command of a slow convoy of merchant
vessels to the Sunda Strait, which separates the islands of Sumatra
and Java, their intended destinations Batavia, the Javan capital, and
beleaguered Singapore in an endeavour to bolster their defence capability. As it later transpired the convoy arrived too late to make any
meaningful difference, and was the last to reach either port, where
the ships, their crews and cargoes for the most part passed into the
hands of the Japanese.

The waters of north-eastern and central Indian Ocean, hitherto
regarded as an area of relative safety, were steadily assuming a more
threatening aspect, with reports being received of submarine attacks
on merchant shipping, and of the growing menace of forays by surface warships. These concerns notwithstanding, a boxing tournament
was arranged during a dog watch on the return voyage to Colombo
from the Strait. This was intended to be, and in fact was, an entertaining diversion, something of a tension breaker for the ship's company.
About a dozen spirited bouts took place in an improvised ring rigged
on the quarterdeck before an enthusiastic crowd of onlookers. My
friend Jock Davidson from Vereeniging in the Transvaal, who was
a boxer with an impressive amateur record, was disappointed in not
being able to compete due to severely slashing his right thumb on a
bandsaw while assisting shipwrights in their workshop. In fact he was
fortunate not to lose the digit altogether. The best bout was between
Harry Stone from East London and Slinger Woods from the UK, both

championship contenders before the war. Their aggressive, all-action display was loudly applauded and while Slinger was adjudged the winner no one would have argued had the decision been a draw. At the conclusion of the tournament, Commander Fair, second-in-command on *Cornwall*, declared, "We have watched and enjoyed some good fights this afternoon but now it's time to return to that other fight that we have on our hands."

The 'other fight' presented us with another convoy almost immediately upon our arrival at Colombo, this time to Rangoon, capital of Burma, which by then was being increasingly infested by the Japanese from across the Thai border. *Cornwall* shepherded the merchantmen almost to within visual distance of the port and then turned about and sped for home, leaving her charges to continue to their assigned destination. They were the last vessels to reach Rangoon before its surrender two weeks later. To what extent the cargoes transported thither were in good time for effective use by the defenders is conjectural but probably a substantial portion, as well as the ships and crews that brought it, fell here too into Japanese hands. Dimbleby in his *Turns of Fate* recalls that when *Cornwall* re-entered the harbour at Colombo she flew from the masthead a yellow flag indicative of our having a case of smallpox on board. I do not remember the incident, but even across the subsequent decades I am curious to know who the sick man was, how he contracted the disease, and what became of him.

In the meantime the worst capitulation disaster in British military history had taken place at Singapore, which propaganda had led the public, including many politicians and even top brass in the armed forces, in fact the British Empire and world at large, to believe was an impregnable island fortress. In reality that impression was woefully fallacious. The main fixed-mounted weaponry on the island had been sited to fire southwards to counter an envisaged attack from the sea, and could not be brought to bear northwards across the Johore Strait.

Early strategists had not contemplated an assault of any significance from the mainland, believing that the Malayan jungle was impenetrable to an army encumbered with the heavy hardware essential for the conquest of strongly fortified defences. The backbone of Allied forces in Malaya – British and Australian – had hoped to stem the Japanese advance in the forestry of the Johore peninsula but had been continually and systematically outmanoeuvred by skilful infiltration, bypassing and encirclement tactics of the enemy, necessitating ongoing withdrawals to operate as a coherent force, forfeiting depots and equipment in the process.

Towards the end of January 1942 the decision was taken to withdraw completely from the peninsula and cross over to Singapore island, an operation that was completed by all remaining units, depleted, exhausted and demoralised, by 31 January, whereupon a 25-yard gap was blown in the 350-yard long causeway, the only dry land access route across the Johore Strait from the mainland. This undertaking swelled the number of combat troops on the island but did not, by reason of the wearied condition of the new arrivals and paucity of equipage still retained by them, strengthen the garrison. On the contrary, it seriously compromised the overall situation by making additional, weighty demands on rapidly diminishing reserves of essential commodities, most importantly fresh water. Apart from the approximately 85,000 British, Australian and Indian troops thus accumulated, of which only 70,000 were armed, the island had a civil population of about one million, and there was no hope of relief of any sort from outside.

The Japanese assault across the strait commenced on 8 February, supported by heavy artillery and aerial bombardment. Gradually the defenders were forced to give ground in the face of overwhelming firepower. The enemy soon restored the breach blown in the causeway to a usable condition, allowing tanks and heavy ordnance to cross and engage in the fighting. On Sunday 15 February, with resources of fuel, ammunition, food and water almost expended, General Percival, C-in-C on the island, to avoid wholesale slaughter, surrendered unconditionally, and the great 'impregnable' Eastern bastion of the British Empire, Singapore, had fallen to the legions from the Land of the Rising Sun, who renamed it 'Shoney'.

Reverberations of the disaster spread rapidly far and wide, greeted varyingly among the Allied nations and among neutrals sympathetically disposed, by shock and dismay, and by many of the armchair genre, ignorant of the ramifications, by censure and disparagement. Alarm was felt particularly in India and Australia, who now felt the chill wind of vulnerability in their faces. The Australian government and military command had suddenly, in preceding weeks, been stunned by the realisation that their war, hitherto almost entirely confined to the Mediterranean region, had now 'overnight' loomed up menacingly on their northern doorstep and, more gravely still, that they were at that point singularly ill-equipped to meet the challenge. Their main fighting strength had been committed abroad, three divisions in Egypt and a fourth in Malaya, leaving in the entire Australian mainland fewer than 32,000 enlisted men, including numerous non-combatants. The feeling generated in the hearts of many Australians was that the dominion had been left in the lurch, that their sons had for the most part been inveigled into fighting in the European theatre, leaving their homeland starkly weak and unprotected. John Curtin, their prime minister, an inveterate opponent of compulsory military service, sensitive to the situation and unfolding implications had, during the Malayan withdrawal, telegraphed Winston Churchill brusquely that "After all the assurances... evacuation of Singapore would be regarded here and elsewhere as an inexcusable betrayal," and that "Any diversion of reinforcements should be to the Netherlands, East Indies and not Burma."

This message from the leader of one of Britain's staunchest allies, pillar of the Commonwealth, their own kith and kin, was very hurtful to Churchill, particularly use of the word 'betrayal' and, in the prevailing circumstances, probably unfair and unhelpful. Certainly, however, Australian sentiment towards the Mother Country dropped to a low level over that critical period – "the lowest", according to one satirist, "since Harold Larwood's bodyline bowling in the early 30s" – and sadly there was nothing anyone could do at that juncture to succour the Singapore predicament. Nevertheless the depth of emotion and foreboding felt across the Australian nation was understandable and Churchill, despite extremely pressing needs elsewhere and acutely mindful of hostile propaganda depicting Britain fighting her battles with other countries' manpower, was resolved to do everything possible to alleviate the Antipodean position. Whereas, therefore, the passage of troops from 'Down Under' had, just a few months previously, been across the Indian Ocean to North Africa, the flow and direction was now abruptly reversed so as to return these fighting men to the defence of their native soil. This, of course, seriously compromised the resources of General Claude Auchinlech's Middle East command and the potency of the Eighth Army then heavily committed in Cyrenaica. Conversely, it was unlikely to incur the displeasure of Erwin Rommel and the Afrika Korps.

So it was that when *Cornwall* arrived back in Colombo towards the end of February 1942 she found troopships in the harbour crowded with returning Australian troops. It was not difficult in the circumstances for the 'buzz' specialists to forecast our next commission, and on 1 March we duly sailed with these ships in convoy, destination Fremantle in Western Australia.

Meanwhile the Japanese 'Orient express' careered headlong southwards with vigour and efficiency, almost without check occupying strategic points in Sumatra, Borneo, Mindaneo, the Celebes and Amboina on their eastern flank. Heroic resistance on the island fortress of Corregidor at the entrance to Manila Bay in the Philippines still persisted but, with no hope of supply or relief, that too would inevitably soon cease. On the day we sailed from Colombo, Japanese units landed on Java, their prime objective in the Dutch East Indies, and by the time we reached Fremantle Rangoon had fallen, as had Lae and Salamanca near the south-eastern tip of New Guinea. Earlier on 19 February Port Darwin, the only port of significance in Australia's Northern Territory, had been severely mauled in a carrier-borne aerial attack, effectively neutralising it as an air and naval base for a considerable time. Approximately twelve ships were surprised in the harbour and sunk, including an American destroyer. On 27 and 28 February the disastrous battle of the Java Sea had virtually eliminated Allied naval power in the entire East Indies region.

At Fremantle Reg Peard, my co-sweeper in the Drying Room Flat, and I went ashore together as liberty men and, in common with most others, took a bus to Perth, capital of the state, which lay just a few miles inland and offered more amenities. Paramount among these, for immediate indulgence, would be an establishment catering for the quaffing of a beer or two, and one such was speedily located. The place was crowded with boisterous soldiers from the convoy we had escorted and, observing the name 'HMS *Cornwall*' on our cap ribbons, they showered hearty conviviality upon us. One 'cobber' in particular, having had a head start on us with the local brew, insisted that we visit him at his home in Sydney when the convoy put in at that port "because that's where we're heading, Sport and... " he added with beery prescience "you will be taking us there just like you brought us here." Reg and I hoped he was right. He wrote his name, Bob Uren, on the back of an empty cigarette box for us, together with his Sydney address, then grinning, pointed to his surname on the box and declared, "My name sounds just like the smelly stuff in the pot under the bed but it's spelt different."

On leaving the pub Reg and I got talking at a street corner to two girls, who took us for coffee, probably with a view to counteracting the beer, and we arranged to meet them again on our next 'run' ashore two days later. I corresponded with one of the girls for quite some time subsequently. Two of our shipmates, strolling down a street in Perth, had a moving experience. A middle-aged woman came up to them and said, "May God bless you both and your ship." The two sailors thanked her, somewhat nonplussed. Then, after a moment's pause the woman added, "My son was on the *Sydney*" and then moved on. As earlier related, HMAS *Sydney* was lost with all hands in November 1941.

The harbour of Fremantle bustled with activity and one could not escape noticing the prominent presence of United States craft, especially submarines. Uncle Sam had clearly shaken off his pre-Pearl Harbor lethargy and was energetically on the move. *Cornwall* and the troopships sailed after a stay of four or five days. We had felt refreshed and at home in Fremantle and Perth, very much as if we had been ambling around in Cape Town or Durban, and we all hoped that our acquaintanceship with Australian ports would be prolonged. Sadly Bob Uren's prediction that we would take the convoy to Sydney was wide of the mark, and shortly after clearing the harbour entrance *Cornwall* swung northwards, bound again for Colombo. Developments had ordained that she be given a new role to play.

Astonished and alarmed by the rapid expansion and spectacular successes of the Japanese war machine in its drive to the south and west, and painfully aware of the perilous implications this might have on the Indian Ocean and contiguous territories, the Admiralty in London had set about mustering in the waters encompassing the Ceylon region the strongest naval force possible at that juncture, designated the Eastern Fleet, under command of one of the Navy's doughtiest admirals. Although we on the lower deck were not yet aware of it, *Cornwall* was then on course to join in the convocation of this fleet.

Cornwall's departure was a most depressing experience for one of her crew, ERA (engine room artificer) 'Chippy' Woods. He it was who, during the action with the German surface raider *Pinguin,* as related earlier, had been second-last to vacate the engine-room when heat caused by damaged ventilation had rendered it untenable. As a result, Chippy's lungs were permanently impaired and recuperation unacceptably tardy. It had therefore been decided, when the cruiser put in at Fremantle, that Chippy should receive hospital treatment ashore and so it was that, from his sickbed overlooking the harbour, feeling sick, utterly lonely and deserted, he watched his ship, with all his shipmates aboard, sail out of sight. However, it turned out to be a providential blessing in disguise because a mere few weeks later everyone on duty in that engine-room died. That would have included Chippy had he not been left behind in a Fremantle hospital ward. He was transferred in due course to Baragwanath Military Hospital in Johannesburg, acquired South African citizenship after the war, and married Agnes, one of the young ladies who had tended him in hospital. I met up with him forty years later, and we and our families became close friends. His heat-damaged lungs contributed to his death in 1998.

Cornwall had just slipped her moorings in Fremantle harbour and was about to get underway when the port was struck by a freak cloudburst of such intensity that the cruiser's prow could not be seen from the bridge through the driving rain. It lasted only a minute or two, but the ship had to heave to temporarily.

"What a storm to start the voyage with!" I exclaimed to an 'old salt' working next to me as the weather cleared.

"Bad omen," he muttered gloomily.

* * * * *

12

TO THE EYE OF THE STORM

(Bless 'em all)

Cornwall's return voyage to Colombo was uneventful, but undertaken at a goodly speed indicative of urgency. Clearly the ship was needed at destination without delay. Otherwise it was routine stuff: dawn action stations followed by sweeping, scrubbing and hosing down decks with CPO Standing of the Fo'c'sle Division in top vociferous form – "Come on there, Lofty [Yours Truly]; stop gawkin' around the 'orison and look lively with that broom. Get all them fag ends and matches out what's stuck in the degaussing gear." 'Degaussing' cables had been installed around the perimeter of upper decks on all ships – merchantmen as well as men-of-war – an enormously costly but necessary undertaking to counter the menace of magnetic mines. The cables neutralised the magnetism in the ships' hulls by encircling them with a current-carrying conductor.

Then it was down to the mess deck for breakfast and, for those off watch, up again shortly after for the usual run of forenoon chores. Dimbleby, ever meticulous in description and detail, recalls in his book that the trip took eight days, and while in that short period it produced little for the ship's company to 'write home about', momentous developments were occurring elsewhere. The Japanese continued their expansion and consolidation in South-East Asia and, in the Bay of Bengal, occupied the Andaman and Nicobar archipelagos to support their military northwards drive in Burma; the German armies in Russia retook territory lost during the winter and prepared for their impending conquest of the Ukraine and thrust to the Volga; Rommel in Cyrenaica was marshalling his Axis division with the intention of crashing through to the Nile delta; the fortress island of Malta was tottering under heavy siege and aerial bombardment; the Battle of the Atlantic was raging at its peak; 'Operation Chariot', the brilliant combined operations raid on Saint Nazaire to breach the Normandy Dry Dock had commenced... and the Wrens were given a new hat.

Wrens, anagram for WRNS, or 'Women' Royal Naval Service, were a growing and refreshing feature in the Navy and, as with their counterparts in the other services, they rendered an invaluable contribution to the war effort, often in the face of grave danger. They were visible almost everywhere: in administration, as signal and wireless operatives, motor vehicle drivers, couriers and messengers, maintenance technicians, stores controllers, in-harbour boat crews and boarding parties – the list is seemingly endless. HMS *Wren*, a First World War destroyer, was, on account of her name, informally adopted by the Wrens and after she was lost in 1940 a new HMS *Wren*, an antisubmarine sloop, was built and officially dedicated to the WRNS, upon whose director, Dame Vera Mathews DBE, was conferred the honour of launching her. The same lady, fiercely proud of the Wren image, spearheaded a crusade to change the nondescript cap worn by her charges to a distinguished and stylish hat. It was at the height of shortages and restrictions in Britain but, refusing to be fobbed off by such trivia, Vera Mathews pursued her demand with unshakeable determination, winning support for her cause all the way to their Majesties the King and Queen. The final decision had to be taken at Cabinet level, where the constituent incumbents, fearful perhaps of precipitating a disposition akin to which 'Hell hath no fury', capitulated. The Wrens got their hat and, let it be said, it crowned a uniform than which there was no smarter anywhere. Reinaugurated from scratch shortly before hostilities commenced, the Wrens increased in number to 72,000 by war's end.

Operating in four watches, as we were on that trip, made life a lot easier. One was on watch only one in four, which allowed more leisure time, especially during the afternoons and evenings, made more delectable by news bulletins and entertainment relayed over the broadcast system and supplemented occasionally by the ship's own royal marine band. In most of us, I believe, music leaves an indelible trail down memory lane even if rendered only imperceptibly, perpetuating our recollections of people and events that touched our lives. This is probably more so under emotive circumstances as in times of war and turmoil. The songs sung and music heard during WWII will consistently, if reproduced subsequently in whatever form, recapture nostalgic memories of that era.

This phenomenon was undoubtedly to the benefit of some performing artists who, but for being wartime contemporaries, would not have achieved quite as much lasting fame as they did. Songs that we then heard over and over again – Vera Lynn's 'We'll Meet Again', 'When they Sound the Last All Clear', 'A Nightingale Sang in Berkeley Square', and 'White Cliffs of Dover' are as poignant and nostalgic to us now as they were then, as are Ann Shelton's 'I'll Be Seeing You', 'Don't Cry My Love' and more. Many other ballads and melodies of that time also revive cherished memories, among them 'Maybe' and 'I Don't Want to Set the World on Fire' by the Ink Spots, 'Underneath the Arches' by Flanagan and Allen, 'Don't Fence me In' and 'You Are My Sunshine' with Bing Crosby and the Andrews Sisters. American morale boosters included 'America I Love You', 'The United States Marines' and 'Coming in on a Wing and a Prayer'. The British patriotic anthem 'There'll Always Be an England' was popular. Then, of course, who among us can forget the perennial canteen bawlers, like:

'You'll get no promotion, this side of the ocean
So cheer up my lads bless 'em all'

as well as 'You'll be Far Better off on the Dole', and 'She'll Be Coming round the Mountain when She Comes (Yippie Yippie Yi)'?

The war yielded a potent stimulus to the film industry too, giving credence to the Dutch proverb, carried over into Afrikaans which, loosely translated, says "One man dead means another man's bread.' WWII engendered many memorable motion pictures with a wartime backdrop. Early productions included *Mrs Miniver*, the story of a family in south-east England around the time of deliverance of the British Expeditionary Force from the beaches at Dunkirk, starring Greer Garson and Walter Pidgeon and *In Which We Serve* with Noel Coward and John Mills, about a British destroyer's traumatic participation in the evacuation of troops from Greece and Crete, based on the factual experience of Louis Mountbatten as commanding officer of HMS *Kelly*. Later came *Casablanca*, rooted, as the title implies, in Morocco, featuring Humphrey Bogart and Ingrid Bergman – a gripping tale of secret agents and intrigue, regarded still today as a classic, as is its theme song 'As Time Goes By' sung by the gravelly-voiced Louis 'Satchmo' Armstrong. Another outstanding film was *Dangerous Moonlight* with Anton Walbrook and Sally Gray. Walbrook played the part of a Polish fighter pilot and piano virtuoso whose *Warsaw Concerto* (composed by Sir Richard Adinsell) became an immediate hit almost worldwide. The war of course provided an abundance of material for the filming of actuality newsreels.

Cornwall had its fair share of musical talent on board. Apart from the Royal Marine Band, whose members were all qualified musicians, some adept at more than one instrument, there were a number who could perform credibly on one instrument or another. Others could sing in good voice. One such was Tubby Cutler, as was Peter Versfeld, an engaging fellow of about my age whose home was in

Constantia, Cape Town. Peter was multi-talented in a widely diverse way: something of a dreamer on the one hand who loved music of all shades and, on the other, an exceptional sportsman. At age 18 he had played first league cricket and rugby in the Western Province, and I heard from more than one knowledgeable source after the war that he had been tipped as a future Springbok fly half.

Peter often, when off watch during the dogs, repaired to the fore-cabin flat, a spacious area usually unoccupied at that late afternoon hour. It contained an old upright piano, secured to the deck for stability at sea, and Peter would sit there picking out tunes on the keys, or singing and humming quietly to the strumming of his ukulele. Quite often I joined him to listen and, at his invitation, offer comment and suggestion regarding his compositions, which to my mind were good. One in particular, titled 'On the Wings of a Dream', I thought outstanding, capturing the longing of someone, such as he, for his home and family thousands of miles away. One afternoon I chaffed him about it, jovially yet not without sincerity. "Minstrel Boy," I said, "when we get leave in South Africa you must send that song to *Snoektown Calling*; it will be a great hit." '*Snoektown Calling* – the craziest radio station south of the line' was a popular programme broadcast from Cape Town and, in those warring years, was aimed mainly at the South African forces, both 'up north' in the Mediterranean region, and at home. I recalled, sadly, that particular occasion later:

> The Minstrel Boy to the war has gone
> In the ranks of death you will find him.

When *Cornwall* steamed into Colombo harbour on 26 March 1942, one sensed immediately something different in the air, a feeling that something fateful was afoot. Usually the big cruiser enjoyed a prima donna entrance and sojourn at the Ceylonese port, being the largest and most powerful vessel present, but on this occasion she had to defer pride of place to HMS *Formidable,* a huge aircraft-carrier, and share lesser effulgence with another three-funnelled "County" class cruiser, HMS *Dorsetshire,* the ship that had administered the *coup de grace* to the German behemoth *Bismarck.* In addition there were numerous smaller 'white ensign' ships in attendance and an above-normal clutter of freighters and other craft.

The 'buzz' wizards, who had duly plied their prognosticatory practice ever since leaving Fremantle, now erupted with enhanced gusto, almost unanimously forecasting that *Cornwall,* until then very much an operative loner, would within a day or two join and be part of a new-forming fleet or task force, opinions differing only as regards the specific missions to which the new force would be assigned. It had indeed been rumoured in recent days that, in face of the extremely menacing situation in South-East Asia, drastic measures were a supreme necessity, something which would have been obvious even to insouciant armchair observers. In particular an effective counter had to be found to the eminently efficient Japanese vanguard, their First Carrier task force commanded by Admiral Nagumo and, as already related towards the close of the preceding chapter, the Admiralty sought to do this by piecing together a new squadron, comprising all warships that could somewhere be spared, to operate in the general vicinity of Ceylon. Thus was reborn the Eastern Fleet and, true to the predictions of the 'buzz' merchants, *Cornwall* was to be a component.

I came across the 'old salt' to whom I had spoken eight days previously when departing Fremantle. He was leaning over a guardrail smoking a cigarette, pensively surveying the congested shipping around us.

"Was this what your 'bad omen' was all about?" I chided him.

"Aye, matey," he rumbled. "Storm ahead, and we'll be right in th' middle on it."

* * * * *

13

COUNTER DIMENSION – THE ADMIRAL

("What the hell do you want?")

Early one morning in the mid 1930s the destroyer *Wolsey* lay in Alexandria harbour. This ship was one of a sizeable number of British warships assembled there as a precautionary presence in the eastern Mediterranean. It was a time of tension, Mussolini the Italian dictator having, in defiance of the League of Nations and disdainful of sanctions, launched the invasion and conquest of Abyssinia – an affront to Great Britain in particular. Adding to general unease was evidence of Italian espionage in the Alexandria/Canal region by submarine and other means.

The first lieutenant of the *Wolsey* was indulging in light physical exercise on the still deserted quarterdeck when he observed a skiff approaching, rowed by a man in khaki attire. When only a short distance away, the occupant of the skiff stopped rowing and, resting his arms on the oars, scrutinised the destroyer intently. Suspicion acutely aroused, the officer called out, "Can I help you?" his intonation clearly implying "What the hell do you want; bugger off!"

"No thanks," came the reply. "I'm only taking some exercise like you, and looking around," adding as he rowed away to inspect another ship, "I'm the RAD [Rear Admiral Destroyers]."

Such was typical of the man, named Somerville – in later years Admiral of the Fleet Sir James – unorthodox, unpredictable, innovative. He and Andrew B. Cunningham (ABC to his peers), his friend and teammate from cadet and midshipman days, veterans of the First World War, were arguably the two most outstanding Royal Navy fighting admirals of the twentieth century. Somerville was the man chosen in March of 1942, when at that time a full admiral, to be in command of the British warships then gathering in dire urgency in and around Ceylon and designated to the Eastern Fleet, intended hopefully as a counterpunch against Japan's carrier-centred naval threat in the region.

As a commanding officer Somerville was probably, within human limitations, closest to the ideal as one could wish: master of his trade, intellect of high order, positive in outlook and, in combat, an optimal blend of daring and prudence. Over and above, he was a humanitarian, ever mindful of the safety and welfare of those in his charge and, while allowing no slackness in efficiency and discipline, consistently effused a keen sense of humour and ready wit. Yet this remarkable officer might inconspicuously have been lost to the Navy and his country during the period between the wars, when his health deteriorated and he was relieved of his duties due to suspected tuberculosis, with the prospect of being put out 'on the beach' on early retirement. Fortunately he recovered fully and was reinstated.

Somerville had already gained distinction in the Second World War prior to his relocation to the Eastern Fleet. He had commanded 'Force H' comprising a fleet of interchanging warships including the aircraft-carrier *Ark Royal,* battleship *Ramillies,* battle-cruiser *Renown*, cruiser *Sheffield* and others, based at Gibraltar and largely responsible for naval operations in the western Mediterranean, but also in the Atlantic if need be. In May 1941 Force H had played a vital part in bringing the super-battleship *Bismarck* to bay. The German behemoth was the most powerful battleship then afloat, with a displacement of 45,000 tons, her defensive armour alone contributing 16,000 tons dead weight. She was superbly compartmented to counteract flooding, and had awesome firepower and the most scientifically advanced gunnery control systems yet devised.

Admiral Sir James Somerville

On the morning of 24 May 1941, shortly after first light, *Bismarck* and her escort, heavy cruiser *Prinz Eugen*, were intercepted south-west of Iceland by the British battle-cruiser *Hood,* pride of the Royal Navy, and *Prince of Wales,* their newest battleship. Salvoes from both German warships straddled *Hood* from the start at 25,000 yards, the third from *Prinz Eugen* starting a large fire among ammunition stored in ready-use lockers on the upper deck. *Bismarck*'s fifth salvo, plunging from a high trajectory, struck *Hood* again on her upper deck, where she was most vulnerable, having little horizontal deck armour.

One shell bored through and exploded deep below in a magazine, which, added to multifarious internal explosions thereby induced, tore the mighty battle-cruiser asunder. When the smoke cleared, all that remained was a spreading patch of oil and debris, and only three men survived out of a complement of 1,419. Thereupon *Bismarck*'s turrets swung around to target *Prince of Wales,* her first salvo straddling the British battleship with a hit on the compass platform, leaving the bridge area in a shambles. *Prince of Wales,* which was having problems with her fire control, then broke off the engagement, unpursued by the Germans.

Bismarck and *Prinz Eugen* then separated, the former having sustained some superficial damage affecting her fuel supply. Realising that the advantage of surprise had been forfeited, and that the British Home Fleet, along with all other strategically placed Royal Navy ships, would now be mobilising to hunt down and overwhelm her, she decided to abandon the commerce-raiding mission. Her immediate pressing concern was to shake off her shadowing tormentors and 'get lost'. In this she was assisted by low rain clouds and fog as well as the trailing vessels having difficulty in maintaining radar contact. Although she had sustained a torpedo hit amidships by aircraft from the carrier *Victorious* of Admiral Tovey's Home Fleet, her progress was not seriously impaired and eventually she succeeded in eluding her pursuers completely, whereupon she set an eastward course for the German-occupied French Atlantic seaboard.

The British pursuit, wrongly surmising that their quarry intended to proceed westwards, in fulfilment of her assigned task or, possibly, to return to Norwegian waters on the Iceland/Faroes route, plotted their strategy correspondingly and only after a chance sighting of the *Bismarck* by a Catalina flying boat was the truth revealed, by which time the German battleship had gained a 150-mile head start and was too far ahead to be overhauled by the Home Fleet before reaching the approaches to the French coast and protection by U-boats and the Luftwaffe – unless she could somehow be slowed down. The only means left for doing that lay in the hands of Somerville's Force H, then racing north-westwards from the Straits of Gibraltar on an interception course.

Somerville's squadron did not have the firepower to engage *Bismarck* effectively in a surface confrontation but he planned to launch an aerial torpedo attack from the carrier *Ark Royal* when within range and, preparatory to that, he despatched the cruiser *Sheffield* ahead to assist in monitoring and reporting the German's progress. The torpedo-bombers available to him were still the antiquated Fairy 'Stringbean' Swordfish – slow and ponderous biplanes nakedly vulnerable in any conflict situation but especially during their run-ins prior to dropping their 'tin fish', tending then to be 'sitting ducks' in the face of anti-aircraft fire. A special monument should be erected, if something of the sort has not already been done, in honour of those inelegant, often ridiculed warplanes and the intrepid men who flew in them, whom Admiral Cunningham hailed as "the cream of the Fleet Air Arm".

The first air strike from *Ark Royal* was abortive and almost disastrous. Conditions were wild and bewildering, a gale-force wind, low driving rain clouds and a heavy sea running. In poor visibility the attacking planes happened upon a lone warship which they mistook for *Bismarck* and released eleven torpedoes at her, only to discover too late that their target was the *Sheffield*. To the utter relief of all concerned none of the torpedoes found its mark. At the second attempt fifteen Swordfish took off from the pitching flight deck and were presently directed to the *Bismarck* by *Sheffield*. Pressing home their attack despite murderous fire, they dropped another thirteen torpedoes and achieved at least two hits, the first, as with almost all others, having minimal effect due to the phenomenal armour of the great battleship. But the second hit, which all but missed, struck under the stern, damaging the screws and angularly jamming the twin rudders to the extent that the ship could thereafter maintain an approximate course only with the greatest difficulty by engine manipulation at a slow, wallowing speed.

So desperately did the Admiralty seek to destroy the *Bismarck* – following the loss in combat of *Hood* the reputation and honour of the Royal Navy was at stake – that they ordered five destroyers to leave a troopship convoy to join in the chase. The destroyers, under command of redoubtable Captain (later Admiral of the Fleet Sir Philip) Vian in *Cossack* located the *Bismarck* after dark and kept up continual torpedo attacks on the German throughout the night, scoring several hits which again did not significantly damage the battleship. One suspects an element of panic in the Admiralty's decision to detach the destroyers and would rather not speculate on the outrage – naval, military, political and civil – that would have erupted had one or more of the troopships been sunk by U-boat offensive in the absence of the destroyer escort concerned.

In the event the curtain came down on the *Bismarck* pageant the following morning with the arrival of the British battleships *Rodney* and *King George V* under command of Admiral John Tovey, C-in-C Home Fleet, and they, supported by several cruisers, pounded the stricken German for two hours into a flaming, smoking wreck, but still afloat, her battle ensign still flying, and her decks and superstructure strewn with dead and dying. Heavy cruiser *Dorsetshire,* also having left a convoy to assist in the operation, then moved in close and fired three torpedoes into the *Bismarck*, whereafter she at last sank, only 115 men surviving out of a complement of 2,400. Engineer Officer Gerhard Junack, one of only two surviving officers, declared later that British torpedoes had not sunk *Bismarck* but that she was in fact scuttled and that he had personally, at the end, given the order for demolition charges in the bilges to be detonated. Indeed when the dying monster finally rolled over prior to her death plunge there was no visible evidence that her hull had been holed. So ended one of naval history's most dramatic sagas, and it was only the rudder-jamming torpedo from Somerville's Force H that clinched it.

The Mediterranean Sea was right from the start crucial to both sides in prosecution of the war, but with heightened intensity after the fall of France and entry of Italy into the fray. It was the vital waterway and strategic access route separating, as its name implies, the land masses of Europe and Africa latitudinally, and the Atlantic and Indian Oceans longitudinally. From a naval perspective its stormy pivotal point, roughly bisecting the Sea into western and eastern zones, was the island of Malta, then a British possession lying vulnerably less than 60 miles from Sicily and at the southern entrance to the 'Narrows', the perilous passage between Sicily and Tunisia. For practical reasons the Royal Navy allocated responsibility for the western zone to Somerville's Force H, based at Gibraltar, and the eastern zone to Cunningham's Mediterranean Fleet based at Alexandria.

The Royal Navy's three priorities in the Mediterranean at that time were the maintenance and defence of Malta, obstruction of enemy supplies and reinforcements to North Africa, and neutralising the Italian navy which, on inventory, was formidable indeed. Both Cunningham and Somerville tackled these tasks with vigour and considerable success. They were men of action who refused to be deterred by the immensity of the risks and hazards facing them. Replenishment of stores and equipment to Malta and, to no mean extent also to Alexandria, was routed for logistic and other reasons through the western zone, Somerville's Force H being heavily committed. Convoys had to contend with submarine attacks from the outset at the Gibraltar end, augmented later by aerial bombing as they progressed eastwards. The threat from the sky intensified as the ships negotiated the constricted passage through the Sicilian Narrows which, in addition, was extensively mined.

In disdain of the Italian Navy, Force H swept north and bombarded installations at Genoa, situated at the apex of the Ligurian Sea, while its Fleet Air Arm successfully bombarded Leghorn, Pisa (without, presumably, aggravating the slant to its leaning tower) and targets on the island of Sardinia. For his part, Cunningham in the eastern Mediterranean led his ships in synchronised support wherever practicable. His most spectacular success, however, was achieved on

11 November, 1940, Armistice Day, in Operation Judgement, when twenty trundling Swordfish torpedo-bombers from the carriers *Illustrious* and *Eagle* surprised a large section of the Italian fleet at Taranto at night, and in the space of minutes, despite intense anti-aircraft fire, wreaked, in the Admiral's words, 'more damage upon the Italian fleet than was inflicted upon the German High Sea Fleet in the daylight action at the Battle of Jutland'. The Battle of Jutland took place in the First World War.

Somerville's most dramatic Mediterranean exploit, but which filled him with repugnance, was Operation Catapult. When France surrendered in June 1940 a primary concern of Churchill's War Cabinet was the disposition of the formidable French fleet and the danger of strong components thereof falling into German hands. The terms of surrender had stipulated that all French naval vessels, except minor units required for coastal surveillance and maintenance of order in French colonies, would be demobilised and disarmed under supervision by the Axis powers with the assurance that the vessels would not be used by the latter in their prosecution of the war. The British government held this assurance in utter contempt, and resolute steps were taken to prevent all French warships not then disposed in French ports from moving thither. Powerful French naval units were dispersed among North and West African ports at Alexandria, Mers-el-Kebir, Algeria, Casablanca and Dakar, and some others at Portsmouth and Plymouth, and while the majority of these, due to geographical location, could be contained and posed no immediate threat to British security, those within the Mediterranean did because they were in a position, if allowed, to make a dash for Toulon, the French south-coastal naval base, as ordered by the Petain government-in-surrender (later designated Vichy) under pressure from their German conquerors.

The most ominous situation in this regard was at Mers-el-Kebir, the naval base adjacent to Oran in western Algeria where, among other naval vessels, were four capital ships including two modern battle-cruisers, *Dunkerque* and *Strasbourg* which, if let loose on the high seas with German crews, could wreak havoc upon shipping, whether in convoy or independently routed. Somerville, then vice-admiral in command of Force H, comprising the battle-cruiser *Hood*, battleships *Valiant* and *Resolution,* aircraft-carrier *Ark Royal,* cruisers and destroyers, was ordered to the scene from Gibraltar, arriving off Oran early on the morning of July 2 1940. Four proposals formulated by the Admiralty, designed to place the French ships beyond German acquisition, were put to the local French commander, Admiral Gensoul, with the rider that if all four were rejected the British would be compelled to use force. Gensoul, aboard *Dunkerque,* resentful of the British posture, communicated these terms to the French Admiralty, where the C-in-C, Admiral Darlan, was likewise irked.

The crisis which had thus arisen was bedevilled, firstly on the French side by their inaccurate referral to their Council of Ministers, and secondly by the British War Cabinet in its inflexible resolve and peremptory orders to Somerville which ultimately demanded compliance 'before dark' – the type of signal which, Admiral Cunningham writes in his memoirs, 'should never be made'. On this note it is amusing, even food for thought, to heed the acerbic observation of another admiral, on another occasion, to the effect that Nelson's celebrated victories more than a century earlier were achieved largely because the age of telecommunication had at that time not yet dawned. Wiser counsel would surely have allowed postponement at least until the following day, by when temperatures would probably have cooled and an acceptable accord without loss of face might have been negotiated.

Somerville's squadron opened fire shortly before 6.00 pm, at what was little more than point-blank range, upon the French ships, cooped up in harbour with virtually no space to manoeuvre. The battleship *Bretagne*, hit in a magazine, blew up in a vast display of smoke and flame, the *Provence* and *Dunkerque*, heavily damaged, ran aground but the *Strasbourg* gained the open sea and escaped in the gathering darkness, firing defiantly at her tormentors, evading aerial torpedoes from the *Ark Royal* and eventually reaching Toulon. French cruisers at Algiers, seizing the opportunity to make a dash while the focus was on Mers-el-Kebir, also escaped to Toulon. Somerville, who did nothing to hide his abhorrence at having to bombard his erstwhile allies, did his best not to extend destruction and bloodshed beyond what was essential to achieve the central objective, and he terminated the attack after little more than ten minutes.

These were part of the 'curriculum vitae' that Somerville, the admiral designate, brought with him when, on 24 March 1942, he arrived in Ceylon to assume command of the Eastern Fleet then taking shape. He had travelled from Britain via the Cape aboard the aircraft-carrier *Formidable*. Characteristically, to gain even a few hours of time, he flew the last hundred miles to Colombo in one of the carrier's aeroplanes, impatient to impose his 'hands on' operational authority.

* * * * *

14

COUNTER DIMENSION – THE EASTERN FLEET

(A glorious and majestic sight)

'Hands on', in the context of describing, at the close of the preceding chapter the man chosen to command the Eastern Fleet, implied action, alacrity and dynamism – attributes readily recognisable in the person of Admiral James Somerville. His flagship to be was HMS *Warspite*, which arrived in Colombo the day after we did, and well I remember my thrill in beholding the famous battleship, resplendent in might and magnitude as it nosed in through the harbour entrance. Her proud record dated back to 1913 and her participation three years later at Jutland. Between the wars she had been considerably modernised, resulting in increased speed and improved endurance, and in the present conflict she had already earned distinction in the western Mediterranean and elsewhere, a fighting ship of 37,000 tons displacement.

Almost immediately an undercurrent of expectancy was felt on *Cornwall*; clearly something momentous was afoot and buzzes were soon flying for'rard, aft and athwart on the lower deck. Though varying in detail, the main ingredient in each was the possibility of confrontation with elements of the Japanese navy. Shore leave was cancelled, which almost certainly presaged imminent departure, underscored by the news that *Dorsetshire,* our 'County' class sister cruiser, which had commenced a boiler refit in dry dock, had been ordered to suspend the operation and return as soon as possible to her moorings in mid-harbour, obviously in readiness to put to sea.

The following afternoon, 28 March 1942, *Warspite,* flying the flag of Admiral Somerville, steamed out to sea and veered slightly on to a southerly course, followed by the great aircraft-carrier *Formidable,* the heavy cruisers *Dorsetshire* and *Cornwall,* a couple of light cruisers and, fleetest of the fleet, some destroyers. Shortly afterwards it was announced over the broadcast system that we would, after joining up with other units of the Eastern Fleet, search for and destroy ships of the Japanese navy which, it was thought, might be approaching Ceylon with hostile intent. No more was disclosed at that point. In fact, little more was then available for disclosure. What was not divulged in the broadcast was that an Intelligence report had that day been received indicating the possibility of a seaborne aerial attack on Ceylon on 1 April or thereabouts, but no more, no approximate estimate of the size or composition of the attackers envisaged.

HMS Warspite, *flagship of Eastern Fleet*

The difficulty for Allied Intelligence was that once an enemy strike force had departed the land and its environs, and disappeared over the horizon into the boundless expanse of the oceans, its whereabouts and intentions became largely a matter of conjecture. The days of satellite surveillance from outer space had not yet dawned, and Intelligence had to collate and select a number of factors, some unreliable, to gauge movements of the enemy who, from his perspective, would operate with hermetic secrecy, observing radio silence and avoiding frequented shipping lanes.

After conquest of the Dutch East Indies the powerful Japanese carrier strike force, still under command of Admiral Nagumo, was for a short while bereft of major operational missions and the high-ranking strategists at Combined Fleet headquarters in Tokyo, their planning overtaken and passed by the speedy advance of their armed forces in the Southern offensive, with objectives attained ahead of schedule, began hastily appraising follow-up options. These lay broadly in three directions: eastwards towards Hawaii and the American Pacific Fleet, southwards towards the Solomon Islands, New Hebrides and New Caledonia, threatening New Zealand and Australia and, to the west, targeting Ceylon, the British Eastern Fleet and India, followed by Madagascar and the Persian Gulf.

At that time Nagumo's carrier division was sheltering in Teluk Bay in the vicinity of Kendari on the south-east coast of Celebes, an island lying between Borneo and New Guinea and resembling in shape a deformed starfish.

Nagumo's strike force left Celebes on 26 March – that much was known to the Allies – and then, ominously, vanished. Immediately the alarm bells started ringing. Would Nagumo, when beyond observation limits, swing left or right, eastwards or westwards, or maintain a southerly course? What were his objectives this time? The strike force could materialise suddenly, with lethal effect, at any point within cruising range, and much further if arrangements were in place to rendezvous with tankers for refuelling at sea, or, for that matter, split up into smaller divisions and hit two or more targets simultaneously. What did the signs, if any, portend? America had broken the Japanese naval code but would radio transmissions from Tokyo give anything away, even a hint? Any ship, Allied or neutral, encountered by the strike force would promptly be despatched, probably before it could send a comprehensible distress signal, but a chance sighting by one of our submarines would be a godsend. However, this did not happen. Radioed messages, if any, from agents left behind among the islands, keyed out at deadly peril to themselves would, if picked up, frequently be garbled and have to be evaluated with circumspection. Was such agent still reliable or had he, to save his skin, switched allegiance, or succumbed to the dictum: 'If you can't beat 'em, join 'em'?

Five weeks earlier, on 19 February, the Japanese carriers had struck Port Darwin at the top of Australia's Northern Territory, the continent's most important port north of the Brisbane latitude, wreaking heavy damage upon installations and shipping in the harbour. Could Nagumo now be heading that way again for a follow-up blow?

The British Command had to weigh all the evidence and as far as possible prepare for any contingency. One such would certainly be an air attack on Ceylon, and on that presumption, urgently applied calculations involving distance and speed indicated a probable strike on or about April 1. Only a fool, the ultimate April Fool, would ignore that. Prime measures taken were to place the island's meagre air defences on high alert, arrange for Colombo and Trincomalee to be cleared of shipping as far as practicable, and for units of the newly established Eastern Fleet then present in those harbours to put to sea, consolidate with other units and take up a tactical position in the waters southeast of Ceylon, from which direction, it was assumed, any seaborne attack, if one impended, would emerge.

The grey dawn before sunrise on 29 March, the day following our sortie from Colombo, presented us with a panorama of the new Eastern

Fleet at sea in its entirety. Five battleships now steamed in line ahead, forming the predominant central column, stretching a mile or more, flanked by three aircraft-carriers, seven cruisers and fourteen destroyers (I am indebted to Ken Dimbleby's *Turns of Fate* for the precise composition of lower-order ships), truly a glorious and majestic sight, the stuff that newsreels rejoice in projecting on screens at the movies to the strains of rousing patriotic music supported by glowing commentary. It was the largest muster of British men-o'-war thus far in the war; the biggest assemblage, according to word circulating, since Jutland in 1916. Be that as it may, we felt intensely proud to be part of it and the mess deck at breakfast was abuzz with animated comment. "If the Jap sticks his nose out today," exulted Hedley Beswetherick in my No 9 Mess, "it will be chopped off." We all agreed with joyous enthusiasm and indeed felt at that stage that a protrusion of Nipponese proboscis would be warmly welcome.

The new arrivals had joined us after a night's steaming from Port T, the secret anchorage at Addu Atoll in the Maldives, and comprised four battleships, another fleet aircraft-carrier, two medium and three light cruisers, and eight more destroyers. In addition, the light carrier *Hermes* had likewise rendezvoused from Trincomalee. Had we been better acquainted with the reality of the situation, however, the ebullience at breakfast might have been at a somewhat lower pitch. Our enthusiasm may have waned somewhat upon sober reflection on the limitations in fighting capability and durability of our array of warships, twenty-nine in all, making up the Eastern Fleet.

The four newly-arrived battleships were the *Royal Sovereign*, *Resolution*, *Ramillies* and *Revenge*, each with a main armament of eight 15-inch guns in four turrets. They were collectively known as the 'R' class, of First World War vintage. Their construction was completed during 1916–17 but, unlike *Warspite*, had not been modernised between the wars. Their projected speed was a slow 21 knots, which had been reduced further by the attachment of torpedo-protective bulges at and below the waterline and, of course, by the passing years. Their design had been influenced from First War/North Sea perspective, which did not envisage extended periods at sea or long distances to cover, for which their fresh water and fuel storage capacity was woefully inadequate. Their effectiveness was therefore best demonstrated in home waters, or otherwise within a limited radius from base. They were regarded in upper naval echelons as obsolete, and Churchill, in an unguarded off-the-record aside, described them as "useless" under Second World War exigencies. That was, however, somewhat unfair because their eight 15-inch guns, supported by 6-inch batteries, could deliver a powerful 'wallop' and under medium- to close-range engagement could be a force to be reckoned with, particularly in coastal bombardment.

At the outbreak of hostilities in 1939 there had been five 'R' class battleships but the fifth, the *Royal Oak,* was torpedoed and sunk where she lay at anchor in Scapa Flow, the great naval anchorage in the Orkneys, during the night of October 14 of that year by the German submarine U47, captained by Gunther Prien, which had overcome strong tidal currents and other obstacles, breached the defences and ultimately made good its escape in an exploit which even Churchill acknowledged as a remarkable feat of arms.

The two large aircraft-carriers now with us, *Formidable* and *Indomitable*, were the cream of the Eastern Fleet, having been completed as lately as 1940–41, displacing 23,000 tons, with speed in excess of 30 knots, and each with accommodation for up to 60 aircraft. In construction they compared favourably with any afloat, especially in one respect, namely flight deck armour. As a class aircraft-carriers were, due to their importance and size, invariably priority targets under attack from the air, and were particularly vulnerable to devastating fires because of the large quantities of high-octane aviation spirit aboard, both in aircraft and in storage. These hazards were appreciably reduced in carriers with armoured flight decks, such as in *Formidable* and *Indomitable*, this having been proved by their sister ship *Illustrious*, which had survived savage pounding by German Stuka dive-bombers in the Mediterranean. Their major weakness, however, was the quality of the aircraft they carried, which at that stage of the war was far inferior to that of the Japanese.

The third carrier, *Hermes*, was some seventeen years older, with an aircraft capacity of about 20, and at 11,000 tons displacement only half the size of the other two. She was the first ship specifically designed by the Admiralty as an aircraft-carrier.

Six of the seven cruisers were veterans of the Royal Navy, having made their debut over a period ranging from the First World War to the late 1920s and, had the Second not intervened, several would no doubt already have exited via the shipbreakers. *Dorsetshire* and *Cornwall* were the two 'County' class heavies at around 10,000 tons each, with powerful main batteries of eight 8-inch guns and conspicuous by their three tall funnels. The two 'middleweights', *Emerald* and *Enterprise*, came at 7,550 tons, their main punch in the form of seven 6-inch guns. Also with three funnels, they were immediately recognisable by the unusual position of their third stack abaft the mainmast. Although old-timers of 1919–1920 vintage, they were still among the fastest cruisers in His Majesty's Navy. Two light cruisers, *Caledon* and *Dragon*, displacing something in excess of only 4,000 tons, were of the oldest in the Navy, having been commissioned during the 1914–1918 hostilities, their main armament also comprising the ubiquitous but trusty 6-inch guns. The seventh cruiser, the *Jacob van Heemskerck,* flying the ensign of the Royal Netherlands Navy, was relatively new, having been completed just two years previously in a British shipyard. Her principal ordnance consisted of ten 4-inch, high-angle guns which, together with ample weaponry of lesser calibre, made her primarily an anti-aircraft ship.

The fourteen destroyers allocated to Somerville ranged in lifespan from old to new, two of the latest being *Paladin* and *Panther,* still in their first year of service. Among them was another welcome and ardent Netherlander, *Isaac Sweer.* While the Eastern Fleet on that morning of 29 March looked imposing and powerful it had, apart from the age of most vessels, two other weaknesses. Firstly, most of the ships were in need, to a greater or lesser degree, of major repair. *Dorsetshire* in fact had already commenced a refit in Colombo before the current urgent operation had been sprung on us. Secondly, the ships' companies had had virtually no experience of inter-fleet battle procedures with which one would expect us to be fully conversant should we meet a Japanese force of comparable composition. Accordingly Somerville determined to put us through our paces vigorously and educate us as much as possible in the few days of grace available and, with characteristic drive and enthusiasm, he wasted no time in tackling the task.

HMS Dorsetshire

The admiral shepherded his flock through a continuing series of manoeuvres and battle simulations, with a keen eye for detail and aberration, drilling and disciplining with parade-ground similitude. He kept everyone in the fleet on tenterhooks, especially executive officers and communication ranks, with a stream of peremptory and critical signals by flag and lamp and, as is not uncommon under mental agitation, errors occurred which under more relaxed conditions would not have. At one point the ships steaming in line ahead were forewarned by hoisted flags on the flagship *Warspite* that they would be required to turn 90 degrees to port en masse, simultaneously. All ships, having hoisted their answering pendants, had their eyes glued to the flagship awaiting the signal to execute and, when this was given, the whole fleet turned to port in compliance – the whole fleet, that is, except *Dorsetshire*, which perpetrated the monumental bloomer of turning to starboard!

The blunder was immediately realised by the culprit and countermanded but it took several embarrassing, red-faced minutes before the big cruiser, racing at 'full ahead', was able to wheel about and regain her rightful station, now in line abreast. Somerville's immediately flashed signal read simply – 'TUT TUT'. It was sent in typical good humour but the commanding officer of *Dorsetshire,* Captain Augustus Agar VC, by repute a martinet of correctitude, was apparently not amused and had considerably more to contribute in admonishing every crew member whom he adjudged even remotely responsible for the boob. The incident naturally caused much amusement on *Cornwall's* mess deck, where it was suggested that, on the day, Agar's VC stood for 'Very Cross'.

Ships' companies were kept partially, if not fully, closed up at Action Stations for the dual purposes of simulation drill and preparedness in case the real thing suddenly burst upon us. The latter contingency was an ever-present possibility although little information had come to hand to corroborate or elaborate upon the Intelligence warning received earlier that the Japanese carriers had put to sea and that Ceylon should logically be regarded as a likely target. Guns' crews and defensive mechanisms were put through 'dummy runs' from time to time, when men in exposed positions were required to don their 'tin hats', otherwise this headgear had to be kept within easy reach. The tin hat of that time was still the identical 'hand-me-down' from World War 1, shallow with outward-bent, wind-catching rim, and kept in place with an adjustable chin strap which, if the hat was blown off by an explosive blast, was known to have broken the wearer's neck. It afforded a measure of protection only to the crown of one's head and to us on anti-aircraft mountings, whose gaze was mostly skyward, it was continually tilted backwards, and soon caused a painful strain on the neck. "After this war," quipped one of our pom-pom crew, "I'll take me tin 'at 'ome and give it to the missus for a piss-pot."

Inflatable 'Mae West' lifebelts had to be worn in deflated state at all times; thus being in position to be blown up immediately should the need arise – too late then to go looking for them. Extra lookouts were posted and at mealtimes men were released from their stations in batches to visit their messes. We, up on the pom-pom platform, two flights above the main deck, had a grandstand view of all fleet activities which, to novices in this respect like myself, were most intriguing. I was especially fascinated when *Cornwall* was screening an aircraft-carrier abreast and watching aircraft taking off and landing back on again, admiring the skill of their pilots, in particular at night when all ships scrupulously observed blackout provisions except for flight deck landing lights. Somerville exercised his air-crews continually in an urgent endeavour to achieve proficiency as expeditiously as possible. The Japanese were expected to emerge at any hour but in the absence of any concrete indication this could not be a certainty. Nor could the enemy strength, if he came, be more than conjecture. It was furthermore anticipated that, if he came, he would choose the shortest, or near-shortest route, via the Java Sea, entering the Indian ocean either through the Sunda Strait separating the islands of Sumatra and Java or, alternatively, through the Straits of Malacca between Sumatra and the Malayan Peninsula, his logical target Ceylon but specifically the two main ports and naval bases of Colombo and Trincomalee. It was surmised that if Trinco on the east was to be attacked first then this approach could possibly be via Malacca but that move would allow shipping then in Colombo harbour to escape westwards. It was felt, therefore, that a Japanese attack would be aimed first at Colombo on the west so that shipping then at Trinco, if it put to sea, could be trapped in the Bay of Bengal and systematically demolished. Having regard to all these considerations it was presumed that the approach, if it materialised, would probably be through Sunda.

On the other hand, both of these routes had, from the perspective of a Japanese tactician, the disadvantage of passing through a channel which, at its narrowest point, was only a few miles wide, rendering the ships, in daylight especially, observable from shore and consequently vulnerable to clandestine radio transmissions warning the British command of their coming. The danger of discovery by an Allied submarine likewise increased in these constricted waters, begging the question – might not the Japanese decide to come another way altogether? It would seem in retrospect that the feasibility of that was not seriously considered by the British naval command – in the event, a grave oversight.

Somerville, urgently striving to inject a modicum of battleworthiness into his ageing and incommensurate, though impressive-looking squadron, manoeuvred it into a position to the south-east of Ceylon, adjacent to the enemy's anticipated line of approach. His main obstacle to formulating strategy lay with the unknown, the veil of obscurity covering the size and composition of the Japanese incursion, if indeed one was impending. It could be of relatively minor potency, a fast exploratory sweep by cruisers and destroyers with perhaps one carrier or, in diametric contrast, a powerful aggregation of battle-ships, fleet carriers, cruisers and smaller craft. Prudentially the British admiral had to assume the latter, in which case he knew a daylight confrontation had to be avoided. Enough was known at that stage of Japanese naval proficiency, of their overwhelming superiority in numbers, quality of equipment, particularly aircraft, and training and experience to recognise that a head-on, fleet versus fleet encounter in the revealing light of day would invite a British disaster of the greatest magnitude. He therefore formulated plans to launch his attack under cover of darkness, to strike a crippling blow at night when impaired visibility hopefully neutralised his adversary's ascendancy.

Assuming that Japanese aircraft would, as customary, fall upon their intended quarry – on this occasion Colombo or Trincomalee – during early morning, Somerville identified the probable stretch of sea that his adversary's ships would traverse during the preceding night, where hopefully a surprise aerial torpedo assault could be delivered. He had, in this regard, one advantage, that of radar, a technology in which, at the time, the Japanese were still some distance behind. In retrospect, however, these plans were extremely risky, if not foolhardy. The essential element of surprise would be hard come by: precisely locating the enemy without being detected in return, torpedo-bombers thereafter probing in the dark for the blacked-out opposing ships, pressing home the attack at close range and then returning unerringly to our own carriers which would perforce need to linger in the danger area until it could reasonably be adjudged that all our still-airworthy planes were back. Another factor, as yet not fully comprehended on the Allied side, was that the Japanese navy had developed exceptional expertise in night fighting, something the Americans were to discover to their discomfort in later months. Furthermore, if our bombers failed to put all enemy carriers out of action we could expect to have their winged emissaries buzzing about our ears like angry hornets soon after first light.

However, Somerville, while professionally circumspect in weighing the odds, was inherently a man of action, not one to stand idly by in the face of danger, and a man who knew that in time of war, calculated risks had to be taken. His quandary, as has been said, was the unknown. If, as hoped, the opposing force, were there one, contained only one carrier or perhaps two, then his plans, resolutely executed, had a reasonable chance of success. The entire Japanese carrier fleet had departed the Celebes – that much was known – but where it was now headed, or whether or not it had split up into smaller sections, with different assignments, was unknown. There were numerous attractive targets from which the Japanese could choose, including Australia's eastern seaboard.

The reality, had it been known to the British, would have been alarming in the extreme – a fast-approaching hostile, carrier preponderate force of cataclysmic potential was only two or three days distant and Britain's Eastern Fleet, which Somerville had planned to position strategically and undetected on the enemy's flank, now in fact lay almost directly in its path.

* * * * *

15

DETERMINANTS OF DESTINY – MARCH 1942

(Most dangerous moment)

The reality, in fact, was a Japanese naval task force substantially the same as that which, four months earlier, had devastated Pearl Harbor, five fleet aircraft-carriers now forming the nucleus as opposed to the six which had assailed Pearl, but its tally of fast battleships increased from two to four, with supporting cruisers and destroyers much as before. It was again under the command of Admiral Chuichi Nagumo who, at that stage, was arguably the world's most experienced fleet commander, his assignment to bombard Colombo followed by Trincomalee and, in the process, destroy British naval and air strength as well as merchant shipping in the area. The five fleet-carriers were Nagumo's flagship *Akagi plus Hiryu, Soryu, Shokaku* and *Zuikaku*. Only *Kaga*, the sixth carrier of Pearl Harbor participation, was now absent. A separate, correlative reality, also unsuspected by the British at the time, was developing at and around the port of Mergui on the west coast of the Malaysian Peninsula, where a subsidiary task force under Admiral Ozawa, comprising a light carrier, cruisers and destroyers, was preparing to debouch northwards into the Bay of Bengal through the Straits of Malacca, coinciding with Nagumo's attack on Colombo. It would range far and wide, preying on merchant shipping and, if circumstances provided, seek coastal and other targets as well.

Hence on the last two days of March and the first two of April the stage was set for an epoch-making encounter between two opposing fleets, together the largest numerically since Jutland and occurring furthest from land up to that time, with inevitably a disastrous defeat for the British and potentially calamitous consequences for the Allied cause. This period was, in the mind of Winston Churchill the 'most dangerous moment' of the war. The author Michael Tomlinson, in his superbly written and researched book by that title, relates how the great statesman, at a function in his honour in the United States in March 1946, expressed, after serious deliberation, that view to be his considered opinion. By then, some six months after war's end, the echo of the last shot having died away, the impact of particular events, the highs and the lows, the profound emotions and ultimate euphoria of victory having abated and, to some extent at least, taken their rightful place in dispassionate assessment overall, Sir Winston was enabled to respond to a question put to him as he thus did.

It is generally conceded that had the two fleets made contact, Britain's Eastern Fleet, miracles excluded, would have indeed been vanquished. Times had changed and Britain had been the slower to move with them. In little over a hundred years naval combat had developed dramatically. Men-o'-war under sail no longer walloped each other with cannonball and musket, a stone's throw apart. In the First World War iron-clad warships propelled by steam turbines engaged one another over distances of 15 miles or more with armour-piercing explosive projectiles, most of which fell into the sea; and, circumstances permitting, at much closer range with warheaded torpedoes, launched mainly by destroyers and submarines. These procedures carried over almost intact into the Second World War, and although the aircraft industry and research had made phenomenal strides during the intervening twenty-one years the top brass in all the navies of the world, by and large, still regarded the battleship as the prime determining component, the backbone of the fleet – all, that is, except that of Japan, where air-minded high-ranking elements within their ranks exerted strong influence and direction. For years prior to the outbreak of war they had assiduously developed and expanded their naval air arm, modernising and increasing their carrier capacity, improving their range of seaborne aircraft and perfecting the training, expertise and tactics of their flyers, the entire programme conducted almost completely under a cloak of secrecy.

Although the aeronautical trend was, to a greater or lesser degree, also gaining ground in other major navies, it was the Japanese, ironically long regarded as copyists, who had taken a commanding lead. There were still heavily-braided admirals around the world who doggedly clung to the belief that aircraft were no match against the firepower of a battleship, yet the reality was that by 1941 ascendancy in naval conflict had passed from ship to aeroplane. The devastation wrought by carrier-based aircraft at Pearl Harbor, and by land-based planes upon the capital ships *Prince of Wales* and *Repulse* off the Malaysian seaboard two days later, was to demonstrate this decisively.

In the looming clash between the fleets of Nagumo and Somerville the former held all the aces. Nagumo's aircraft would have a numerical advantage of about 3 to 1, approximately 300 to 100, but that was not the main factor. Somerville's antiquated Swordfish and Albacore biplane torpedo-bombers would be hopelessly outmanoeuvred, outsped and outgunned by the Vals, Kates and Zeros of the Japanese aviators who were, in addition, better trained and vastly more experienced, many having already cut their teeth in the Sino-Japanese war, by then four years underway. Their Aichi 99 dive-bomber in particular, dubbed 'Val' by the Allies, was lethally effective and, at that stage of the war, probably the world's best, outperforming even its German counterpart, the Ju 87 Stuka. Their Zero naval fighter plane had yet to meet its match anywhere. Accordingly the predictable sequence of events was that Japanese bombers, amply supported by fighters, would swarm over the Eastern Fleet in overwhelming numbers, concentrating first on the three British carriers which, if not immediately despatched to the bottom, would be totally incapacitated, preventing their unlaunched aircraft from taking off, while leaving those already in the air with nowhere to land. The attack would then be pursued on the battleships, cruisers and destroyers.

It must be acknowledged of course that the collective anti-aircraft fire of the Eastern Fleet would be prodigious and the fighting spirit of the men behind the guns would not be found wanting. The Japanese flyers therefore would suffer considerable losses, but by sheer force of numbers coupled with their finely-honed skills, not only in accurate bombing but also in avoiding the arc and elevation of defensive fire, they would ensure that few if any of Somerville's ships survived. The final curtain of the tragedy would come down when Japanese surface craft moved in to finish off the cripples by gunfire and torpedo.

Predictably the Eastern Fleet would simply cease to exist, possibly every ship sunk and, having regard to distance from land and the unlikelihood of succour from that or any other quarter, sunk with all hands – a catastrophe unparalleled in naval history!

At this point, assuming the foregoing prognosis to be not improbable, I leave, for the time being, the two fleets surging inexorably towards one another. I shall now endeavour to assess the consequences of elimination of the Eastern Fleet, in effect the Royal Navy, from the Indian Ocean, the impossibility of replacements, the far-reaching situations that would follow locally, regionally and globally, and the impact these would have on the further course of the war. To grasp and understand the full significance and implications of the unfolding situation one must look at the broad picture of the entire conflict, determining factors as revealed at that critical period in March 1942 and, as a secondary consideration, whether HMS *Cornwall* played a deviatory role.

Here, at the risk of protraction and some repetition, is an outline:

At sea overall

Little if any assistance in the Indian Ocean could be expected from the United States, which was still desperately trying to regain strength in the Pacific after the devastation suffered at Pearl Harbor three months earlier, her array of battleships in ruins, her other units strenuously committed to contesting Japanese expansion southwards.

The Royal Navy had sustained grievous losses almost from day one and her available resources in fighting ships were stretched beyond tenable limits. She too could not be expected to fill any sizeable void precipitated in the Indian Ocean. Just two weeks following declaration of war she lost the aircraft-carrier *Courageous*, torpedoed by a U-boat south-west of Ireland, with the loss of half of her crew. In June of the next year her sister ship, the carrier *Glorious*, during the evacuation of Allied troops from Narvik, ran foul of the German battle-cruisers *Scharnhorst* and *Gneisenau* and was obliterated by shellfire, some 95 per cent of her crew perishing. The carrier *Ark Royal*, several times wrongly claimed sunk by German radio propaganda, was eventually, on 14 November 1941, sent to the bottom by a single torpedo from a U-boat which had penetrated a screen of seven destroyers, undetected, in the western Mediterranean. Valiant efforts were made to tow the stricken *Ark* to Gibraltar some thirty miles distant but finally, almost within sight of the Rock, she foundered, mercifully with the loss of only one man. The carrier *Eagle* was doomed to suffer the same fate a few months later. In March 1941 the fleet carrier *Illustrious* had sustained horrific damage by German Junkers 87 dive-bombers in the Straits of Pantelleria, central Mediterranean, and was fortunate to reach Valetta, Malta, where she also had to withstand further trauma during bombing of the island. Subsequently *Illustrious* was able to slip away and cross the Atlantic to Norfolk in Virginia, where she underwent extensive repairs. Roosevelt's lend-lease agreement became law in the same month, and this greatly facilitated the repair of British ships in shipyards of the United States, who at the time was still nominally neutral.

The fortunes of His Majesty's battleships had hardly been better than the carriers. The *Royal Oak*, as already related, was torpedoed and sunk whilst lying at anchor in Scapa Flow within the first month of hostilities. In May 1941 *Hood*, the acknowledged pride of the Royal Navy, blew up while engaging the German *Bismarck*, only three of her crew surviving. Six months later, in the central Mediterranean *Barham* was hit amidships by three torpedoes fired at point-blank range by a U-boat, which again had penetrated a strong destroyer screen. Within minutes an induced internal explosion rent the battleship apart, costing the lives of three-quarters of her ship's company. Among those who survived was Vice-Admiral Pridham-Wippell, the squadron's commanding officer.

German battleship Bismarck

HMS Hood, *British battle-cruiser*

On 10 December 1941, just three days after Pearl Harbor, the newest battleship *Prince of Wales* and battle-cruiser *Repulse* were sunk by land-based bombers off the east coast of Malaysia, as more fully described in a previous chapter. Churchill received the news by telephone while opening his morning mail, still, as was his wont, in bed. He relates that in his shocked state he was glad to be alone.

Barely a week later, on the night of 18 December, an Italian submarine launched three 'human torpedoes' off Alexandria harbour, with two men riding astride each 'torpedo'. They succeeded in breaching the boom defences when these were opened to allow for the passage of ships. Displaying laudable skill and daring, the Italian 'charioteers' attached to the bottom of battleships *Queen Elizabeth* and *Valiant* time-bombs which detonated some hours later. Both veteran 'battlewagons' sank to the harbour floor, fortunately at shallow depth enabling them eventually to be refloated and repaired, but the damage was severe and both warships were out of commission for months. When, shortly afterwards, the *Malaya* too was torpedoed, badly damaged and withdrawn from service, the Royal Navy was left without a single operational capital ship or aircraft-carrier in the Mediterranean.

Britain had paid a heavy toll in smaller naval vessels as well. This had markedly been the case during evacuation operations, as at Dunkirk, Narvik, Greece and Crete. The Mediterranean, at no time since the war's beginning a safe and peaceful retreat, had, with the Luftwaffe increasingly active from the toe of Italy, Sicily and Pantelleria, become a high-intensity danger zone with, in addition, the constant threat of U-boats, E-boats and minefields, not to mention the large and potentially powerful Italian fleet. Sustaining the Eighth Army and Allied forces in North Africa via the Straits of Gibraltar and the Mediterranean had to be forsaken and diverted to the long and time-consuming haul around the Cape.

However, the navy had other vital obligations, requiring passage across the Mediterranean, which could not be avoided. Plumb in the centre of the great inland sea, less than 100 miles from Axis airfields on Sicily, lay the island of Malta with its naval and air facilities, indispensable to the Allied campaign in North Africa and indeed the defence of Alexandria and the Canal zone. Strategically situated, it provided a splendid platform for aircraft and submarines based there to interdict and destroy Axis shipping transporting troops and material across to Africa, otherwise forcing the enemy to sail by widely circuitous routes, usually attracting other hazards. When Malta operated from a position of strength about 40 per cent of Axis shipping making the crossing were sunk, but when badly weakened by aerial bombardment the percentage dropped as low as 5. Inevitably the island was subjected to bombing, at times on a massive scale by German and Italian aircraft in an attempt to isolate and neutralise it completely, sowing destruction and death, particularly in the harbour and airfield areas as well as at defence installations and infrastructure generally. The Royal Navy for its part strove wherever possible and by whatever means and at great cost to run in essential supplies of every sort. In the darkest period fuel and ammunition were delivered to the island by submarine. Indeed it was said that the safest craft in the Mediterranean travelled below the surface. Nevertheless Malta remained a source of intense frustration for Erwin Rommel, the dynamically brilliant commander of the German Afrika Korps, whose burning aspiration was to drive through to Suez.

Malta fought back resolutely against towering odds, its fighter aircraft at one stage reduced to three outdated Gloster Gladiator biplanes dubbed, by irrepressible British humour, "Faith, Hope and Charity"! The wrecked remains of one of them are, I believe, still preserved in a Maltese war museum. It would have profited the Axis powers handsomely had they captured Malta, and indeed they set a target date to do so, but Hitler, during one of his characteristic mood swings, and obsessed as he was with the Russian front, postponed the plan, which in the end was never implemented. The operation would of course have involved German paratroops to a large extent, and the heavy losses inflicted upon this elite corps on Crete must certainly have given their high command pause for thought. In recognition of the stout courage and resilience of the island's population King George VI conferred on Malta the George Cross, Britain's highest decoration for civilian valour. The honour was richly deserved. At the height of the onslaught the island withstood 200 to 300 air-raids per month and in March 1942 alone its 95 square miles of terra firma absorbed 6,700 tons of bombs. The civilian population, numbering about 200,000, as well as the armed forces at hand, were approaching starvation point and during the same month a convoy of four ships with essential supplies was despatched from Alexandria, supported by diversionary attacks by the British North African forces. Two of the ships made Valetta harbour but both were sunk at their moorings next day by aerial bombing, with only a fifth of their cargoes salvaged. Subsequently the Royal Navy launched two convoys simultaneously, one from Alexandria and the other from Gibraltar, comprising together seventeen supply ships. Only two reached Malta.

Fighting at great sacrifice to bring supplies to desperately beleaguered Malta was not the navy's sole preoccupation in the Mediterranean. Comparably important was the function of the inshore squadron of small ships, including some of the South African navy, engaged in supporting the fluid forward position of the Eighth Army along the North African coast. They did invaluable work under highly dangerous conditions running in a wide range of supplies and, in the case of Tobruk, transporting thousands of troops to and from the Libyan port during its eight-month siege. The Tobruk run alone cost 27 naval and 6 merchant vessels sunk, plus many more damaged. Plainly in those circumstances the Eastern Fleet, if it met with extreme adversity, would not be able to look to the Mediterranean for replacements.

On a much larger scale still, and infinitely more worrisome, was the Western Approaches life link transportation across the North Atlantic to the British Isles. Rudyard Kipling expressed it succinctly in verse, albeit at a less stressful time, in his poem titled 'Big Steamers':

> They are brought to you daily
> By all us big steamers
> And if anyone hinders our coming
> You'll starve.

The U-boat menace, which Churchill in his memoirs singled out as "the only thing that ever really frightened me during the war", was at its peak. In the month of March 1942 shipping losses from this cause alone reached almost 800,000 tons, the third highest recorded. The situation was extremely critical, both sides exerting every sinew to gain ascendancy, improving tactics, introducing new weaponry and countermeasures. Germany achieved her highest number, 235, of U-boats on active service, many organised into lethal 'wolf packs'. She developed the *Schnorkel*, which enabled U-boats' diesels to 'breathe' and her batteries to be recharged while submerged. She unleashed the 'Gnat' torpedoes, designed to home in on ships' propellers. Britain for her part robustly improved her support (hunter) groups at sea, her asdic and radar detection, and brought to bear innovations such as the 'Hedgehog' which could project ahead a pattern of twenty-five mortar bombs. Increasing support from the Royal Air Force and the U S Navy helped considerably, but it was not until April/May of the following year that the U-boat tide began to turn. Added hereto were sinkings by aircraft, surface raiders, and mines. Merchant vessels were being despatched to the seabed faster than they could be replaced, and casualties among skilled crewmen were mounting.

U-boats were not the only concern. The German super battleship *Von Tirpitz*, pocket-battleship *Scheer*, cruiser *Hipper* and others were potentially poised to sally forth from Norwegian fjords into the Atlantic shipping lanes, while the battle-cruisers *Scharnhorst* and *Gneisenhau* along with heavy cruiser *Prinz Eugen* had been sheltering at Brest on the northern tip of the Bay of Biscay, a point much closer to the critical convoy routes, posing a constant ominous threat. However, the three warships at Brest had forfeited their strategic advantage in February 1942 by returning to Germany, but in the process had inflicted an embarrassing psychological blow to British pride by dashing northward through the Straits of Dover in broad daylight under the nose of British coastal guns and nearby airfields. The Germans had succeeded in effectively jamming British radar, and attacks by torpedo-bombers and small naval craft on the three Germans, when they were belatedly discovered, were decisively beaten off. The three warships reached home havens almost unscathed, amid jubilation in Berlin and humiliation in London. The pill was all the more bitter to swallow because Brest had repeatedly been a target of the RAF, and BBC bulletins had left the impression that German warships sheltering there had been heavily damaged.

The problem of conveying supplies across the Atlantic was not

confined to the British Isles; there was also the extremely demanding Russian exigency. The Soviet Union had for nine months suffered
the main fury of the German war machine, and the situation along
the entire length of territory from the Baltic to the Black Sea was
extremely grave. Stalin was constantly and vociferously calling on the
western allies to open a second front to reduce pressure on his harried
armies in the east and was scornful of the reasoned counter-arguments
of the American and British governments, who plainly were in no
position at that point to launch an invasion of continental Europe. The
latter nevertheless recognised the urgent need, in their own interests
as well as those of the Soviets, to extend whatever assistance possible
to Moscow and accordingly set in motion Arctic convoys laden with
war material, routed around Norway's North Cape to the Kola Inlet,
Murmansk and Archangel, sailing as far north as the ice barrier, which
advanced or receded according to season, would permit.

The Arctic convoys comprised a conglomeration of cargo vessels,
including tankers, heavily laden with the sinews of war, many with
additional deck cargoes, escorted by a mix of naval vessels, cruisers,
destroyers and trawlers. On the outward run the ships converged on
Iceland as the staging point from American ports and from Loch Ewe
in Scotland, thereafter proceeding eastward above the Arctic Circle
to their intended Russian destination. Convoys were code-numbered
consecutively, prefixed PQ on the outward voyage and QP on the
return (later changed to JW and RA respectively) usually returning
in ballast. Iceland had been protectively occupied by Britain, with the
consent of its inhabitants, after its co-state Denmark was overrun by
Germany in April 1940.

The Russian convoys, it was widely acknowledged, were the
worst, fearsome even without the attentions of the enemy, with
howling gales, driving rain and snow, tumultuous seas, dense cloying fog, temperatures plunging twenty degrees below zero, water
and spray cascading over the bows and hurtling aft to cloak fo'c'sle,

guns, railings and superstructure with ever-thickening ice that had constantly to be assailed and dislodged with chipping hammers wielded by parties of men in duffel coats, oilskins, balaclava helmets, knee-high seaboots, scarves and whatever other procurable clothing, to safeguard the ships from becoming top-heavy and capsizing. Men who had the misfortune to land in the 'drink' at those extreme latitudes froze to death within two minutes. Add to this attacks by U-boat 'wolf packs', bombers from German airfields in occupied northern Norway, minefields and, for good measure, the threat of heavily-armed warships striking from strategically adjacent fjords, then one comprehends why author Ewart Brookes chose as the title to his correlated book *The Gates of Hell*.

The cost in ships and cargoes lost in aiding Russia was grievously heavy, as was the forfeiture of human life: 1,840 sailors of the Royal Navy plus many hundreds of merchant seamen. From PQ 17 alone only 12 ships out of 36 reached Russia, including less than 23 per cent of vehicles, tanks and aircraft consigned. Nearly 1,000 ships sailed for Russia in the Arctic convoys, carrying almost six million tons of war material; 91 merchant and 19 naval ships were sunk and it was a matter of deep disappointment to Churchill and Roosevelt that their countries' massive contribution around the North Cape evoked scant appreciation from the Kremlin. On the contrary, Stalin's response was increasingly demanding, even contumelious, while the treatment meted out to British personnel arriving at Russian termini bordered on hostility. Eventually a telegram so vituperative was received from Stalin that Churchill refused to accept it and handed it back in an envelope to the shocked Soviet ambassador in London. Thereafter interaction between the two leaders improved somewhat.

The circumstances thus delineated (though I fear I have digressed a little) will make it clear that from here too in the Atlantic theatre, the Eastern Fleet would not be able to recoup losses incurred. The Royal Navy's resources in fighting ships were stretched beyond reasonable limits. Her operational battleships worldwide, should the Eastern Fleet be eliminated, would be reduced to five, including a battle-cruiser, with two more under construction.

In early 1942 the only armed forces of any significance contesting Japanese expansion through the Dutch East Indies were a motley mix of American, British, Dutch and Australian army, navy and air force units. These were incorporated into the 'ABDA Forces' under overall command of Britain's General Archibald Wavell, the naval contingent, basically comprising elderly cruisers and destroyers, operating under Dutch admirals Helfrich and Doorman. ABDA's continuance, sadly, was short lived. After Singapore surrendered on 15 April 1942 the main focus shifted to Java, the 'crown jewel' of the Indies, which was soon strongly invested by the Japanese, who rejoiced in overwhelming strength on land and afloat, with complete mastery in the air. The ABDA warships, desperately striving to prevent enemy troops coming ashore, fought gallantly but forlornly in the protracted Battle of the Java Sea against impossible odds and, virtually entrapped among surrounding islands, were almost completely destroyed, including HMS *Exeter* of River Plate acclaim. The survivors of all Allied ships sunk in the Java Sea were fated to fall 'into the bag' as Japanese prisoners of war. The Eastern Fleet could therefore expect no back-up from that last quarter either, the blunt, conclusive truth being that it, the sole Allied naval bastion in the Indian Ocean, was on its own and, should it disappear under the might and supremacy of Nagumo's approaching carrier armada, the void thus created could not be filled – except and inevitably by the Japanese. The road to the Persian Gulf and beyond would then be open and clear for Japan and Germany.

On land overall

From an Allied viewpoint, the territorial picture at the end of March 1942 was daunting in the extreme. In the Far Eastern and Pacific theatres Japan had, as we have seen, overrun everything before her and now stood astride the entire Dutch East Indies, the Philippines, Indo-China, Malaysia, Singapore, Burma and the Andaman Islands. She had established herself in New Guinea and the Solomons, and had created a vast defensive perimeter of Pacific islands. India, Ceylon and Australasia were now under threat.

Continental Europe was almost completely subjugated by Germany, and even including Italy, her Axis partner. Only Sweden, Switzerland, Spain and Portugal, plus two or three tiny principalities, remained independently neutral. The entire European coastline stretching from beyond Norway's North Cape, less than 100 miles from Murmansk, down to the Franco-Spanish border near Biarritz and again from Cerbere on their Mediterranean frontier, right across to Turkey and the Black Sea, including Crete and the Greek islands, was under Axis control. Only the island fortress of Malta stood out as a bastion of valour and hope in all the waters separating Europe from North Africa. Malta, however, was herself in dire straits, with provisions of every description dangerously low, under constant aerial attack and, indeed, targeted by the Axis leaders for invasion at an early date.

On the North African front the position was ominously fluid – Auchinleck's 'Operation Crusader' had failed to drive the enemy out of Cyrenaica and Rommel, benefiting from intensive bombing of Malta, had received considerable replenishment of equipment, nutrition and petrol by sea, and now sat poised to strike from the area west of Agheila/Gazala. The 'Desert Fox', master tactician of mobility and thrust, ever daring and unpredictable, had a weakened Tobruk garrison and the Nile delta in his sights.

But the most crucial territorial area of all from a global perspective was the Soviet Union. Indeed upon it more than any other depended the outcome of the war. In March 1942 the German armies on their eastern front, having consolidated after the rigours and reverses suffered during the winter, held a line stretching roughly from Leningrad on Lake Ladoga in the north, upper Baltic area, to Rostov in the south at the tip of the Sea of Azov, offshoot of the Black Sea, giving Moscow a narrow 70-mile berth along the way. Intelligence reports left no doubt that as soon as weather conditions improved a major German drive would be launched in the southern sector, its primary objectives being the capture of Stalingrad on the Volga river and Astrakhan on the Caspian Sea, followed by the Caucasian oilfields and the littoral ports of Batum and Baku. Success in their planned offensive would effectively deny the Russian heartland and its war machine vital oil supplies while the Ukraine, bread basket of the USSR, would be in German hands – factors which, it was believed, would sooner, rather than later, bring about the collapse of the Soviet Union. Should that come to pass, the entire prospect of the war would change dramatically.

The consequences if Japan won dominance of the Indian Ocean
By March 1942, having achieved her primary objective: conquest of the islands spread across her southern aspect with their abundance of natural resources, notably oil, Japan had, in the matter of further expansion and enhancement, five clear options for consideration and resolve – firstly, to forego expansion altogether, at least for the time being, and to devote her energy instead to consolidating and strength-ening her newly-begotten gains; secondly, to secure her back door by mounting an all-out decisive offensive against Chungking on main-land China, effectively to eradicate opposition from that quarter for the foreseeable future. Her third option was to isolate and neutralize Australia, possibly establishing a bridgehead on the antipodal conti-nent which, as remarked earlier, evoked serious concern among the population there, for whom it would be impossible to defend compre-hensively their enormous coastline, the cream of their fighting men being thousands of miles away engaged in hostilities on foreign fields. The Australian navy had suffered crippling losses and her home-bound air force, at that juncture, was weak. The major Australian cities were

vulnerably sited along the coast within easy reach of seaborne aircraft, indeed within range of naval gunfire. The fourth and most compelling option was to seek and destroy the remainder of the American Pacific Fleet which, notwithstanding the demolition of battleships sustained at Pearl Harbor, providentially still retained its aircraft-carriers and most of its cruisers and destroyers, and disturbingly gave evidence of a vigorous revenge-driven resurgence. The vast and exposed oil-storage and repair facilities at Pearl, amazingly neglected by Japanese bombers of December 7, still beckoned.

That left the fifth option, namely to gain command of the Indian Ocean. For strategic and logistical reasons this choice had been left relatively dormant but it obviously revealed prodigious possibilities. Obstacles preventing immediate implementation were demands in other areas which at that point were adjudged more pressing and, in addition, the knowledge that despite the loss of their capital ships *Prince of Wales* and *Repulse* in the South China Sea and other war-ships in the Java Sea, Britain had succeeded in assembling in the Ceylon region a fleet which, according to Japanese estimates, was formidable. Clearly that force, the newly-constituted Eastern Fleet as we knew it, had to be removed before this fifth option could be fulfilled but, if that were done, then a panorama of electrifying opportunities for Japan would unfold. With no opposition of any consequence left the Japanese navy would reign supreme over all the waters between Africa in the west, and Australia, the Dutch East Indies, Malaysia and Burma in the east, threatening their peripheral coastal areas and having the islands encompassed within, there for the taking. First to be seized would be Ceylon, the gemstone of the Orient with her abundance of beaches custom-made for landing invasion troops, her two excellent harbours, Colombo, man-made to the south-west and Trincomalee, natural and extensive to the north-east, plus her appreciable facilities and infrastructure. Ceylon's puny defences would be summarily swept aside and to all intents and purposes the island would be in Japanese hands within two or three days. This objective could be achieved without the commitment of vast numbers of men or quantities of material and, once there established, the invaders could to a large extent live off the land, thus attenuating problems of supply and reinforcement.

Ceylon under Japanese control would be perfectly positioned as the hub and nerve centre of their entire Indian Ocean agenda, a base from which action and enterprise could be initiated in all directions. Subsidiary bases could be established at the Seychelles, Mauritius and Reunion to provide, *inter alia*, staging posts for submarines, and mooring and anchorage for seaplanes and support vessels. Of still greater anxiety to the Allies, particularly Britain, should Japan gain ascendancy in the region, was Madagascar, where the governing authorities were, nominally at least, subject to vanquished France's Vichy government but unlikely to offer serious resistance in the event of an invasion from whatever side. It was known that Japanese ocean-going submarines were already probing the area, the prime objective obviously Diego Suarez, a magnificent and immense natural harbour at the northern tip of the island, from where a dominating influence over the Mozambican Channel could be applied – a threat to shipping as far south as Durban. In that regard few Durbanites, then or since, were or have been aware that a Japanese aircraft launched from a submarine flew along their beachfront one night in May 1942, checking the layout and admiring the lights shimmering on the water.

Exercising surveillance of movement across the Indian Ocean would, in the circumstances envisaged, be relatively easy and inexpensive for the Japanese navy. With no antagonists to contend with other than perhaps an occasional submarine, a small Japanese detachment comprising, for example, a light aircraft-carrier such as *Ryujo* and one or two cruisers could impose iron rule over large tracts of the ocean which, Churchill observed at the time with deep concern, was the main access route to India and the Middle East, carrying in manpower alone some 50,000 per month on average, the Mediterranean being effectively closed for this purpose.

India was now directly under threat. The Japanese invasion of southern Burma in January had succeeded two months later in taking the strategic port city of Rangoon, thereafter swinging northwards towards the Indian border some 300 miles distant. This at the same time imperilled the Burma Road, supply artery to the Chinese forces under Chiang Kai Shek, and American General Stilwell, fighting the common foe on the continental mainland. Britain felt honour-bound to support India to the maximum possible, but was heavily committed in other theatres as well. On the one hand Australia was gravely menaced, circumstances which, as we have seen, had strained relations between the two countries and which needed to be remedied as expeditiously as possible. Providentially the United States was in her own interests increasingly strengthening lines of communication, co-operation and sustenance with Australia from across the Pacific.

However, the most devastating consequence of Japan's gaining mastery in the Indian Ocean lay over the western stretches from the Mozambican Channel up into the Arabian Sea. It was across those tropical waters that the great troopships of the Allies conveyed reinforcements and freighter convoys carried arms, munitions and all the military impedimenta, wheeling around into the Gulf of Aden and up the Red Sea to sustain and expand the Eighth Army locked in mortal combat with the Axis armies under Erwin Rommel. It would be impossible to maintain that indispensable lifeline if a Japanese carrier supported by cruisers was allowed to gallivant off the Horn of Africa. That would render unthinkable any suggestion of committing troopships in particular to blockade-running of such suicidal proportions and in turn place the whole Allied disposition and planning in North Africa in jeopardy. It would hardly be feasible as an alternative to transport significant numbers of men and quantities of war material overland up the continental spine from South Africa, or across the northern spread from Freetown or thereabouts in West Africa.

Japanese dominion over the upper stretches would, in addition, cut off the Allies' crucial source of oil from the Persian Gulf, at the same time making this all-important commodity available to the Axis partners and Japan. It would also, in reverse, interdict British and American aid to the Soviet Union along the only functional access route apart from the Arctic convoy passage. Overall hung the spectre of a German–Japanese link-up at the Gulf. This had long been a consideration espoused by both countries, discussed at ambassadorial and military liaison levels but, due to developments of a more immediate nature, had, for the time being, not been advanced further – relegated, so to speak, to the 'back burner'. Each side, it would seem, while recognising the strategic advantages to be gained, hesitated to take the first positive step towards a link-up, tending to wait and see how the worldwide picture unfolded.

The German vision extended beyond the Gulf states to the Caucasian oilfields within the USSR: Groznyy, Maikop, Batum on the eastern shore of the Black Sea and Baku on the Caspian but, as we have seen, Hitler's priority was to win this prize from the north at the culmination of the German drive by army groups A and B through the Ukraine and across the River Don to the Volga in the summer of 1942. He was fixated on this course by an obsession to capture Stalingrad – which bore the name of his most hated enemy – with the seizure of Astrakhan to follow. In this he was supported by his inner coterie of Goering and Generals Halder and Jodl but there were others among the hierarchy, better qualified to take a dispassionate, practical view, who favoured the Persian Gulf route. Among them were General Rommel and the naval C-in-C Admiral Raeder, both of whom tried desperately to convince Hitler of the preferability of the Middle East option.

Rommel, as a precursory move in that direction, was straining at the bit to launch an all-out attack on the Nile delta, Alexandria and

the Suez Canal, thereby isolating and eventually enforcing the surrender of the remaining British and Commonwealth forces in Egypt and
thereafter thrusting across weakly defended Palestine, Trans-Jordan
and Syria, the latter having been wrested by Britain from the Vichy
French. From there he envisaged proceeding through the northern
regions of Iran and Iraq to invade the Caucasus from the south, at
the same time detaching a contingent to occupy Basra at the upper
extremity of the Persian Gulf. He believed that such a development
would induce Turkey to co-operate with the Axis forces, if not enter
the war on their side. This whole concept, of course, presupposed an
unfailing back-up of essential supplies to maintain momentum.

Raeder too, on more than one occasion, earnestly entreated Hitler
to grasp the Middle East opportunity, pointing to the spectacular
Japanese successes since Pearl Harbor, predicting further strategic
conquests, in particular Ceylon, key to control over the entire northern half of the Indian Ocean. Now was the time, argued the admiral, for Germany to grasp the hand of her Asian ally and establish
a supremacy in the region that would strangle the enemy in North
Africa and eventually bring about the downfall of the Soviet Union.

I digress somewhat from the chronology of the *Cornwall* story
but do so advisedly because the occurrences herein mentioned elu-
cidate the eminently critical situation threatening in the Middle East,
an impending crossroad at which the whole course of the war could
change direction. And specifically, as the subtitle of this book insinu-
ates, could *Cornwall* provide the key to such change of course? If the
Soviet Union were defeated, as foreshadowed above, and her armed
forces vanquished or driven beyond the Ural mountains into Siberia,
the bulk of German divisions confronting them, together with their
armour and supporting Luftwaffe squadrons, would be redeployed to
defend their dispositions in France, the Low Countries and elsewhere
as well as regenerate offensive operations against the British Isles.
In that event it may with some conviction be assumed that Operation

Overlord, the invasion of Normandy by Anglo-American troops, would not have come to pass on 6 June 1944.

The consequences and ramifications, immediate and prospective, of a Soviet collapse in 1942–3 can be argued and speculated upon at great length but beyond doubt the course of World War II, had it happened, would have changed and, from the Allied perspective, for the worse. To national leaders of vision the perils inherent in developments in and around the Persian Gulf were plain to see. Churchill was extremely apprehensive of them; Roosevelt recognised them; General Smuts, whose counsel was eagerly sought and highly valued, warned against them. Why then had Germany and Japan, who had already conferred positively on the prospect, not yet pursued the Middle East option with vigour and determination? The answer, it seems, lay with their top command's preoccupation with other events in their respective areas and a neglect of liaison in regard to the proposed pincers link-up. Each appeared to wait for the other to make the first move.

Hitler fully recognised the importance of the Gulf region in its relevance to the Soviet's Caucasian underbelly and, by extension, to the prosecution of the war on his eastern front. He listened to and, at least during receptive mood swings, empathised with arguments advanced by men like Rommel and Raeder who held that the Caucasian goal would best be achieved via Egypt, Palestine and the Arabian states. He promised Rommel sufficient reinforcement of men and supply of material from across the Mediterranean to enable his Axis forces to complete their drive to the Canal and proceed beyond. Once Syria was subjugated, supplies and reinforcements would be channelled through that country. To this end he undertook to liquidate Malta, which remained a painful thorn in the side of Axis convoys to and from North Africa, even setting a provisional date for invasion of the island. However, and fortunately for the Allies, Hitler's moods were frequently far from receptive. He remained infatuated with the grander vision of surging through the Ukraine, capturing its vast granaries, eliminating enemy salients and dispositions along the way, herding thousands of prisoners 'into the bag' and grabbing Stalingrad. In consequence the invasion of Malta was postponed and, ultimately, cancelled. Of Rommel's promised reinforcements and supplies only a fraction materialised – a myopic dereliction which persisted even later when Rommel, having seized the initiative in Cyrenaica, refused to relinquish momentum and, despite frustration and in contravention of orders, crossed the border into Egypt in pursuit of the British Eighth Army, finally coming to a halt through lack of logistic support at, so to speak, the gates of Alexandria. When Rommel arrived there at El Alamein he had left only twelve serviceable tanks while 85 per cent of his transportation consisted of captured British vehicles. Had he then had at his disposal a fresh division with panzer and motorised components, backed by fuel, water and other essentials, the outcome might, for the Allied cause, have been disastrous. In fact it might have changed the course of the war. In the event Rommel, one of the war's most able generals, had, due to his commander-in-chief's ambivalence, reached the end of his tether.

The other claw of the pincers lay with the Japanese. Their high command too, while engrossed in other developments, saw the enormous strategic potential in establishing dominion over the Indian Ocean and gaining control of the Persian Gulf. Everything had gone their way from the outset and, having achieved their primary objectives, they were, by the first quarter of 1942, well braced to give serious consideration to embarking upon this inviting enterprise. Only one obstacle appeared to stand in their way – the Royal Navy's Eastern Fleet. Their strategists had a fair estimate of the composition and potency of the opposing British force but were justifiably confident it could be disposed of entirely if brought to bay by their own First Carrier Fleet. Thus with greater sanguine insight and less prevarication than their Nazi counterparts, they decided the time was right to 'go for the jugular', smash the Eastern Fleet in or around its Ceylon bases, and take the spoils. Accordingly, as we have seen, the powerful Carrier task force under command of Vice-Admiral Nagumo sailed from Kendari in the Celebes on 26 March and commenced closing in for the kill. The die was cast and nothing, it would seem, could now save the Eastern Fleet from destruction nor, consequentially, prevent the subjugation of Ceylon and Japanese dominion over all the waters stretching from the Straits of Babel Mandeb on the Red Sea to the Persian Gulf, to India and on to the East Indies and Australia – indeed, in practical terms, over the Indian Ocean.

In amplification of the peril, this turn of events would certainly jerk Hitler and his sycophants into cognisance of the need for immediate fulfilment of the link-up with their Nipponese ally so as not to be sidetracked in the deal. That would mean providing Rommel rapidly with everything needed for his African troops to slice through to Suez, down to Basra and up to the Caucasus, thus bringing to reality Churchill's nightmare of German and Japanese forces conjoining and securing a stranglehold in the Middle East.

It may be said then that Nagumo's sortie from the Celebes on 26 March set World War II on a new course, one that, if the operation achieved its immediate goal of extinguishing the Eastern Fleet, would by its sequel impact on every theatre of the global conflict.

What, if anything, could be done to ward off the impending catastrophe, to change the course once more, this new fateful course that had suddenly come into being? In actuality what could be done to prevent contact between the fleets of Somerville and Nagumo? One may venture to say, in retrospect, that the only hope reposed in brilliant, unsuspected strategy and, not least, in amazing luck – continual, repetitive luck, or to define it more correctly, the abiding grace of God.

*   *   *   *   *

16

GOOD FRIDAY

(...in the nick of time)

Brilliant strategy and amazing luck! Those, we have surmised, were the only elements that could possibly ward off a collision between Somerville's Eastern Fleet and Nagumo's Carrier task force when, as dawn broke on Good Friday, 3 April 1942, the two were but a day's steaming apart. One more day would, unless the unexpected intervened, bring the two mighty antagonists to the point of mutual discovery.

In the event the unexpected did happen. During the night Somerville had decided to call off the search and leave the area. No Japanese warships had been detected by aerial reconnaissance or by radar and still less had Colombo or any other target in Ceylon been attacked on or about 1 April as foreshadowed by Intelligence. Somerville concluded that it had been a false alarm and that no enemy was heading our way. For a commander, astute and battle-seasoned by repute, his decision was astonishing. True, Intelligence had lost track of Nagumo's fleet since it left the Celebes and which by now could feasibly be anywhere from the Coral Sea to home waters, but a computation of probabilities had, after all, pointed to Ceylon and, presupposing a direct approach via either the Sunda Strait or Malacca Strait, had arithmetically determined April 1 as the logical strike date. Nevertheless two days beyond was surely too soon for the admiral to arrive at his conclusion but ironically his miscalculation was a major stroke of luck, one of perhaps ten that contributed to the deliverance of the Eastern Fleet from annihilation. It allowed the British fleet to be moved out of harm's way in the nick of time, if only temporarily.

However, Somerville's hand was in any case forced by other circumstances. The four 'R' class battleships under his command were old, of mid-World War I vintage, and had been designed to meet the exigencies of that period: to defend British shores against Germany's High Seas Fleet, entailing sorties into the North Sea of comparatively short duration and within practical reach of their home ports – quite the opposite of what was now required of them. Consequently by April 2 their resources of fuel and, more importantly, fresh water were in urgent need of replenishment. Here was another stroke of luck, in the absence of which Somerville might have tarried in the search area for a while longer, perhaps for another twenty-four hours – and paid the price! Again it is ironic that structural weaknesses in the battleships in question actually led to their salvation.

These were not the first manifestations of luck that significantly affected the flow of events. The first had, unbeknown to the Allies, already occurred when Nagumo set sail for Ceylon from the Celebes on 27 March. Contrary to expectations he did not take the direct, shorter route through the Straits of Sunda or Malacca but proceeded on a southerly course towards the Lesser Sunda archipelago, which extends out eastwards from the lower tip of Java like stepping stones. There he slipped through the Ombai Strait between the islands of Timor and Flores, where the passage of his ships was likely to attract less notice, if any, on land, and entered the Indian Ocean. (See diagram 2.)

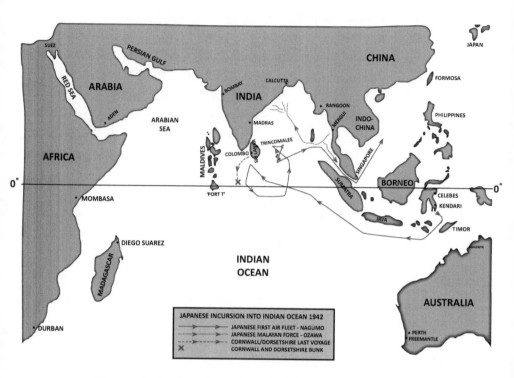

Diagram 2: Japanese incursion into Indian Ocean, April 1942

He chose therefore, in the interests of secrecy, a longer, roundabout course which would bring him to his goal a few days later. Here once again we are struck by the irony of the situation where Nagumo's decision to approach by a circuitous route, which anyone would agree was shrewd, resulted in the event in his quarry evading him. That the possibility of Nagumo approaching around the bottom end of Java, as he did, apparently eluded the thinking of Intelligence and Naval Command (who one assumes would consider every feasibility) is to me, with hindsight (and the smug sagacity of an armchair critic) still strange. The result was that Nagumo's strike date was delayed several days beyond April 1. (See diagram 3.)

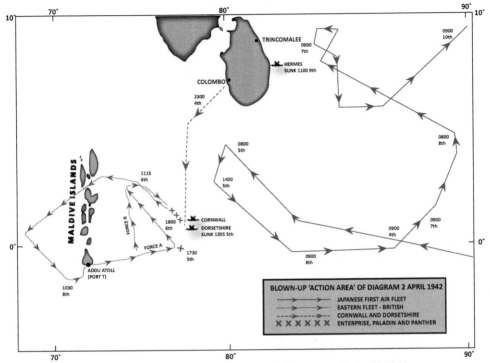

Diagram 3: Blown-up 'action area' of Diagram 2, April 1942

'Lady Luck' was to continue her bestowal of favours on the Eastern Fleet and we shall keep recognising these in turn as they occur, but it is perhaps opportune now to consider the other factor essential to dodging destruction: that slender thread of hope, namely brilliant strategy. This too had already happened – an idea long conceived at the Admiralty but only recently, and just in time, implemented. The strategy at issue has already been described in the earlier chapter titled 'Robinson Crusoe Revisited'.

The establishment of a secret naval base at Addu Atoll among the Maldives, a profusion of coral islands virtually untouched at that time by progress with languorous climate, almost pristine in natural features, largely unexplored and uncharted, lying spread up to 600 miles south-west of Ceylon, was indeed brilliant strategy. Quite as brilliant in this context was the achievement in preserving secrecy about the base, code-named 'Port T'. Very few, even among the top brass, knew of its existence and, providentially, neither did the Japanese. For that is where the Eastern Fleet, with the exception of four ships, had gone when, soon after, Nagumo launched his air strikes on Ceylon and, to his great disappointment, did not find his prime target at or in the vicinity of Colombo firstly, or later at Trincomalee, at which two localities it should logically have been found. For the Royal Navy, therefore, the strategy had worked brilliantly, at least for the time being, but for the Japanese Carrier task force it meant, to a great extent, mission unaccomplished.

On Good Friday morning the two 'County' class sisters, *Dorsetshire* and *Cornwall*, were ordered to Colombo, and the light carrier *Hermes* with destroyer *Vampire* to Trincomalee. If Somerville had misjudged the enemy's intentions and whereabouts he was, if anything, outperformed by the C-in-C Ceylon, Admiral Sir Geoffrey Layton, the latter's reputed ability and dynamic character notwithstanding. He too did not know where the enemy was and in his uncertainty should, one would think, have played prudently and prepared for the gravest contingency: an imminent attack. Instead *Hermes* and *Vampire* were detached in anticipation of an operation in Madagascan waters; *Cornwall* was to await the arrival of a troopship to be escorted to Australia; while *Dorsetshire* was to recommence engine-room repairs in dry dock which had been interrupted by participation in the Eastern Fleet's reconnoitre just ended. Dry dock and dismantled engines would not be the most desirable situation in the event of an air-raid, in which case she would, to adapt a dubious metaphor, be "caught with her panties down".

All four ships would within a week be in 'Davey Jones' locker', on the sea bottom, but the diversion of the two cruisers under these indiscreet deployments by top command would, ironically again, prove to be the fourth stroke of luck to smile benignly on the Eastern Fleet, which in the meantime dropped anchor at Port T.

Reverting to 'brilliant strategy' it will be recalled that I concluded 'Robinson Crusoe Revisited' by recommending that a monument be erected on Addu Atoll (if not already done) honouring the person or persons whose brainchild it was to establish a secret base there. The memory of illustrious, epoch-making events down the road of history is rightly perpetuated by memorials of some design or another, as massively done at Waterloo in Belgium, on a smaller scale at Delville Wood in France, and at many more locations around the globe. However, there were numerous other occurrences less proclaimed, faded in the mists of time and today virtually unknown, which deserve recognition. One such, in my opinion, was the Royal Navy's exploitation of the coral-encompassed anchorage at Addu Atoll in the Maldives which, it has been accepted, saved the Eastern Fleet, possibly averting in the manner of a chain reaction the elimination of British power in the Indian Ocean; subjugation of Ceylon; defeat in North Africa of the Eighth Army, its lines of supply extirpated; link-up of German and Japanese forces in the Persian Gulf; conquest by them of the Middle East and Caucasian oilfields; and defeat of the Soviet Union.

If, therefore, a monument were raised on Addu Atoll, the inscription thereon might appropriately be headed by these words:

TARRY HERE BUT A MOMENT, WAYFARER,
AND REFLECT, FOR UPON THIS ISLAND IN 1942
DEPENDED THE OUTCOME OF THE SECOND WORLD WAR.

* * * * *

17

EASTER SATURDAY

(Something momentous was afoot)

Dorsetshire and *Cornwall* arrived at Colombo during the forenoon on Saturday, April 4 1942 and secured for'rard and aft to buoys in the harbour. I still recall the complacency that seemed to pervade generally, filtering down from the upper structures of command despite their awareness that a Japanese fleet, almost certainly of powerful composition, was at sea somewhere and was therefore bound to reappear somewhere, anywhere, at any time, and strike! Yet, as if to say that was nothing to worry about, all-night shore leave was given to *Cornwall*'s port watch, in effect, half the ship's company. *Dorsetshire* was similarly unperturbed and, as if to reinforce her equanimity, proceeded to dock and continue the dismantling and refit of her engines.

But why should breezy, happy-go-lucky Jack concern himself with such trivialities? Leave that to the big shots, the guys with 'scrambled egg' all over the peaks of their caps. They know what they're doing. Obviously it was all a false alarm; how often had that not been the case? In the meantime the vibrant, colourful city of Colombo beckoned, its shops, bazaars, bars, streets filled with intermingling pedestrians, hooting cabs, carts, black scavenging crows, beer and cheap nourishing meals at the Fleet Club, with leisure facilities and even beds for overnight stay.

True, aerial reconnaissance conducted by the Eastern Fleet during its five-day patrol south of Ceylon had not revealed any sign of an approaching enemy but since that operation had for the time being been called off, reliance had to be placed solely on land-based aircraft scouring along an arc some 300 miles south. Resources for this purpose in Ceylon were extremely inadequate, long-range reconnaissance having recently been reduced to one serviceable Catalina, an American-built flying-boat. Catalinas had already won acclaim for their performance over the North Atlantic, highlighted by tracking down the German super-battleship *Bismarck,* and would continue to excel in other theatres. The Consolidated Catalina was powered by two engines mounted on a wing of exceptional span, the two extremities of which folded down vertically to double as stabilising floats when the craft was on the water. The underslung fuselage was large and cumbersome but comfortable, with sleeping bunks, ablution and cooking facilities for use by its nine-man crew. It was equipped with a formidable defensive armament but its overriding merit lay in exceptional endurance. Catalinas could stay aloft for thirty hours, giving them a range, out and back, of some 4,500 miles.

Catalina flying boat

At about the time that *Dorsetshire* and *Cornwall* returned to Colombo a few more Catalinas reached Ceylon, hastily despatched thither by Britain, alarmed now at the threat of an imminent Japanese invasion. These aircraft and their crews were pressed into service almost immediately upon arrival, there being hardly a day to spare for 'shakedown' exercises.

I took an early liberty boat with Jock Davidson, who was my most frequent 'oppo' on runs ashore. We wandered for some while in the central business area, known as 'The Fort', and then moved away in search of a suitable place to indulge in liquid refreshment. Finding a rather sumptuous hotel, somewhat above our class I suspected, we seated ourselves at a table out on a covered verandah. Nearby a wide aperture in the roof revealed a bright tropical sky and shed sunlight upon a luxuriant palm growing directly underneath. A waiter materialised alongside, resplendent in livery, turban and sash, tray in hand. He eyed us with the doleful mien consistent with contemplation of a puny tip, if any. Jock was proudly conscious of his Scottish ancestry, in deference to which he liked to start proceedings with a Caledonian distillation. We ordered whiskeys. Coincidentally, some 350 miles south-sou'east from where we sat savouring the taste and fragrance of the golden liquid, one of the most electrifying incidents of the war was unfolding! (Diagram 2)

A Catalina newly arrived from the frigid Shetland Islands and hurriedly propelled into hot tropical service, was nearing the end of its reconnaissance patrol at a point slightly above the equator and was preparing to return to its base at Koggala, a lagoon in southern proximity to Colombo. A final sweep with the binoculars revealed a spot on the horizon due south and Squadron Leader Birchall, captain of the 'Cat', turned to investigate. To his and his crew's pulsating excitement the spot emerged as the vanguard of an armada of battleships, carriers, cruisers and destroyers – the long-expected Japanese attack force. Birchall headed for home as fast as the lumbering flying boat could go – about 180 mph – and his wireless operator commenced with utmost urgency to transmit a message to naval headquarters in Colombo giving estimated enemy position, course and conjectured composition.

But the Japanese had seen the Catalina and within minutes six Zero fighters were launched in pursuit, overtaking at around 350 mph – twice the speed of their quarry. Inevitably the flying boat, fiercely assailed from all sides, pounded by a murderous fusillade of bullets and explosive cannon shell, was shot down, six of her heroic crew surviving, including Birchall and the wireless operator, all injured, to be picked up by a Japanese destroyer and roughly interrogated, thereafter spending the rest of the war as prisoners of war. However, the wireless message, substantially intact, had been received in Colombo, handed to the C-in-C and from thence passed on posthaste to all services, including Admiral Somerville, whose Eastern Fleet had arrived at Port T.

The wireless transmission from the doomed Catalina had ceased abruptly during a repeat and headquarters in Colombo concluded, correctly, that Birchall's plane had 'bought it'. Another Catalina, commanded by Flight Lieutenant Graham, was despatched to the stated sighting area to locate and report on the enemy fleet. By then night had fallen and at about 1.00 am Graham radioed that he had seen an enemy destroyer. With the benefit of hindsight it seems to have been foolish and needless to send out a second vulnerable and precious flying boat and crew when Command already knew that the Japanese had arrived, their whereabouts, that their obvious objective was Colombo and the probable time of their intended attack next day. What more did they need to know? Graham's message also went dead during transmission and neither he, his crew nor aircraft were seen or heard from again.

In reassessment, had Birchall turned for home five minutes earlier, or had the Japanese arrived five minutes later at the point sighted, discovery would not have happened. Furthermore, Nagumo was at that very time moving his force westwards to gain a run-in bearing due south of Colombo, a run-in which he believed would be more likely to escape detection by British aerial patrols. A few more miles further west and again Birchall would have missed him. In the nick of time, therefore, the Eastern Fleet had its fifth stroke of luck because, had the enemy force not been detected, *Cornwall* and *Dorsetshire* would have been dealt with next day in Colombo harbour by Nagumo's aviators, and would not have been able to play the saving role they were fated to do later at sea.

Jock Davidson and I had downed probably three tots of Scotch apiece and were in jovial mood when the imposingly attired waiter came over to our table with the purposeful stride of someone who was about to make an announcement, but Jock beat him to the draw. "Another two whiskeys," he called.

The waiter shook his head. "No more; I'm sorry. You must return to your ship at once," he pressed, and then continued, "All sailors have been ordered to return to their ships, now."

"Why?" we exclaimed.

The man grimaced and gestured in the air with his arms. "Air-raid," he said.

We both laughed and Jock, looking up at the sky through the opening, protested loudly, "I don't see any airplanes up there," then grinning – "Perhaps a bomb will fall through there and hit that palm bush of yours. Who told you we all have to go back on board? That's nonsense. We've been given all-night leave. Now be a good chap and bring us another round, please."

The waiter became agitated. "The bar is closed. No more drinks. All our customers are leaving, and you must too."

"Come on," Jock said to me, "let's go and find some place else. Bloody nonsense."

We left the hotel and, walking in a roughly northern direction we entered an unfamiliar run-down neighbourhood. Presently we found a sleazy-looking tavern and went in. The customer area comprised a single room containing four or five tables with chairs, and the wall opposite the entrance lent access to anterooms of sorts through a door and a serving hatch, the latter presumably the passage through which liquor would come forth. We seated ourselves at one of the tables, the only customers at that time. A sour-faced man wearing a dead-pan expression and dirty apron came across to us and when, upon enquiry, he indicated yes, they stocked whiskey, Jock ordered two 'doubles'. To me he explained, "Got to make up for lost time." The doubles duly emerged, courtesy of the serving hatch.

As minutes ticked away and more liquor flowed we became jollier and noisier and Jock, switching his accent to broad Scots, as was the custom among the Davidson siblings under their parents' roof, started singing lustily, "Ah belang tu Glaskie, guid auld Glaskie toon", sup-plementing this by dancing swayingly around and between the tables, knocking over a chair. Jock was never a troublemaker in an abusive way, and was as good-natured as anyone could wish, but the booze, of questionable quality served in that dive, did have a boisterous effect on him, while I just sat there laughing my inebriated head off. At one stage Jock tossed his empty glass, for refilling, towards a face peering through the service hatch, missed the opening, hit the wall and shattered the glass. "I'll pay, chum, don't worry," he guffawed at the terror-stricken face.

Soon afterwards Jock made it known to the man who had been serving us and whose facial expression had by then changed from deadpan to choleric, that he needed to visit a toilet, and was ushered out through the door to the back. When Jock reappeared a few min-utes later, grinning from ear to ear, he was riding a bicycle. Even in my befuddled condition I reasoned that this was taking things too far, having blurry premonitions of smashed furniture and broken limbs, so I staggered up and grabbed the handlebars. "No, Jock," I said, "that's enough. Come on, let's go."

"Wait," Jock remonstrated. "I'm just having a little ride." But I held on, fearing that we were nearing the point of serious trouble. I was mistaken. That point had already been reached.

I was vacantly aware in my bibulous state that the room had somehow filled with people, Indian men, probably ten or twelve, but attached no significance thereto. What my bleary vision did not register was that each of the men was armed with a long stout stick. Suddenly, without warning, Jock and I were set upon by the newcomers, blows raining down viciously on our heads, shoulders and backs. We bolted for the exit but the walloping continued unabated until we were out in the street. As I rushed through the door behind Jock another Indian came in from the opposite direction and instinctively I swung a punch at his head, feeling a stab of pain in my right thumb, but whether the unfortunate fellow had come to join in with our assailants or was an innocent outsider, I shall never know.

The attack had been executed in a swift, efficient manner by what was obviously a well-trained bouncer squad but we wondered subsequently why it had been found necessary in our case. There had been no aggressive behaviour on our part. Over-frolicsome certainly, but no antagonism. We had paid for our drinks and for the broken glass. Had we been asked to leave, we would have done so without much ado. However, as a quick-fix remedy for curing drunken conditions I can affirm authoritatively that there is nothing more effective than a one-minute assault with heavy sticks, or similar, wielded by ten or twelve irate assailants. Forget black coffee and cold showers. Once in the street Jock and I were as stone-cold sober as a bench of judges at a state funeral.

It was now dusk and sensibly we made our way towards the harbour to rejoin our ship, having abandoned any inclination to sleep at the Fleet Club. As we approached, the long, timber-constructed passenger jetty came into view and we realised immediately that something momentous was afoot. The jetty was a-bustle with sailors, moving with urgency, crowding into liberty boats jostling alongside, spurred on by Petty Officers shouting and gesticulating. The waiter at the hotel had obviously not lied – there had been a general recall.

In fact, an air-raid alarm had sounded. We broke into a run. "Come on you two, get a jerk on," yelled one of our own POs. "That's our pinnace over there. Jump in, or you'll be adrift." We did as we were bid, the coxswain barked an order, the bowman released his boathook from a mooring ring and pushed the prow away, the engine burst into life and we chugged off across the darkened anchorage, past the black indistinct shapes of ships, gangways rigged outboard, topped by lights directed down the steps on to patches of shimmering water, and so on to where *Cornwall* lay near the gap in the outer mole of the harbour. There was an undercurrent of excitement and expectation among the returning liberty men. They too sensed something big in the offing and speculated loudly among themselves, quite in contrast to the laughter and singing to which sailors customarily gave vent when returning from shore leave.

Back on board the cruiser we were not made much the wiser. Our shipmates who had not gone ashore knew little more than we did except that the ship was due to sail in company with *Dorsetshire* as soon as the latter, which had been in the process of dismantling engines and was now feverishly reassembling them, was ready for sea. That was expected to be at about 2200 hours, or 10.00 pm. Everyone assumed that the Japanese were, in some form or another, the cause of the commotion but more explicit information could be expected only over the broadcast system and that, as always, would not be communicated until after the ship had left port. However, *Dorsetshire*'s temporary disablement was, for the Eastern Fleet, a sixth lucky stroke. Had she been ready to set sail with *Cornwall* an hour or two earlier, then the two cruisers would not on the morrow have been at the right place at the right time to play their crucial part.

The liberty boat continued to ply between ship and jetty as long as time allowed to bring back every possible latecomer. If the naval authorities had earlier been remiss in their appraisal of the Japanese threat they were, after receipt of Birchall's wirelesed signal from the stricken Catalina, swift, decisive and thoroughly efficient in reaction. The entire island of Ceylon had to be alerted, its meagre defences brought to a state of readiness, and shipping in port, wherever possible, despatched and dispersed at sea. As a priority *Cornwall* and *Dorsetshire* had to leave Colombo with utmost celerity. Recalling off-duty personnel from across the city and its environs was a masterpiece of organisation and application, sailors in particular having frequently to be winkled out from seedy out-of-the-way joints in backwater areas. When *Cornwall* sailed that night only two out of her then complement of approximately 700 were missing. *Dorsetshire* reportedly did even better.

At approximately 10.00 pm *Dorsetshire* was ready, and the two cruisers prepared to leave. Lieutenant-Commander Grove, a Capetonian, was in charge of the bows-mooring operation and at the right moment shouted down to the Ceylonese buoy attendant to slip the mooring cable. The attendant demurred and protested loudly in his own tongue. Precious seconds ticked away. Neither Grove nor buoy-man could understand what the other was saying and patience at the bows and on the bridge was reaching breaking point. "Another bad omen" flashed through my mind. Eventually Grove boomed, "Bugger off", the gist of which was apparently grasped down on the buoy, and the mooring wire was let slip. The bridge telegraph clanged and *Cornwall* edged away towards the harbour exit in the wake of her three-funnelled sister.

Minutes later the broadcasting system crackled into life, informing the ship's company that units of the Japanese navy had been discovered heading for Ceylon, and that the two cruisers were proceeding at speed to rejoin the Eastern Fleet the following afternoon.

That seemed to break the tension; the uncertainty was dispelled and we sped off into the black night.

* * * * *

18

EASTER SUNDAY

(That was a near one)

The grey dawn of April 5 1942 found *Dorsetshire* and *Cornwall* cleaving a calm sea at approximately 28 knots, close to the maximum of which the two ageing cruisers were still capable, their twin white and foaming wakes stretching far astern towards the horizon. (See Diagram 3.) *Dorsetshire* was on station one mile ahead of *Cornwall* and 45 degrees to starboard. The weather promised to be sunny and windless with some scattered cloud. It was Easter Sunday, Day of the Resurrection. The ships' companies, which had, since leaving Colombo, operated in two watches – one half of the defences manned – had now closed up to Action Stations – all defences fully manned – in the pre-dawn darkness. This was standard practice at sea before dawn, the order to 'secure' normally coming shortly after sunrise, but today that directive never came and the men remained in full battle readiness.

Obviously the situation was regarded at command level as highly menacing, something that could strike suddenly without warning, something demanding thorough, unremitting preparedness. The previous evening's announcement that units of the Japanese navy were approaching Ceylon presupposed the assumption that they would include one or more aircraft-carriers, with the sequential threat of air strikes. The enemy when reported was plotted somewhere to the south of Ceylon, heading northwards and, contingent upon its later movements, could possibly now be within strike range of the two cruisers over to the west racing south. *Cornwall* had not yet been fitted with radar, in the present circumstances a serious defect, and although a set had been installed in *Dorsetshire* it was regrettably small and substandard. The two ships strove to alleviate this handicap by posting extra lookouts and maintaining mutual, visual communication.

The men at Action Stations broke away to breakfast in quick shifts, returning to their station promptly thereafter, otherwise obtaining permission to slip away to the heads (toilets) or to fetch a fanny of tea from the galley. My station was the port mounting of 8-barrelled pom-poms high up amidships, in fresh air and sunlight with a 180 field of vision – more pleasant than most. We were dressed, apart from the officers, mostly in blue overalls with inflatable Mae West lifebelts harnessed around the chest, and white anti-flash helmets and gloves stuffed in pockets or otherwise close at hand. Those in exposed positions, as on the pom-poms and other anti-aircraft armament, had regulation tin hats also within easy reach for wearing during action. By and large the men showed little concern; this sort of thing had happened scores of times with seldom any excitement befalling. Mostly they lolled about, swapping yarns, smoking or reading magazines. Mailbags had as usual come aboard after our arrival in Colombo and there was much reading matter, apart from private letters, in circulation. The general feeling was that this was just another wild goose chase of which we had experienced many in the past.

However, at about 9.00 am something of a flutter spread throughout the ship when it was learned by radio that Colombo had been attacked an hour earlier by carrier-based bombers. It brought home the realisation with something of a jolt that, this time, there was indeed an enemy within striking distance and, moreover, in considerable strength. For a short while the banter and wisecracks fell silent but soon the pervading sentiment seemed to be: Well, that was a near thing. Lucky we were away in time. Whistling in the dark?

So the morning wore on, the sun burning hotter as it climbed towards the meridian, until suddenly there was a new development that caused more than just a stir. Signals were exchanged with *Dorsetshire*, whereafter several pairs of binoculars on and around the bridge turned to sweep the sky above the horizon astern. Arms pointed. Soon the word passed along and excitement flared. "Spotter aircraft above the horizon astern, elevation 15 degrees, almost certainly hostile." If so, then this was it! Not only was the enemy within strike range but he had, without any doubt also discovered the British ships and was hardly likely to leave them unmolested. The significance of this development was not lost on the men manning the guns. One could discern this in the facial expressions.

The spotter was indeed hostile, a float-plane launched from a Japanese cruiser, reconnoitring a sector to the west of the Nagumo force to which it immediately radioed its find. Doubtless the crew of the spotter were exhilarated yet their vigilance was ironically a tragedy for the Japanese because, their attention arrested and held by the two cruisers, they surely missed the exceedingly bigger prize not much further on. Japanese search planes of this type worked sectors to a radius of approximately 300 miles, at the end of which they flew a 'dog leg' to left or right of 60 miles before returning to their parent along a new 300-mile radius. (See Diagram 4.) This one had found the cruisers long before reaching its 300-mile range extremity and had immediately abandoned further search in order to keep tabs on its new-found prey. Had it proceeded to the end of its assigned sector the chances are almost certain that, flying at around 2,000 feet, it would have made a far more sensational sighting – that of the faster division of Somerville's Eastern Fleet, which was converging at speed and only a few hours' steaming away! Inasmuch as the float-plane's decision, or instruction from Nagumo, to remain in contact with the cruisers instead of completing its search sector was a crucial misjudgement by the Japanese, it was conversely a major stroke of luck

– the seventh – for the Eastern Fleet, which thereby again escaped discovery by its greatly superior adversary.

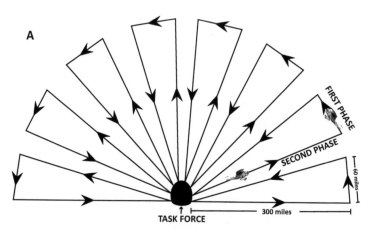

Typical aerial search pattern used by Japanese naval task forces, consisting in this case of eight sectors, each basically of 300 miles radius and 60 miles 'dog leg' at extremity. Illustrative only, as the parent ship of an aircraft returning after perhaps four hours may have travelled 100 miles from point of launch. In reality the pattern flown by a search plane would presumably conform more closely to the diagram at B below where, for convenience and on a larber scale, only one sector is illustrated.

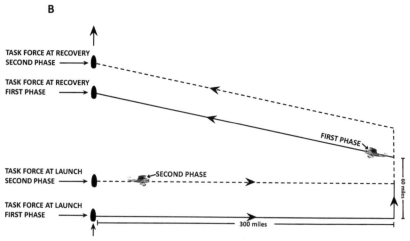

Single sector of search pattern assuming in this illustration that the task force has kept a straight course throughout the launch and recovery period.

Diagram 4: Japanese naval search pattern

The eighth stroke of luck, perhaps the most vital of them all, followed shortly afterwards in the form of an astounding miscalculation. When the presence of the two cruisers was first radioed by the reconnaissance plane the first thought of Nagumo and his staff was that these British warships were advancing to attack their fleet, which might have had serious consequences as a large component of Japanese air strength was at that time away bombarding Colombo. However, that concern soon evaporated when the Japanese command arrived at the astonishing conclusion that the cruisers were in fact 'running away'.

Nobody can categorise the Japanese as stupid; in point of fact they rank amongst the most efficient and astute nations on the planet. Nevertheless, the occasional blunder, oversight, not 'seeing the wood for the trees', call it what you will, sneaks in to bedevil even the best once in a while, especially if an eminent distraction comes into play, and in this instance the Japanese, in their elation at chancing upon the two British heavy cruisers, missed the cue, their perceptions, temporarily at least, inhibited. This was all the more remarkable because the Nagumo force boasted an abundance of brainpower: discerning, analytical and highly experienced officers, including Rear Admiral Tamon Yamaguchi; his Chief of Staff, Rear Admiral Ryunosake Kusaka; Captain Mitsuo Fuchida, overall Flight Commander; and Commander Minora Genda, brilliant planner of the Pearl Harbor attack. None of these apparently queried the assumption that the cruisers were 'running away'. A little sober reflection should have posed the question on the Japanese flagship: "Why, if they are running away, are they steering the southerly course they do, which at best skirts perilously close to the known area of operation of the Japanese task force, whereas the logical direction of escape would be somewhere in the region of north-west, a variant of 90 degrees or more? Surely, therefore, the cruisers are not running away but are pursuing this present course with a purpose – a rendezvous perhaps."

Indeed the two warships were blazing a trail straight to Somerville's Eastern Fleet but Nagumo, his staff and commanding subordinates failed to recognise it: a truly profound stroke of luck – the eighth to save the Eastern Fleet – and brought about by *Cornwall* and *Dorsetshire.*

At around 11.00 am a short Sunday service was broadcast by the ship's chaplain, Lieutenant Reverend J Bird, to the men at their Action Stations, wherever they were, throughout the length and breadth of the ship as it sped onwards. Under normal, calmer circumstances Sunday religious services were held for off-watch personnel on the quarterdeck (Catholics and Jews at other shipboard venues) but imminent peril rendered this impossible on that Easter Sunday. The voice of the chaplain, one of the most respected officers aboard, crackled slightly through the loudspeakers, calm and deeply moving. Not a man stirred until the last words of prayer were spoken which, to us up on the pom-pom platform were whipped away in the ship-driven wind and lost in nothingness over the foaming wake '…through Jesus Christ Our Lord, Amen.' Tragically, that prayer was fated to be the padre's ultimate homage to Him 'who alone spreadest out the heavens and rulest the raging of the sea'.

At noon *Cornwall's* lower deck men started down to dinner on the mess decks in quick, small shifts, gulping their food down, egged on by Petty Officers and Leading Seamen, and then hurrying back to their stations as fast as possible. I bumped into genial Tubby Townsend from my home town, an older man in his thirties who never seemed to be flurried.

"They really seem to think we'll be in action today, Tubby. Where do you think the safest place will be on the ship?"

"Safest place?" laughed Tubby. "No such thing. If your number's up then you'll cop it no matter where you are. I'm a fatalist – if a bomb or shell or bullet has my name on it, then I've had it; nothing I can do about it. If my name is not on it then I'm safe where I am."

The daily rum issue, which normally took place shortly before midday mealtime would, it was announced, be postponed until suppertime when, it was hoped, the danger would have diminished. When I left the mess deck to run up the companion ladder the last man eating his dinner in my No 9 mess was Hedley Beswetherick, also from my home town. It was to be his last meal.

At the same time a group of eighty type Val dive-bombers, led by Lieutenant-Commander Takashige Egusa, Japan's leading dive-bomber ace, was approaching from the east at 200 knots.

* * * * *

I climbed the vertical iron ladder linking B Gun Deck with the pom-pom platform and for a few seconds peered over the shoulder of one of the gun's crew sitting there who, I remember, was paging through a magazine named *The Outspan*, a popular South African publication of those days. The communication rating on the mounting, who, wearing earphones, was on line to Air Defence Control in the director, called out matter-of-factly, "Radar warning from *Dorsetshire* close-up." Lazily we took up our positions on and around the 8-barrelled pom-poms and in keeping with drill donned our anti-flash, asbestos impregnated balaclava type helmets and gloves, as well as burdensome tin hats. We had suffered several of these 'close-up' alerts during the forenoon, and in the midday heat and scorching sun it was becoming tiresome.

Then. a high-pitched whine obtruded suddenly upon the senses, growing in the space of a second or two to an ear-shattering roar, and passed overhead and away. In what must have been one hundredth of a second the notion flashed through my mind that *Dorsetshire*'s Walrus reconnaissance plane had overflown us. That absurdity was shattered almost immediately as the ship shuddered violently with the muffled crack of an explosion deep down. Even before stunned realisation took hold, the scream of the second dive-bomber rent the air, followed again by the horrendous concussion as the bomb detonated somewhere below.

Men were recovering from the initial shock and moving to do the things they had repeatedly been taught to do. Someone shouted, "For God's sake, get those guns going" just before the third bomber hurtled down in a deafening crescendo, preceding again the sickening tremor of a direct hit – three out of three so far! Guns were firing back now, gouts of flame belching from the twin muzzles of the 4-inch high-angle guns, and the multiple pom-poms coughing in staccato bursts. I was vaguely aware, amid the pandemonium, of blowing some air into my Mae West lifebelt.

But the planes plummeted down in a continuous stream, barely seconds apart, raking the bridge and superstructure with machinegun fire in addition to delivering their bombs. A near miss detonated in the sea some ten yards off the port bow, sending a mass of discoloured water towering skywards. "That was a near one," I said, hoping to sound nonchalant. The erupted enormity of water hung seemingly motionless in the air for a moment, and then crashed down upon the cruiser with the force of a massive waterfall, drenching the men in exposed positions. Already *Cornwall* was listing appreciably to port and the guns on that side could not elevate sufficiently to compensate so as to hit back at the steeply diving attackers, but one Japanese bomber, in the process of pulling out, veered into the depressed field of fire of our port pom-poms, and Dobson, captain of the mounting, gave it a burst. Muzzle smoke obscured our view but I was vaguely aware, in a detached sort of way, of someone shouting, "Well done, port pom-pom!" Able Seaman Duncan from Cape Town, who was positioned further aft, later declared that the Japanese plane had burst into flames and crashed into the sea astern. At a reunion celebration fifty-six years later Duncan reaffirmed to me that he had seen the wrecked craft, bearing the 'Rising Sun' insignia, in the water. He was not a mendacious type prone to exaggeration, so I believe my mounting was entitled to 'chalk one up'.

Dense black smoke was billowing from the cruiser's funnels and out of other openings on the upper deck due to havoc wreaked in the vicinity of the engine and boiler rooms, swirling and wreathing among the men labouring at their tasks. Another explosion wrecked hydraulic power to gun turrets and mountings, and amidst the smoke and clamour men wrestled to switch controls from power to manual. Training and elevating the cumbersome pom-poms then entailed strenuous physical effort and much slower manoeuvrability, hardly the answer to fast-flying aircraft. A hit in close proximity to the transmitting station, the ship's electronic combat centre, rendered co-ordinated defensive action impossible. Scenes of devastation and carnage between decks were abundant, in the marine mess deck and sick bay locality among others. On the upper deck, in and around the superstructure, hostile machine gun fire and flying shrapnel were continuous murderous hazards. One wayward piece of metal activated the ship's siren on the for'rard funnel, the released steam producing an ear-shattering banshee wail. At a certain point I shot a glance out to sea and beheld the *Dorsetshire* about a mile away – naught for my comfort there. She too lay low in the water and on fire – no prospects for rescue from that quarter.

As each dive-bomber screamed down, men crouched instinctively, hoping, and then rose again to their tasks after the bomb had ripped into the ship or alongside. One diabolic missile, exploding on impact, hit S1, the 4-inch, twin-gunned anti-aircraft mounting, starboard side for'rard, sending up a fearsome wall of searing flame, thirty to forty feet high, roaring skywards and over the pom-pom platform, from which the two gun crews fled for their lives, climbing or jumping to the deck below on the port side opposite. Only the location of the pom-poms, one deck higher and disposed inboard from the overhang, saved their gun crews from the inferno. No member of the S1 crew survived, although the less fortunate did not die instantly. The enormity and ferocity of the flames prompted a suggestion that the device had been an 'oil bomb', and this soon became general belief. However, I do not concur. There is little evidence that the Japanese Vals carried, on that occasion at least, anything other than their standard 500 lb bomb, nor for that matter that 'oil bombs' as incendiaries existed at all. In close proximity to the S1 guns were vertical, ready-use lockers, crammed with 4-inch 'fixed' ammunition – veritable powder kegs. In addition, ammunition would have lain in readiness on loading trays or would have been physically carried by supply ratings. It is my contention that the intense heat generated by the bomb exploding on impact actuated secondary explosions among ammunition in and around the ready-use lockers, particularly their cordite content, resulting in the ensuing conflagration. But, whatever the case, it put the pom-poms in addition to S1 out of contention.

When I reached B Gun Deck immediately below, the two 4-inch port-side batteries, P1 and P2, were still firing and I made my way along the tilting deck to the latter, situated further aft, with a vague intention of assisting there. The stricken vessel was now burning fiercely and listing ominously, her hull breached and taking water fast. The steep lean-over threatened to burst open the doors of the ready-use ammunition lockers close by P2 and a few of us, including Tubby Townsend, battled to secure the door handles to prevent the heavy cartridged projectiles from spilling out and careering across the deck. Again came the scream of a diving bomber and we crouched low, waiting. The bomb slashed the edge of the iron deck a mere five yards from where we ducked down, and deflected into the sea. By the grace of Providence it did not explode. Possibly the angle of con-tact sufficed to bring the fuse slightly offline, perhaps by a millimetre or two. Had the bomb detonated when it hit, then the disaster at S1, with ammunition lockers again exposed, could have been replicated. Tubby, I and the others around us would either have been reduced to red splotches or been incinerated. Had the bomb exploded in the water against the ship's hull she, *Cornwall,* already listing thirty degrees to that side, would almost certainly have capsized. In the event we were simply transfixed, staring blankly at the jagged, tortured metal on the edge of the iron deck where the bomb had struck a glancing blow.

At last the bombardment stopped after, one must assume, forty bombers had assaulted each ship. Captain Mitsuo Fuchida, overall Wing Commander in the Japanese carrier division, was later to write, 'The dive-bombers scored hits with close to 90 per cent of their bombs' and 'rather than feel exultation over the proficiency of Egusa's bombardiers, I could only feel pity for these surface ships assailed from the air at odds of forty to one'. I would regard Fuchida's estimate as conservative because only one bomb, I feel safe in saying, completely missed *Cornwall* along her port side of which I had a grandstand view. Clearly she absorbed at least thirty-five hits, which must rank among the most severe aerial batterings suffered by any ship during the war. The same can be said of *Dorsetshire*. Apart from the accuracy of their bombing one cannot but admire the skill of the Japanese aviators in approaching their quarry, because despite *Dorsetshire*'s radar, albeit inadequate, and the posting of numerous lookouts, the two cruisers failed to detect their attackers virtually until the lead planes dived down.

HMSs Cornwall *and* Dorsetshire *under attack (*Dorsetshire *at right foreground,* Cornwall *in background - Japanese photograph)*

Cornwall was sinking fast, bows dipped under, upper deck awash along the port side almost to the quarterdeck. She had come to a dead stop in the water, her engine-rooms a shambles, all means of propulsion gone. Some of the 4-inch, high-angle guns were still firing defiantly in a desultory, ineffective manner, hoping that an exploding shell, fuse set to minimum, might somehow score a lucky hit among the planes milling around above. All able hands began applying themselves feverishly to preparation for abandoning ship, cutting ropes that lashed Carley floats to the upper works and throwing overboard anything that would float: lifebuoys, planks and other wooden material that could possibly give a measure of support to men in the water.

Most of the boats had been smashed in the attack, the saddest loss being the great pinnace, which could have held a hundred men, but which I watched helplessly as it broke up on its chocks with a protesting rending of timber and metal as seawater surged past and around it. Groups of seamen managed to launch a 27-foot whaler, normally propelled by five oarsmen, and a cutter, some six feet longer and broader in the beam. The steeply listing decks were now crowded, as men came up from below knowing that the cruiser's minutes were numbered. Many of them were injured and some obviously dying. Lifeless, crumpled bodies lay strewn about and a party of ratings under direction of medical officers lowered the dead over the side.

The sky was full of Japanese aircraft, wheeling and circling around for a grandstand view of the death throes, among them the float-plane that had shadowed us during the forenoon. One flight of five or six bombers came down in 'follow-the-leader' line ahead formation, only about twenty feet above the sea, flying slowly down *Cornwall*'s port side from stem to stern and only some twenty yards from the doomed ship's side, open canopies for better viewing. We could see the faces of the pilots and observer-gunners clearly. It was an amazingly foolhardy manoeuvre on their part because for the privilege of a ringside seat they rendered themselves vulnerable to any small arms fire that the cruiser could still bring to bear. Presumably they believed we had nothing left to throw at them. In the event, a mounting of four vertically aligned Vickers .5-inch machineguns atop the hangar was still operative and as the Vals winged their way aft the .5s manned by Able Seaman Pickering opened up on them with long withering bursts at point-blank range. Astonishingly the aircraft flew straight on, unwaveringly, without a tremor, apparently unharmed, but they must have taken numerous hits. Fortunately for them the pom-poms with their graze-fused explosive shells were by then out of action. (See Diagram 5.)

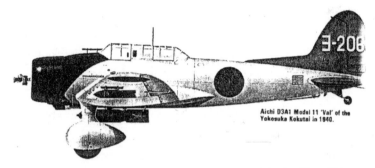

Aichi D3A1 Model 11 'Val' of the
Yokosuka Kokutai in 1940.

Navy Type Aichi 99 Carrier Bomber, code named 'Val' by the allies which was, with variants, the standard Japanese naval diver-bomber. Throughout the Pacific conflict, sinking, inter alia, HMSs *Cornwall, Dorsetshire* and *Hermes*. Armament: two 0,303 inch fixed forward-firing machine guns and one 0,303 inch machine gun on flexible mount in rear cockpit. Bomb-load: one 551lb and two 132lb. Maximum speed level flying 239mph.

Diagram 5: Japanese naval dive-bomber, Type Aichi 99, codenamed 'Val'

'Abandon Ship' was now in full process and men everywhere were 'leaving home', boarding available boats and Carley rafts, some stepping or jumping into the water, others supporting, even carrying injured comrades. Once overboard they paddled or swam to put distance between themselves and the battered warship, lying low, smoking and burning on the water. I joined about a dozen others in their endeavours to launch one of the largest Carley floats, which lay flat on B Gun Deck. It was an extremely heavy and cumbersome contraption which refused to budge towards the ship's side despite all our pushing and pulling, and notwithstanding the favourable downward list. With much heaving and unrefined utterances we lifted upwards the side of the float furthest from the water to vertical, then flipped it over to crash down on the deck with a crack. One more flipover would land it three-parts in the water already lapping over the deck's edge, and make it launchable. Another gasping heave plus reinforced invective, a mighty splash, and the float was sluggishly buoyant.

Ominous rumbling and shuddering from deep down in the ship came as a forewarning that the end was near, and instinctively we stepped into the Carley raft that we had set afloat, and cast off, helping others in the water to crawl on board. Looking back, we could now see into the top open ends of *Cornwall*'s three funnels belching thick black smoke. The last men physically able to leave were now jumping or lowering themselves, or helping shipmates, into the sea. A white-uniformed figure splotched with blood on upper torso appeared suddenly high up on the starboard quarterdeck, clutching the guardrail, and a score of voices on the water took up the cry, "There's the skipper!" Releasing his grip, Captain Mainwaring slid and rolled down the steeply canting quarterdeck into the brine, and nearby swimmers splashed to his assistance.

Minutes later *Cornwall*'s bows dipped deep under, her stern rising ponderously skywards until, almost perpendicular, one screw still slowly rotating, White Ensign flying, she slipped slowly beneath the surface, leaving for a few moments a patch of bubbly turbulence, taking with her some 180 souls. A mile away *Dorsetshire* had fared no better, having in fact preceded her sister *Cornwall* to the ocean floor.

HMS Cornwall *sinking (photographed from a Japanese aircraft)*

The leader of the attack planes still orbiting above, his bomber distinguishable by a red tail-fin, fired a triumphant burst of tracer across the serene, tropical sky, whereupon the Japanese flyers, taking up formation, droned away into the distance, became a cloud of tiny dots, and then disappeared out of sight. Their departure left me momentarily with a queer feeling of being deserted, left helplessly alone in the ocean hundreds of miles from anywhere. I was almost sorry to see them go. Our assailants had been superbly efficient and thoroughly ruthless in driving home their attack but they abided by the rules: men in the water were not machinegunned or otherwise harassed. With the passage of time one had grudgingly to admire their proficiency. On the other hand, *Dorsetshire* survivors reported some instances of being fired at in the water.

*   *   *   *   *

255

Alone! Alone in mid-ocean – it was a queer, if momentary emotion, the realisation that we, approximately five hundred survivors, were left spread over a wide area, about half a mile square, swimming, bobbing, clambering into Carley floats, of which perhaps six or seven had been successfully launched, or clinging to all manner of planks and other flotsam, including a makeshift wooden raft and portion of the wooden foremast which fortunately had snapped off; realisation also that we were a mere pinprick on the vast Indian Ocean, proverbially a needle in a haystack, and that no friendly body as yet knew of our predicament.

But those thoughts were immediately relegated to the back reaches of the mind as there was much urgent work to be done. Apart from the floats and flotsam aforesaid, two boats – the whaler and cutter already mentioned – were saved and soon filled to capacity. In addition one of the ship's two motorboats had blessedly, miraculously floated free. It rode higher on the water, and was therefore more visible, and the logical rallying point. It had a canopy covering a small cabin which provided a measure of shelter for the most seriously wounded. It was towards the motorboat that the entire multitude of widely scattered castaways now strove to converge. That was no easy task. Carley floats were like giant, bulky doughnuts, an outer ring on which the occupants were expected to sit; the inner space filled by a loosely tied wooden grating functioning as a footrest. They were designed, as the name implied, to float, not travel around. Nevertheless, among other articles lashed to the floats were some puny paddles and with these we endeavoured to propel ourselves in the direction of the motorboat. Very soon, with more and more swimmers climbing on board, filling every available space, or hanging on from the outside, our Carley float supported an estimated seventy men, more than double its theoretical capacity, the weight of human cargo causing it to submerge completely. In the circumstances it seemed a miracle that the paddlers could make it move at all.

Our immediate, most serious concern was for the wounded, many with frightful burns, some gashed and mutilated by fragmentation or shot up by machinegun fire, some unconscious or nearly so, and a number clearly close to death. These were not the injuries that, up to then, I would have pictured: the typically illustrated figures found in adventure books for boys – the soldier with a white bandage around his forehead, a red spot of blood seeping through, or his arm in a sling. These were different. There were charred faces, charred limbs, the skin from their upper arms peeling off and hanging loosely below their hands, overalls burnt and in tatters. In our float only Freddie Grimster from Durban revealed some likeness to the storybooks: he had a flesh wound on his forehead from which blood was trickling. I was supporting a badly burnt sailor whose blackened face I did not recognise. "Hold on, mate," I said to him, "You'll be OK once we get you on the motorboat."

"You're lying, Ging," the black face muttered, addressing me by nickname, and I realised with shock that I was supporting Hedley Beswetherick, my messmate whom an hour earlier I had seen eating his dinner in the mess. Hard up against my left side stood Able Seaman Maurice Williams, at first glance apparently uninjured but, at second, obviously in severe pain. I tried the same approach with him, hoping to convey a small measure of encouragement. I had long been an admirer of Williams, a senior AB, master of everything he did, warm, friendly and helpful, belying an inner strength and steely resolve. "You'll be fine, Bungey," I said to him, "once we get you onto the motorboat."

He shook his head slightly, forced a smile and answered, "No, I'm dying," then after a moment's pause, "but I'm not downhearted." Had I looked less perfunctorily at his overalls before speaking I would have seen that they were riddled with bulletholes. He had manned a Lewis machinegun on the bridge, hopelessly outgunned by the succession of diving attackers, firing until he dropped. Williams was made of the stuff that, given the right time and place (and the right recommendation) would merit the award of the Victoria Cross.

Another complication which manifested almost immediately after the *Cornwall* foundered was bunker fuel oil. It came welling up from the depths in vast quantities, thick, black, and slimy, suffocatingly pungent to the nostrils. Very soon it covered everything, saturating men in the water, clothing, faces, flesh, hair and wounds. To grip anything, be it a paddle, piece of timber or an injured comrade was an extremely slithery, difficult task.

Gradually the widely dispersed men, in boats and Carley floats, or clinging to flotsam, managed to draw closer together and presently Commander Fair, *Cornwall*'s second-in-command and, in normal times, dapper and spruce, clambered onto the motorboat, his erstwhile white, tropical uniform black with crude oil, to address what remained of his ship's company. Captain Mainwaring, he announced, had survived, although wounded in the chest and arms. He urged all floats, boats and men in the water to merge into one large body as quickly as possible so as to make detection from the air easier because, he said, the two ships would already have been missed at their intended rendezvous, and air searches from our carriers would be launched. The Carley floats and boats should be loosely tied to one another to prevent their drifting apart, and the seriously wounded were to be put in the boats, those of a more critical nature in the motorboat, which afforded a modicum of shelter. The commander exhorted the men to be of good cheer but advising against singing ('Roll out the Barrel', 'There'll Always Be an England' and others had been sung lustily since the ship went down) as this could aggravate thirst, and we might be in for a long wait.

But the afternoon was well advanced before the entire company of black and bedraggled men had assembled more or less in one cohesive body, accomplished by prolonged and tiring effort. But then lifting the badly wounded and burned out of the black, oily water up into rocking boats was laborious in the extreme and exceedingly painful for the victims, although some of them were past caring about it. Beswetherick was a limp, inert body when we passed him up, and it is my belief that he was already dead. Bungey Williams endured the agony of being hoisted into the motorboat with hardly a murmur, but his death too was near.

Although nearly all who had abandoned ship eventually managed one way or another to reach and merge with the main body in the vicinity of the motorboat, there were one or two groups which had strayed. Low down on the water as we were, our range of vision was limited to a few hundred yards, but, alerted by their cries, the men in the motorboat spotted them, and our whaler was despatched more than once to bring the stragglers in.

Reg Peard, self-effacing athlete from my home town, spotted an unoccupied Carley float some distance away which had apparently been detached and had floated free when the ship foundered. A strong swimmer, Reg struck out for the float, clambered aboard, untied a paddle secured thereto and proceeded to urge the ponderous contrivance towards the clusters of foundering oil-blackened men in the water, where it would be worth more than its weight in gold. The first group he reached included an officer, although hardly distinguishable as such in the muck, and, as Reg wryly remarked later, so ended the only seagoing command that came his way during the war.

It was about this time, perhaps half past four, that a biplane, one of our own Swordfish or Albacore, suddenly arrived on the scene, swooping down low over the jubilant, waving throng, Aldis signal lamp flashing. It circled once or twice above us and then winged away towards the setting sun. Once more Commander Fair climbed aboard the motorboat to tell us that the aircraft had signalled help was on the way. The knowledge that we had been discovered by a search plane from our own fleet was of immeasurable comfort and relief to us, and made all the difference to our frame of mind and morale during the hours that followed.

Speculation was rife as to how long it would be before rescue ships arrived but as the sun sank lower and finally dipped below the horizon came the realisation that help could not be expected before the following day and that a cheerless night in the water lay ahead. As the last light of day faded in the sky another aircraft was seen a long way off and very high, but there was no way of knowing whether it was friend or foe. I suspect the latter. It disappeared into the gathering gloom and soon there were only the stars.

The plight of the wounded was in many cases desperate. The surgeon-commander and his assistants did what they could, but with the limited supplies of dressings and medication found in the motorboat, woefully insufficient in the prevailing circumstances, that was very little. The worst cases began to die and, as the surgeon pronounced them dead, their bodies were lifted from where they lay or sat and lowered gently over the side to sink into the darkness. Most of the men in the water suffered to a greater or lesser extent from fuel oil affliction in their eyes, causing painful irritation and burning. Eventually some could not open their eyes at all.

The night wore on. The vast majority who were not in boats were up to their armpits in water, even those of us on Carley floats which, overloaded, were completely submerged, but still supportive. The water had been comfortably warm all afternoon but now turned cold, and men huddled closer together in quest of warmth. Chatter and wisecracks died down. Some smoked, having managed to salvage sodden cigarettes and matches by sticking them in their hair to dry in the sun – remarkable resourcefulness to satisfy an addiction! The sea was blessedly calm.

Those who could, dozed fitfully in whatever position they found themselves. Every now and then a voice would cry, 'Light on the horizon', or 'Ship ahoy'. But it would only be a rising star. In the boats the surgeon's torch flashed from time to time, and once in a while came the soft splash and ripple of another body consigned to the deep. One corpse was reluctant to sink and floated for some time in amongst its shipmates in the water… and still the night wore endlessly on.

Sailors are not renowned for devotion to prayer and religious supplication, but I do believe that most of us, at some time during that fateful night, and in some manner, raised our minds briefly to God, perhaps glancing upward through oil-stung eyes at the starry firmament above, each breathing a silent SOS to the Creator of the universe. I think I said an 'Our Father', or part of it – also a 'Hail Mary' – I'm not sure. My mind was wandering from the present to far, far away and to ages long departed. I recaptured at one point the image of a boy, six or seven years old, in the little sandstone church of our home town in the Orange Free State, my father towering sternly above me, my mother gently playing the organ. Snatches of time-honoured hymns, lyrics and melodies drifted back into my subconscious. Words from one hymn to the Blessed Virgin seemed singularly apt:

> Mother of Christ
> Star of the Sea
> Pray for the wanderer
> Pray for me.

Dozing off again – the sound of lapping water and the foul stench of fuel oil – immersed chest-deep in the thick black slime – head on a shipmate's shoulder – five or ten minutes' oblivion – sweet dreams.

* * * * *

19

EASTER MONDAY

(If one comes close, splash)

Dawn came at last, the transition from darkness to light almost abrupt, as it usually is near the equator, and spirits rose anew. It was Easter Monday and, for some, a public holiday. Cramped and shivering, the men longed for the warming rays of the sun and scanned the horizon and sky for signs of rescue, but there was only the sea and the grey, turning to blue vault above – disappointing. We had hoped…

At around breakfast time all available foodstuffs were mobilised and a rational distribution was organised. These came from emergency stores, which at all times were stowed in boats or lashed to Carley floats. They consisted mainly of tinned corned beef, unsweetened condensed milk, South African canned fruit and fresh water. A controlled number of cans were prised open and each man hooked out a small chunk of bully-beef and half an apricot with an oily finger, and took a sip of fruit juice. To facilitate operations of this nature, naval issue tin openers were also stowed with the foodstuffs. These were formidable appliances which, if need be, could be turned to good account in hand-to-hand combat. At one stage we were each allowed a sip of fresh water but this and the condensed milk was carefully husbanded and reserved mostly for the wounded.

We had yearned for the sun to rise but it was not long before we changed our minds. As it rose in the heavens the sun blazed hotter and hotter and men scooped up seawater to douse and cool their unprotected heads. Oil in the eyes was still torture to many, but by now the thick black layers on the surface had started to dissipate and patches of clear water began to appear. However, welcome as this was, it soon evoked an interest of rather less comforting dimensions, because what had hitherto been out of sight beneath the oil slick, and therefore largely out of mind, now obtruded gracefully into view in the translucent depths below – a white streamlined shape, gliding effortlessly, and another and another. Far down in the gloom were others, indistinct, merely white shadows, ghostlike.

An officer spoke up. "Sharks are mostly only curious creatures. We are safe enough if we stay together in a bunch. Don't stray far from the main body. If one comes close, splash." I doubt whether any of us had unquestioning faith in the officer's expertise regarding matters pelagic, specifically in respect of the natural inclination of sharks when they happen upon a body of five hundred sailors on the surface. However, we had no better advice to put forward, and did what we were bid. The sharks did not come too close but they were always there, sometimes singly or in twos and threes, sometimes a dozen or more, patrolling continuously, silently – waiting? Only curious? Perhaps.

The new menace injected added urgency to speculations concerning rescue. Why was it taking so long? At the time of the Japanese dive-bomber attack we were reportedly only hours away from the point of rendezvous. Surely Somerville would have initiated a surface search as soon as it became clear that we had met with adversity. It should not have been difficult for him to determine our probable position, par-ticularly after the return of the Swordfish airplane that had located us. That in turn raised fears that the plane had failed to return, shot down perhaps or, God forbid, that the Eastern Fleet had been discovered by the Japanese. We were to learn the answers to these questions later.

Midday came and went, sun burning pitilessly, unremittingly. But the gallantry of the men in the water and boats, their good-natured banter, unselfishness and courage, never waned. Captain Mainwaring, though suffering painful wounds, refused to leave the water for the comparative comfort of one of the boats in which lay or sat most of the seriously injured, cramped and in torment from the heat, some showing signs of delirium. I had long since vacated my seat in the crowded Carley float, jammed to capacity as it was, preferring to be on the outside, where I could move around more freely. I still wore my half-inflated Mae West, which provided ample buoyancy.

An officer organised a measure of relief for some of those swimming on their own by allowing them a spell in the cutter for, perhaps, half an hour, and I also had a turn. I squeezed on to one of the thwarts and was handed a baler, a shallow dish with a handle, with which to bale out sea water which leaked in through the clinkers or lapped in over the gunwales. It was not strenuous work but the heat from sun's rays was extreme. There were several injured men in the cutter, one obviously critical, and an officer who had suffered extensive burns and, mercifully perhaps, was semi-comatose. After a while all sign of life in him ceased and the surgeon-commander, summoned from the motorboat, swam across and confirmed that he was dead. I helped to lift the lifeless body over the side and watched as it sank in the now crystal clear water. What I then beheld would ordinarily have caused me to cry out in horror but in my mind-numbed state I merely stared. A large shark drifted right up to the sinking body, surveyed it for a second from a distance of two inches, and then with a flick of the tail glided past. The deceased officer, I was later told, was the nineteenth to die and be buried at sea since the ship sank.

Mid-afternoon and still no sign of rescue – surely not another night in the drink! Back in the water, one hand holding on to a loop of cordage drooping from a Carley float, my sleep-starved brain was wandering again, back home to East London where my folks – dad, mother and sister Pat – would still have no inkling of my situation. It would be about lunchtime there, I thought, the three sitting at table.

Perhaps they were talking about me, and I knew that each in his or her own way and in own time would pray for me, especially my mother, whose waking hours were characterised by intermittent, silent invocations. Words of that evergreen ballad dating from the First World War drifted back:

Every tear will be a memory
So wait and pray each night for me
Till we meet again.

Suddenly, at about 4.00 pm, a great shout went up and everybody was waving and cheering. Again a double-winged Swordfish or Albacore was droning around in a tight circle above us, Aldis twinkling until, message completed, it flew off for a repeat performance a mile or so away where the *Dorsetshire* survivors were in similar straits. Commander Fair, unflappable as always, archetypal British naval officer albeit begrimed with oil, once again ascended the motorboat and amid lusty cheers announced that help was near at hand. Some while later, to our indescribable joy and relief, three ships hove into sight: His Majesty's cruiser *Enterprise* and destroyers *Paladin* and *Panther*, their rescue boats already swung outboard on their davits for lowering. *Enterprise* headed for the *Cornwall* throng and hove to about 100 yards away, her two destroyer escorts making for the *Dorsetshire* group.

Soon their boats were among us. The motor-powered pinnace secured our motorboat side on, at the same time filling her spacious interior with men from the water, and then drove back to the cruiser, where eager hands helped to get the wounded up the gangway. The pinnace returned immediately to bring in the cutter and whaler with their occupants. The remaining rescue craft were oar-propelled and as they filled up with swimmers and men on Carley rafts they would row back to the cruiser to discharge their cargo, and then return to us. The pick-up operation proceeded in an orderly, competent manner but of necessity took some time – an hour perhaps. Eventually I observed that I was one of a last small group in the water and for a moment was gripped by panic, feeling that by some mischance we would be missed and left behind. However, we too were eventually helped into a whaler – the last of the survivors plucked from the sea in which we had been immersed for nearly thirty hours.

Cornwall *survivors in the water awaiting rescue*
(photographed by British carrier-borne aircraft)

I cannot express enough praise for Captain Annersley of the *Enterprise* and his ship's company for their magnificent, helpful support in every way. They had men on the gangway to assist those of us with unsteady legs, and a half-mug of drinking water was waiting for us when we reached the top. We were ushered to the washrooms and helped to get the grime off our bodies with buckets of hot water and soap. The clothing we were wearing, overalls and the like, impregnated with fuel oil, had to be discarded. The ship's 'slops', or clothing stores, were thrown open and garments, mostly shorts, distributed. Their lower-deck ratings dug into their lockers and kitbags to help cover the nakedness of the survivors they had rescued and who had caused the population of their ship to almost double at a stroke, so to speak. One of their seamen handed me a pair of coarse drill trousers, part of what was routinely referred to as 'Number 5s', which I gratefully accepted. That, together with a pair of old canvas plimsolls which materialised from somewhere, were to comprise my entire ensemble for the next several weeks. The name imprinted on the trousers was 'Catchpole' and I intended to write him a letter of thanks in due time but, to my discredit, I did not get around to doing so.

In what was apparently the counterpart of *Cornwall*'s forecabin flat, a relatively spacious area between decks, the injured were laid out on the corticine underfoot to receive attention and treatment by medical personnel, doctors and sick bay 'tiffies', including our own from *Cornwall*. The more serious cases were accommodated in the sick bay and other improvised 'ICU' locations. Numerous survivors who were suffering from painful inflammation in the eyes caused by fuel oil, but otherwise uninjured, queued for eye-drop treatment.

Next came plates of heaven-sent hot food and mugs of tea in the seamen's mess decks, which areas were placed at our disposal. Where the *Enterprise* lads ate and slept that night, having been displaced by us, I did not know nor, in my exhausted state, did I care. Bone-weary men were starting to doss down wherever they found space: on mess tables, benches, lockers or the deck. I managed to grab a place and lay back using my partially-inflated Mae West as a pillow. The time, I thought, was about 9.00 pm. I closed my eyes and was gone, oblivious to the world.

Survivors three in makeshift clothing
(left to right - Reg Peard, Peter Pare, author)

The same three survivors sixty years later
(left to right - the author, Peter Pare, Reg Peard)

20

AND THE DAY AFTER

("Three cheers for the skipper")

"Nine o'clock," called a voice distantly. "Still only nine?" queried my fractionally percipient brain. Then other sounds drifted in, other stirrings, other voices, the clink of metal utensils and crockery, the familiar hum, throb and vibration within a ship underway. I opened my eyes. Bright sunlight was streaming in through the portholes, their deadlight flaps having been lifted in accord with the piped command to 'undarken ship'. The mess deck was packed with scantily-clad humanity, some still asleep, others in various postures of gradual physical and mental arousal.

Presently another voice boomed, "Wakey, wakey, lads. Show a leg. Hands to breakfast – bread and jam and...," the voice added, "tea's wet." Several *Enterprise* seamen brought in 'pusser' navy tea kettles – monstrous metal cylinders containing boiling water and having concentric, sieve-like receptacles in which were tea leaves hanging down their central interior. Ah! Life-saving tea! It was now Tuesday, April 7. I had slept dreamlessly and unstirringly for 12 hours.

Through the portholes one saw that we had rejoined the Eastern Fleet, or part of it, and were steaming at high speed obliquely away from the ascending sun, presumably on a north-westerly course, and at about that point one began to piece together a picture delineating and elucidating the movements of the two opposing fleets, British and Japanese, on the two preceding days, how these impacted upon *Dorsetshire* and *Cornwall* up to and after their sinking, and understanding why we were not rescued from the sea sooner than we were.

Somerville, it will be recalled, after patrolling an area south-east of Ceylon for three days to challenge a 'possible' Japanese attack on the island from that direction, decided that it had been a false alarm and retired westwards with the Eastern Fleet to Port T at Addu Atoll in the Maldive Islands. Apparently so assured were he and the C-in-C Ceylon in this belief, that his two heavy, big-gun cruisers, the light aircraft-carrier *Hermes* and a destroyer were detached for other assignments. It would therefore have come as a startling shock to Somerville when, late on Saturday afternoon in the midst of refuelling and provisioning, he received the radio transmission from Colombo conveying the import of Birchall's sighting signal from the ill-fated Catalina.

The British admiral had divided his fleet into two parts, Force A being the fast division, the core of which was his flagship, the battleship *Warspite* and the large fleet carriers *Formidable* and *Indomitable*. Force B was the slower division, its core comprising the four old 'R' class battleships *Resolution, Royal Sovereign, Ramillies* and *Revenge*. Somerville, man of action, prepared immediately to put to sea with Force A, arranging to rendezvous with *Dorsetshire* and *Cornwall* the following day, Sunday afternoon, and then to probe eastwards with the intention of intercepting the Japanese force returning from its presumed attack on Colombo. His Force B, which had still to refuel and rewater, would follow as soon as possible thereafter under command of his second-in-command, Vice-Admiral Algernon Willis.

At that stage Somerville still had no explicit knowledge of his enemy's strength and composition but, while prudence warned against underestimating in that regard, he persisted in the hope that the odds would not completely rule out his plan to strike an aerial torpedo blow under cover of darkness. He therefore set his Force

A a course roughly east-north-east from Port T, which would enable *Dorsetshire* and *Cornwall* to rejoin the following afternoon on schedule and hopefully place him in a position favourable for inflicting a telling blow on his unsuspecting adversary some hours later – in retrospect unmerited optimism.

On Sunday morning Somerville, along with many others, was electrified by the radio announcement from Colombo of the Japanese air attack on that city at approximately 8.00 am. The weight and extent of the bombardment left him in no doubt that the opposing force was large and powerful, vastly dominant in aircraft-carriers, clearly at least four, (in fact five), indeed indicating odds that should not be trifled with. The British admiral nevertheless continued on course, hoping to receive information from time to time about the enemy's movements, having not yet discarded the proposition of launching an aerial torpedo attack that night. In any case he was still committed to a rendezvous with *Dorsetshire* and *Cornwall* in the afternoon, and could not risk breaking radio silence to alter that arrangement. He was concerned that the course followed by the two cruisers might bring them too close to the operating area of the Japanese but anticipated, optimistically again, that the latter, having dealt with Colombo, would immediately turn eastwards to address the situation at Trincomalee, thus widening the distance between themselves and the two cruisers as well as the Eastern Fleet's Force A.

Nagumo, however, did not oblige in that way but swung instead westwards, and then chose a southward retirement course roughly 100 miles further to the west, surmising no doubt that the Eastern fleet might be found lurking at a distance offshore in that direction – not ill-advisedly as it happened. The Japanese admiral's decision also brought him 100 miles closer to the path of *Cornwall* and *Dorsetshire* and was therefore a contributory factor in facilitating these ships' discovery and destruction, thus once again shielding the Eastern Fleet by what may grotesquely be regarded as its ninth stroke of luck.

Dorsetshire's captain, Augustin Agar VC, wisely deemed it necessary in late morning to break radio silence to inform Somerville that his ship and *Cornwall* were being shadowed by a Japanese reconnaissance plane, indicating that the enemy had obviously not yet turned eastward and that the sighting portended an imminent attack. Tragically the message was delayed and distorted, arriving on the flagship only in early afternoon. It did, however, go some way towards clearing the picture for the admiral and his staff on *Warspite,* but presented also an agonising predicament. His plotting table would now show, in the light of Agar's report, that the present course of his Force A and the apparent course of the Japanese were converging and, if not altered soon, would inevitably lead to mutual discovery. Should he play safely as possible, reverse course westwards, meet up with Force B following in his wake and take all his ships out of danger? This would, under the constraints of radio silence, mean abandoning *Cornwall* and *Dorsetshire* to the perilous vicissitudes of the moment. The cruisers, if still afloat, would arrive at the point of rendezvous, find nothing, be nonplussed, perhaps linger needlessly in the face of growing jeopardy, arrive at their own conclusions and hopefully pursue well-reasoned, independent procedures from then on.

Somerville gallantly, if ill-advisedly, decided to proceed to the appointed position and, on arrival, there being no sign of the cruisers, his disquiet deepened. An aerial search, in itself a risky undertaking, was ordered and when, in mid-afternoon the Swordfish (or Albacore) biplane came upon the two oil slicks, each containing its human conglomerate as earlier related, the truth was known. When the aircraft reported back to Force A Somerville's worst fears were realised – his two heavy cruisers had been sent to the bottom and, re-evaluating from this basis the probable present location, course and speed of the enemy, the admiral knew that if his Force A did not vacate the area posthaste, both it, and by extension Force B too, would be entrapped by the much more powerful antagonist and suffer substantially the same fate.

He therefore set out immediately at full speed on a north-westerly course, away, he hoped, from hostile detection, at the same time taking his fleet far to the north of Port T to avoid its discovery by the enemy should the latter follow in pursuit. Somerville had no intention of abandoning the men in the water, planning to rescue them next day as soon as confirmation was received that the Japanese had moved away from the area. Even so he was not sure that he had escaped the trap, that his ships had not also been spotted or that the telltale wakes of Force A, at 'full ahead', stretching for miles across a calm sea, had not given the game away.

In the event, Somerville and the Eastern Fleet, Forces A and B, *had* escaped, but for a different reason – the last and, by my reckoning, the tenth amazing stroke of luck. The prime objective of Nagumo's incursion into the Indian Ocean had been the destruction of British naval power, the Eastern Fleet which, it was assumed, would be found in Ceylonese waters within the operational compass of Colombo or Trincomalee or both. As might be expected, the Japanese commander opened his offensive on Easter Sunday at Colombo on the west coast but found no sign there of his principal quarry which, he then concluded logically, would be uncovered in and around Trincomalee on the other, eastern side of the island. Trinco, one of the world's greatest natural, deep water sanctuaries, could in any case accommodate far more vessels than Colombo. So he would steam thither as quickly as possible, providing only on the way for a reconnaissance sweep some hundred miles to the west. It was during the course of this sweep that the Japanese discovered *Dorsetshire* and *Cornwall*, which, due to a fortuitous mental lapse, they deemed to be 'running away', yet too important to be allowed to 'get away'.

Nagumo accordingly maintained his southward course to remain in contact with the cruisers but, as soon as they had been despatched he swung 45 degrees to port to commence a wide, extended arc eastwards. He was anxious to prevent the Eastern Fleet, now confidently assumed to be in the Trincomalee locality, from escaping southwards through the broad gap between Ceylon and Sumatra. He may also have feared that the British might overwhelm Ozawa's small foray into the Bay of Bengal from Mergui on the Malaysian Peninsula, which had been planned to coincide with the bombardment of Colombo. Nagumo's sharp change of course eastwards, executed at approximately 2.00 pm was crucial because the foe he hoped to bring to bay in the Bay of Bengal lay, before he turned, directly ahead of him, virtually within the radius of his reconnaissance aircraft – for the Eastern Fleet the closest of shaves! Thereafter, unbeknown to their commanding officers, the two opposing fleets drew further apart and the danger receded with each passing minute. The deadly game of blindman's buff had come to an end and due to the brilliant strategy of a secret naval base and at least ten interventions by Lady Luck, the Eastern Fleet survived. If a guardian angel was assigned to the Eastern Fleet, he or she had worked overtime!

But Somerville's worries were not over. Manoeuvring his fleet – Force B having rejoined – well north of Port T during the night and forenoon of April 5–6, his thoughts were constantly with the men in the water – a thousand or more at a guess – and with the chances of rescuing them. He had received no confirmation that the Japanese had left the area; on the contrary, both the C-in-C Ceylon and the Admiralty in London had signalled their belief that the enemy was still lingering thereabouts, implicitly discouraging any British attempt to return there. It was a recognised stratagem for the victor to tarry near the point of sinking of his vanquished adversary in the hope of also destroying would-be rescue vessels, and this possibility could not be ignored. Should the *Cornwall* and *Dorsetshire* survivors therefore be abandoned to their fate to minimise the risk of the Eastern Fleet being discovered? The principle was accepted in the

Navy that, in extreme circumstances, the few must be sacrificed to save the many.

Seldom has a naval commander had to make such an agonising decision. At around midday on 6 April, Easter Monday, still in the dark about Japanese movements and against the advice of most of his staff including his second-in-command, Vice-Admiral Willis, Somerville, with immense moral courage, elected to dash to the aid of the survivors still keeping body and soul alive in the sea. He knew full well that with another night under those conditions, with virtually no reserves of food, water and medication, far fewer would see the sunrise on the following morning.

The fast cruiser *Enterprise* and destroyers *Paladin* and *Panther* were sent on ahead to search, find and do the pick-up, aided by a Swordfish biplane from one of the carriers and, as related in the previous chapter, did, in the words of Admiral Somerville's congratulatory signal, a 'magnificent job', rescuing more than eleven hundred men. What was not generally known until years after was that the rescue ships were, because of the extreme danger perceived, ordered not to proceed beyond a specified point at which, if the survivors had not been found, the ships were to abandon the quest, turn about and retire at speed. That point, point of destiny, was in fact reached without any sign of the survivors and it was only intervention by the navigating officer on *Enterprise,* who pleaded for an extension of ten minutes to the search, that saved us. It was during those few, fateful minutes that we were found – talk about guardian angels!

*   *   *   *   *

Forward again to Tuesday, 7 April on board HMS *Enterprise* – breakfast and tea, a quick wash of hands and face and the uninjured survivors felt and looked, except for their makeshift attire and two days' stubble on cheek and chin, almost no worse for wear. Our

Petty Officers had no intention of allowing us to idle around and soon organised us to do light chores, such as clearing up mess decks and other areas that we had temporarily invaded, and assisting the exhausted medical teams of both ships in caring for the wounded in the 'forecabin flat' or recreation space. Two of the rescued men had succumbed to their injuries since being brought aboard, and were later accorded a formal burial at sea.

According to naval convention the bodies were sewn up in canvas, weighted at the feet and, at the appointed time placed on boards on the upper deck, overlapping the ship's side and at right-angles to it, each body covered with a White Ensign. The ship would heave to, and ship's company not engaged in other duties would be in attendance and brought to attention. A guard of honour – messmates if available – would take up positions next to their fallen comrades. The chaplain (failing whom, the captain) would read the traditional prayer, whereafter the guard of honour would lift the inboard ends of the boards, allowing the bodies to slide overboard from under the ensigns and be consigned to the deep. Those in attendance would then be dismissed and the ship would proceed underway.

I spoke to Tubby Townsend, who had also survived, and asked, "Tubby, remember that bomb that struck the edge of the deck at P2 but did not explode?"

"Could I forget?"

"But, like you said, the bomb didn't have our names on it."

Tubby considered that for a second or two and then replied, "I think it did have our names on it – it was so damn close – but that our names were misspelt."

In the afternoon all uninjured and 'walking wounded' *Cornwall* survivors were piped to assemble on the quarterdeck to be addressed by our captain. He arrived in spotless, white tropical rig, provided by Captain Annersley of the *Enterprise*, who accompanied him. Captain Mainwaring's arm was in a sling and his torso was bandaged under his shirt. Ruggedly handsome, thickset, facial expression connoting dogged resolve, master of his profession, he stood out as a leader. A man of few words, his message was invariably clear, rational and authoritative. His first words in his address to us, I remember, were, "You have seen the enemy and how ruthlessly efficient he is." Dimbleby in *Turns of Fate* commenced his description of the occasion thus: "In the words of one of the survivors..." Since I am the survivor referred to I feel I am not taking undue liberty by repeating my 'words' here:

"He gave us as stirring an address as I've ever heard. He spoke for only a couple of minutes but the morale of everyone present was boosted tremendously. If there had been any despondency among his men before he spoke, everyone wanted to fight the Japs by the time he had finished. He thanked and praised everyone for their courage and forbearance in the water, and also expressed gratitude to *Enterprise* for picking us up."

One of our Chief Petty Officers called for "three cheers for the skipper" and the men responded with enthusiasm in full voice. Thereafter three cheers were given with equal gusto for "the captain of *Enterprise* and his ship's company." Never has lusty approbation been more richly deserved.

Somerville, who still had no reliable information concerning the whereabouts and movements of the Japanese task force, shepherded his flock well clear to the north-west of Port T, the existence of which he was anxious to conceal from the enemy, eventually approaching the base along a wide circuitous route, arriving there only at midday on Wednesday, 8 April.

An attempt was made to compile accurate lists of men killed, as well as wounded and unwounded survivors, and we were queried by Petty Officers appointed to the task regarding those we could name with certainty as killed. The latter were eventually classified in official announcements as 'missing, believed killed' which, in many cases gave rise to false hopes amongst next-of-kin. We were acutely aware of the anxiety that our families at home would suffer as soon as news of the sinkings broke and of our utter inability at that stage to alleviate their fears.

I was one of a party assigned to assist the overworked medical personnel in attending to our wounded billeted in the 'forecabin flat', or recreation space, where they lay stretched out on the corticine deck and made as comfortable as possible. My duty watch was the 'first', that is from 8.00 pm until midnight on Tuesday. Our unskilled job was to cater for the ordinary needs of our injured shipmates who could not adequately help themselves – adjust their positions, administer approved food and drink, facilitate urination and so on. I helped a stoker whose upper body, including arms and hands was swathed in bandages, to smoke a cigarette and it seemed to me that many of our patients, if interested in partaking of anything at all, were more attracted to cigarettes than to food. Looking at the rows of bandaged and elastoplastered comrades lying in the flat, many in pain, some sedated, brought home to me how fortunate I was with not a scratch, the only slightly tender spot being my right thumb, a leftover from the Saturday afternoon's ejection from the drinking dive in Colombo with Jock Davidson. I thought about personal possessions lost. In my locker were, apart from clothing, ten South African one-pound notes, equal value in those days to their British Sterling equivalents; a Kodak camera and more than a hundred photographs and snaps; and a few items of jewellery and other souvenirs.

A young *Enterprise* officer was engaged in preparing a supply of lime juice for the patients by decanting lime concentrate from a bottle into a fanny of iced water. Obviously he was wholly inexperienced in performing this task, with not the vaguest idea of the ratio required, and after a tentative trial he poured a little of the mixture into a cup and handed it to a dour-faced, middle-aged seaman in attendance. "Here," he said, "try this and tell me if it tastes like lime juice." The seaman did as he was bid, ruminated with furrowed brow for two or three seconds, his gaze, had it not been for the intervention of the ship's hull, stretching to the far horizon and beyond. When he had at last reached a decision he replied, his speech leaving no glimmer of doubt as to where his ancestral roots lay, "Och aye, Surr," he said, deadpan, "it's juice 'a richt, but ah dinna ken aboot the lime."

So ended the long Easter weekend. And so, too, except for memories, ended the odyssey of the 'Three Funnelled Bastard'.

Two Dorsetshire *survivors sixty years later*
(left to right - Ray Lock, Vernon Brill)

* * * * *

279

POSTLUDE

1

AFTERMATH

(I had improved my performance fourteenfold)

When the Eastern Fleet re-entered the anchorage at Port T at midday on Wednesday 8 April 1942, Somerville still suffered incognisance regarding the whereabouts of the Japanese strike force, last encountered by *Cornwall* and *Dorsetshire* on Easter Sunday, three days previously. Admiral Layton, C-in-C Ceylon, and indeed their Lordships at the Admiralty in London, were no whit wiser and, in the circumstances, equally on edge. Apparent to all was the grave danger for the time being of the Eastern Fleet remaining in the vicinity of Ceylon, given the Japanese navy's overwhelming dominance in strike power and mobile capacity, and plans were already afoot to execute a general withdrawal to healthier climes.

Somerville decided, as a first step, that his Force A, with *Warspite* and carriers *Formidable* and *Indomitable* as nucleus, would set course for Bombay to cover the strategic area south of the Persian Gulf; and that the slower Force B, under command of Vice-Admiral Willis, predominated by the four "R" class battleships, would retire to Mombasa for further deployment in defence of the East African sea routes. The uninjured survivors from *Cornwall* and *Dorsetshire* were hastily distributed amongst the ships of Force B, and I found myself part of the draft to the battleship *Revenge* on passage to the Kenyan port. The wounded survivors were at the same time given temporary accommodation on a supply ship in the anchorage, there to await the arrival of a hospital ship for transportation in due course to Durban.

The four 'battlewagons', with escorting cruisers and destroyers, sailed on 9 April, heading west, and to me it was a thrill to walk the decks of one of Britain's battleships and marvel at the eight great 15-inch guns housed in four turrets. On board *Revenge* we were again treated with utmost consideration, especially after their captain had addressed the ship's company over the broadcasting system, giving a brief account of what had befallen the two three-funnelled sister ships and paying tribute to the "gallantry" of the men in the water. It did much to uplift our dishevelled egos. Even more stimulating it was to savour again the midday tot of rum, 'Nelson's blood', which for what seemed an aeon extending all of five days, the fates had denied us.

I was one of a group of survivors standing in the port waist on the upper deck when a signalman came down from the bridge bearing a signal pad. "This may interest you, lads," he said, and he showed us the text of a decoded signal from C-in-C Ceylon to the Admiralty in London reporting the loss of *Dorsetshire* and *Cornwall* at a position 1 41 north 77 51 east. Later we heard the announcement of the sinkings on the BBC news broadcast and, on the following day, that Trincomalee had been heavily attacked by Japanese carrier-borne aircraft. The rough picture of Nagumo's incursion into the Indian Ocean now began to take shape. Still later came the news that our erstwhile companions in the Eastern Fleet – the light carrier *Hermes* and destroyer *Vampire* – had been sunk off the East coast of Ceylon. They, it will be recalled, had also been detached from the fleet earlier, but had now been caught heading south from Trincomalee, *Hermes* without her own aircraft, which had been flown off to bolster the port's defences. Many of us had friends on board *Hermes* and hoped that they had survived. The old carrier and her escort had been only five miles offshore and, unlike *Dorsetshire* and *Cornwall*, foundered in relatively shallow water. It has been reported by fishermen that on exceptionally calm and windless days, when the surface of the sea assumes a mirror-like resemblance, the dim spectre of *Hermes* can be seen on the bottom through the crystal clear water.

In due time the full story emerged, including the rampant peregrinations of Vice-Admiral Ozawa's smaller secondary force which sallied into the Bay of Bengal from the Burmese port of Mergui to coincide with Nagumo's bombardment of Colombo and in two days raised havoc between Madras and Calcutta along the east coast of India, sinking twenty-three merchant vessels. Thereafter both Nagumo and Ozawa decamped from the Indian Ocean and, at the dictate of subsequent developments, never returned. Thus the anomalous situation came about of two opposing fleets, having searched vainly for one another in the waters off Ceylon, retired unbeknown one to the other in opposite directions, leaving the intended decisive battle area deserted. The Eastern Fleet reassembled and returned to Ceylon only in September 1943, still under command of Admiral Somerville, but later was substantially incorporated into the Pacific Fleet under Admiral Sir Bruce Fraser.

With the announcement by the BBC of the sinkings we realised that the news would be breaking at home as well, and our thoughts were very much with our families, who would suffer a prolonged period of anxiety pending arrival of the fateful telegrams. I visualised in particular the anguish of my mother during the long days and nights of waiting and praying. In this connection it is worth recording a case of endearing decency, redolent of the milk of human kindness. On the evening of Sunday 26 April, sixteen days after the news broke, the telephone rang in our home in East London. My mother answered and the conversation proceeded along these lines:

"Hello," said my mother.

"Is that Mrs Muller?"

"Yes."

"Mrs L Muller?"

"Yes," apprehensively.

"Mrs Muller, I have some very good news for you... Hello, are you still there?"

"Yes," almost inaudibly.

"Mrs Muller, I am in the telegraph office at the post office. There is a telegram for you from Simonstown which will be delivered tomorrow but I thought I would let you know what it says tonight. Your son Walter E Muller No RNVR(SA) 67291 is a survivor from *Cornwall*... Hello, are you still there?"

"Yes, yes," between sobs. "Oh thank you, thank you! You are a darling! Thank you – and thank God."

The considerate telegraphist would make several other similar calls that evening but, alas, in at least two cases he would not 'phone.

I had survived, but the war had not ended. In fact, although I did not know it at the time, the war had not yet reached the halfway mark. My length of service was destined to extend until after hostilities finally ceased and along the ongoing way I had some interesting, and at times exciting, experiences – but they are another story. I shall therefore restrict the post-*Cornwall* episode, insofar as I was affected, to a 'fast-forward', sketchy account.

The four 'R' class battleships duly arrived at Mombasa and we survivors were transferred to the troopship *Mendoza*, converted from a captured French, passenger-cum-cargo vessel, slow, rust infested and uninviting, which was to carry us to Durban. Once at sea we were assigned watch-keeping and other duties and in my case, as an AA trained gunner, I was put in charge of an ancient American Hotchkiss machinegun, a type I had not seen before and which I fervently hoped would not need to be put to use. I suspected it posed more danger to the user than to the targeted enemy.

I cannot recall whether we had an escort during the voyage to Durban but we were painfully aware that enemy oceangoing submarines, Japanese and German, were operating around the South

African coast and up eastwards into the Mozambique Channel. To add to our unease we encountered a heavy head-sea in the Channel which caused *Mendoza* to pitch wildly, groaning and protesting, bows rising steeply on the crested swells and crashing down again into the following troughs with an impact that at times realistically simulated a torpedo explosion. Had we indeed been torpedoed in that heaving sea, I fear there would have been little hope of survival for anyone, with or without an escort. I did derive a glimmer of comfort from the fact that I still had my Mae West inflatable lifebelt, which I took off only in the washroom and when I lay down to sleep, using it then as a pillow for my head. (I still have that Mae West to this day.)

We were all relieved eventually to see the Bluff, Durban's conspicuous headland, jutting out to sea. (The hapless *Mendoza* did not last long after that voyage, sunk by a U-boat six months later just 95 miles north of Durban.) There followed a brief sojourn in Wentworth Camp, billeted in bell tents, and within a few days we were fully re-kitted with uniforms, other essential apparel and appurtenances, and also received some very welcome back pay and token compensation money.

Survivors four being photographed for new identity documents
(left to right - Tubby Townsend, the author, Louie Spencer, Jock Davidson)

Then dawned the glorious excitement of proceeding on a month's leave, which, in the case of about eight East London sailors, included a two-day train journey, culminating in joyous family reunions. While at home I visited the widow of Hedley Beswetherick, who had still clung to the belief that, somehow, Hedley was still alive and would one day return. With her was their baby daughter, already learning to walk, who tragically would never see her father. I also wrote to the parents of Peter Versveld in Cape Town to express my condolences as a close friend.

Back in Durban for redrafting, a large group of us were surprised to find ourselves again entrained, this time for Port Elizabeth to undertake, as far as we could gather, specialised shore duties. On arrival at our destination we were bundled into an army truck and transported out to the north of the city almost to the Zwartkops River and deposited at what appeared to be a hotel of moderate size. It was in fact a health spa now leased by the Royal Navy, established on the site of a hot mineral-water spring which until shortly before our arrival had been open to paying members of the public seeking a natural curative for a variety of ills. Water from the spring, hot with a sulphurous odour and taste, was piped into a swimming pool and to all baths and handbasins in the building. Fresh water was also on tap for drinking, cooking and laundry. A glass or two of the hot mineral water was claimed to be a speedy antidote for constipation. We were allocated comfortable double bedrooms, comparable to what one might expect in a country hotel, beds with sprung mattresses, and good meals were served in a dining room by competent kitchen staff – luxury by sailor standards. That was the good news.

The bad news was that we were to do guard/sentry duty on a 4-hour on, 4-hour off basis for spells of 48 hours followed by 24 hours off. The Royal Navy had decided to establish an ammunition depot about two miles distant from our 'hotel', and we were to guard it. A massive warehouse, property of the British Wool Commission, was leased for the storage of naval cordite charges and fixed, cartridge-cum-shell ammunition. About half a mile away from the warehouse an extensive dump had been built to stockpile shells of various calibres, ranging from the 16, 15 and 14-inch battleship projectiles down to those fired by all manner of smaller weapons, while a little further on separate storage was provided for detonators because of their volatile propensities. A single-track railway line connected the depot to the docks.

The 48-hour periods were tiresome, monotonous drudgery exacerbated by sleep deficiency, but the 24 hours off that followed were refreshing. One could bus or thumb a lift into Port Elizabeth, book a bed for the night and enjoy low-cost meals at the Services Club and take in some of the pleasures on offer in the town from dancing or the movies to singing or brawling in a pub. We, officially dubbed the 'RN Guard', were kept there for several months. It was at a dance in the spacious Feathermarket Hall, I recall, that music and jollification were interrupted to permit the announcement that Stalingrad had been relieved and that 90,000 demoralised and exhausted Germans had been taken prisoner – a major turning point in the tide of war. However, a long road still stretched ahead, bestrewn with setbacks and tribulation. Churchill's offer in May, 1940, of 'blood, toil, tears and sweat' still applied.

Another short interval of home-leave, whereafter it was off to the tented transit camp at Hay Paddock bordering Pietermaritzburg, capital of Natal Province. I had not long to wait for my next draft but, to my chagrin, found myself separated from my *Cornwall* and *Dorsetshire* mates. My next ship was HMS *Manchester City*, an impressive name which belied the unflattering characteristics of the vessel, an old, coal-fired passenger-cargo steamer to which the demands of war had no doubt given extended longevity. It was propelled by a single screw, maximum speed at her age, in a following wind, probably not sustainable in excess of twelve knots – a hostile submariner's delight. Her armament comprised two antiquated guns of approximately 4-inch calibre, mounted one on the bows and the other on the stern, her anti-aircraft defence residing in two single-barrelled Oerlikons positioned atop the superstructure on either wing abaft the bridge. As an AA gunner I was put in charge of the starboard Oerlikon.

Words of a lower-deck ditty persistently tormented my mind:

> I wonder, yes I wonder
> If the Jaunty made a blunder
> When he made this draft-chit out for me.

'Jaunty' was naval slang for master-at-arms, who on large ships was chief police officer and in that capacity wielded near-dictatorial power over the rank and file.

Manchester City was classed as a minelayer by conversion but was a far cry from her eminent regular minelaying cousins, such as *Manxman* and *Welshman*, the navy's fastest ships, which could make 40 knots on a calm sea. While the latter two operated largely offensively, often sowing a variety of mines, according to requirements, in enemy-controlled waters, *Manchester City* laid and serviced only defensive mines for the protection of harbour entrances. These mines, huge and bulbous, about eight-foot high on their base mountings, were laid attached at intervals to loops of armoured electric cable stretching across the protected area on the seabed, the number of mines to a loop depending upon the length of the loop. The loops of cable with their attached mines and anchor bases remained on the seabed, perhaps seven to ten loops in total, lying more or less parallel to one another. Between the mined loops were laid indicator loops – devices which could detect any large metal body, such as a submarine, crossing the minefield. All loops, being electrified, led to a control centre ashore where trained personnel kept a 'listening' watch twenty-four hours a day. If the indicator loops showed that a large submerged object, presumed to be an enemy submarine, was entering the minefield, the officer or rating in charge at the control centre could, by throwing switches, blow up whatever loop or loops of mines as was thought necessary to destroy the enemy. Heavy calibre artillery and searchlights were also in place at harbour entrances to deal with any hostile incursions on the surface.

If my memory serves me well the ship, when loaded to capacity, carried approximately 90 mines together with enormous reels of electric cable and other related paraphernalia. A sizeable contingent of specially skilled men rated 'wiremen' undertook all tasks associated with the mines. In the nature of these specialised operations the ship spent long periods in harbour which, when she was in Durban, made for pleasant jaunts into the city, but in most other instances the inclination was rather to stay on board during shore leave.

While at sea *Manchester City* lived a charmed life and, in retrospect, I am surprised that the Admiralty put so much at risk by entrusting the controlled mines enterprise to the old plodding steamer with high, conspicuous freeboard visibility, made additionally noticeable by its inability to curtail smoke emissions. That she never fell prey to an enemy submarine, particularly in the Mozambique Channel, where losses from that source were abundant, is remarkable. Never, as far as I can recall, was she provided with an escort, although such would have been of dubious benefit. A torpedo strike on the old minelayer, or shellfire, would almost certainly have touched off the mines and *Manchester City* would have disappeared in a monstrous cloud of smoke, flame and falling debris.

Digressing briefly, while on the topic of submarine warfare, it is worth noting that the waters stretching from the northern entrance to the Mozambique Channel southwards and around the South African coast held more menace than is generally realised. This was especially so during the years 1942 and 1943 when the Mediterranean was virtually closed to Allied merchant shipping. A voyage from the United Kingdom to Alexandria, which in normal times would take four to five days, had to be replaced by another, around the Cape to Suez, lasting three to four months. Traffic on the long route was heavy – a situation that was exploited by enemy oceangoing submarines, first by the Japanese, then by the Germans, who were later joined by the Italians. It has already been related that on at least one, but probably more, occasions a Japanese seaplane launched from a submarine overflew Durban during June of 1942. Around the South African coast and up as far as Beira 118 merchant ships were sunk by enemy action, nearly all by submarines. During these perilous days the South African ports were overcrowded, especially Cape Town and Durban, so much so that masses of vessels had to lie at anchor in the roadsteads outside harbour awaiting berthing space within, their numbers frequently reaching 50 or more at a time. The enemy must have been aware of these circumstances and it is strange, and hugely fortunate for the Allies, that U-boats did not at night fall upon these defenceless 'sitting ducks' and create mayhem.

But to return to *Manchester City*, controlled minefields were established at Diego Suarez, a magnificent, natural, deepwater harbour with a narrow entrance channel, on the northern tip of Madagascar, at Kilindini, Mombasa, Colombo and Trincomalee, the ship returning from time to time to these ports for maintenance work when necessary. The monotony of long stops in port was broken to some extent by rugby and cricket matches against teams from other ships and shore establishments. *Manchester City* did surprisingly well at rugby and won most encounters, even against much larger ships. A few of us were granted a few days' leave in Ceylon to visit Kandy and a naval rest camp at Diyatalawa in the beautiful, mountainous interior of the island. South Africans among us were intrigued when hiking in the latter locality to discover a small war cemetery, well maintained, containing graves of Boer prisoners of war from the Anglo-Boer War of 1899–1901. We were entertained one evening at the camp by the British singer Paula Green.

The months slipped by, and news bulletins from the BBC were increasingly triumphant. On 7 May 1945, VE Day, Germany surrendered. Hostilities ceased at midday on 8 May and formal ratification was signed in Berlin on the following day. The war in Europe had ended, Italian resistance having ceased back in September 1943 after the fall of their Fascist leader, Benito Mussolini, who was later executed by his own people. In the Far East fighting on all fronts was receding towards the Japanese home islands and the vast United States-Royal Navy armadas were steadily closing in. Eager to be part of the final historic scenario, three of us on *Manchester City*, which was then in Colombo, contrived to secure a draft off the old minelayer, hoping to board another warship. We were transferred to the huge Mayina transit camp on the northern outskirts of the city, but apart from experiencing there some torrential monsoon rainstorms little else happened, and we seemed to have been forgotten.

Eventually I was included in a draft to a destroyer, HMS *Eskimo*, one of the renowned 'Tribal' class, which was then moored in Colombo harbour and under sailing orders. The others in my party, it soon transpired, were all South Africans and it came as no surprise to learn when we came aboard that the buzz was destination Durban. Demobilisation was in the air.

Apart from the fact that the buzz proved correct and that, contrary to our recent aspirations, *Eskimo* was headed in the wrong direction, the voyage home was pleasant and relaxing, with a calm sea and friendly crew. On our arrival in Durban conditions deteriorated abruptly and we soon found ourselves once again behind high barbed-wire fences, this time in sprawling, unlovely Clairwood Camp, with the ubiquitous bell tents in multitudinous array, and overbearing young sub-lieutenants, freshly commissioned, their service heretofore limited to an officers' training college, bellowing orders and threats, causing extreme irritation and an inclination to commit murder. On the news we heard of a new instrument of mass destruction called the atomic bomb, which had been dropped on Hiroshima. I felt unease rather than elation. What was the world coming to?

As usual we were allocated watches and, predictably, mine was duty watch on my first night back in my home country after an absence of two years. For the vast majority of the duty watch there were no 'duties' to be done but they had nevertheless to remain in camp, prevented from going into the city. There was at least a large canteen and after supper three or four of us ex-*Eskimo* new arrivals repaired thither to join the throng, contemplate our lot and drown our sorrows in quart bottles of South African brew. We stayed until closing, by which time I had established my record for one sitting, namely seven quarts or, differently defined, nearly two gallons. As I assailed the last quart, not entirely convinced as to whether I held in my hand one bottle or two, I summoned the perspicacity, momentarily, to recall my first ever pint of beer, in the dining saloon of the train on the day I embarked on active service and which had gone potently to my head. I had improved my performance fourteenfold over the intervening war years, I smirked.

I remember leaving the canteen, someone pointing me in the right direction, but nothing more until I awoke next morning in the tent. Yes, it *was* my tent, I observed with relief, and this *was* my blanket and that's my kitbag against the tent pole. So I had found my way back unerringly amidst hundreds of identical tents and hopefully not tumbled over any guy-ropes. My companions in the tent were bestirring themselves and gave no indication that I had caused any problems when I came in. At the top of my kitbag lay my No 3 uniform that I had worn the evening before, folded perfectly in regulation manner, which was quite an art in order to produce a small, compact bundle for easy storage. For example, each leg of the trousers had to be folded back and forth seven times – the 'seven seas', as the folds were called. And no hangover… not bad, I thought.

The days passed uneventfully, the tedium being broken by 'runs' into town on off-duty days. On one such I tagged on to a huge crowd being addressed by Field Marshal Smuts from the steps of the city hall to mark VJ Day, the surrender of Japan and end of the Second World War. It was the first time I had seen the great leader of world acclaim. He explained among other things that the atomic bomb was a microcosm of the sun. In the same city hall I attended one evening an amateur boxing tournament, Durban versus the mining town of Benoni in the Transvaal. One young tearaway pugilist, 16 or 17 years of age, was introduced as the 'Atom Bomb' from Benoni. His name was Vickie Toweel and he won his encounter that evening. Five years later, in only his 14th professional fight, he ended the 8-year reign of Manuel Ortiz to become the bantamweight champion of the world – South Africa's first world title holder. That was way back in the days when there were just eight weight divisions in the professional ring and eight champions, before these numbers were abrogated by money-driven proliferation.

At long last administrative procedures took effect. Gas masks, tin hats and lifebelts were handed in and rail warrants, where applicable, were issued to return us to our enrolment centres to await demobilisation. Consequently I found myself back in East London where it all started, was certified medically fit and on 22 October 1945, five years and nine months to the day since joining, I was 'demobbed', paid the balance of moneys due to me, and handed a written authorisation to wear my uniform for a further ten days. I looked back with strangely contrasting emotions – aversion yet nostalgia, pride of participation, yet relief at final closure – and, lurking on the fringe of mental awareness, was that nonpareil of sentimental refrains:

BE IT EVER SO HUMBLE,
THERE'S NO PLACE LIKE HOME.

* * * * *

Not infrequently the question is asked by latter-day cognoscenti, pacifists and others, "But was it indeed necessary and right to go to war, to become involved in death and destruction of such immensity? Was it all worth it?" I do not pretend to know the perfect irrefutable answer but my memory inevitably rebounds on such occasions to a wartime concert hall, packed with men and women of the services, and to a large, barrel-chested soldier on stage who, with mounting fervour and characteristic Welsh euphony, sang a song dating back to 1917, words and music by Edgar de Lange and Sam Stept:

I saw a peaceful old valley
With a carpet of corn for a floor
And I heard a voice within me whisper
"This is worth fighting for".

I saw a little old cabin
And the river that flowed by the door
And I heard the voice within me rumble
"This is worth fighting for".

I gathered my loved ones around me
And I gazed at each face I adore
Then I heard that voice within me THUNDER
"THIS IS WORTH FIGHTING FOR".

* * * * *

2

EPILOGUE

(Even the pigeons seemed the same)

It is common for Second World War writers, when summing up, to dwell at some length on the horrors, tragedies and futility of war, and rightly so. Armed conflict between nations, countries, racial and tribal groups, often spurred on by religious disparity, has been with mankind since the dawn of history and, alas, will probably remain with mankind until history's day is done. One contemplates with aversion the dreadful waste of life, not only of those engaged in battle, but men and women of all ages, of children and babes-in-arms, of maimed and broken bodies, the intense anguish and sorrow of loved ones. One thinks also of the devastation of cities, towns and infrastructure, the slaughter of animal life, of refugees in their millions, of displacement, destitution and abject poverty.

With advances in 'blitzkrieg' warfare, aerial and rocket technology, home fronts become front lines. In World War I civilian casualties were estimated at 11 per cent of the total. In World War II this estimate rose to 53 per cent. In World War I Allied shipping losses totalled 12¾ million tons. In World War II the figure rose to 21 and a half million tons. How, one asks, can humankind be so mindlessly cruel, so fixated on conquest and greed, so stupid? Is not the Latin expression *homo sapiens* a misnomer? Should it not rather be *homo stultus*?

But having said the foregoing and without detracting from its truth, would not history without international strife have been dull and uninteresting? Alexander the Great might have been Alexander the Cafe King, intent on expanding his Hellenic culinary enterprises across Asia Minor; Napoleon could have followed his father's footsteps as a lawyer in Corsica, adapting his innate military genius to vanquishing opposing counsel in the courtroom, while Hitler might have guided his burning ambitions towards achieving fame as a painter of the Austrian Alps. Nelson might have appeased his passion for naval combat by belabouring like-minded opponents with oar and boathook in flat-bottomed boats in the Thames Estuary, not perhaps achieving glory comparable to defeating Franco-Spanish fleets at Trafalgar but at least sparing him an eye and arm.

Did the Allies achieve the goals they had set when taking up arms? Was their participation in the war worthwhile? It started with the German invasion of Poland. Britain and France having pledged full support for Poland's independence, in effect against any aggressor, declared a state of war with Germany. Thereafter complications set in rapidly. Soviet Russia overran and occupied Poland's eastern region without precipitating an Anglo-French declaration of war. When the Soviets then invaded Finland the latter received moral and material support from Britain and France, who succeeded in having the Soviets expelled from the League of Nations, for what that was worth.

However, as soon as Germany assailed Soviet Russia in Operation Barbarossa in June 1941 and proceeded to drive the Russians out of Poland and Finland the policy was reversed. Soviet Russia now became a major ally of Britain and France, and later of the United States, while Finland, having permitted German troops to expel the Russians from her territory and continue using it as a springboard, was, technically at least, an enemy.

Poland remained under German occupation and domination until late 1944 when Hitler's armies were in general retreat on the eastern front from the Baltic to the Black Sea and the Russians by early 1945 were surging into Poland and the Balkan countries. Britain and France, supported by the United States, felt honour-bound to liberate Poland, and restore her borders and sovereignty by facilitating there a provisional administration to be followed as soon as possible by a freely elected government. Soviet Russia had given nodding approval of these intentions but, while the attention of the four major Allied powers in the European theatre was focussed on more critical situations, agreement on the future of Poland remained perfunctory.

By January 1945, however, the position was different as the war in Europe was manifestly coming to an end. France was almost entirely freed from German occupation and the Allied armies had advanced to the banks of the Rhine. The liberation of Poland in fulfilment of the Anglo-French pledge in 1939 now assumed extreme urgency as its territory, with the onrush of the Russian armies, was daily falling more and more under the latter's martial control. Furthermore it soon became obvious that the Kremlin's conception of appropriate Polish governance differed sharply from that of her western allies.

The last elected Polish government was operating from London in exile, and it exercised jurisdictional control over 150,000 Polish militiamen fighting with the western Allied forces. They had, for example, played a prominent part in the capture of the Monte Casino massif south of Rome some eight months earlier. Britain, France and the United States were anxious, as soon as circumstances allowed, to return the government-in-exile to Poland to head a provisional national authority there. The Soviets, on the other hand, had already installed in eastern Poland a communist government of their choosing, which came to be known in the West as the 'Lublin Government', and did not disguise their intention to expand its authority eventually across the whole of Poland. Therefore as a matter of compelling concern a summit meeting of the 'Big Three' – Roosevelt, Churchill and Stalin – was, at the instigation of the first two, convened to formulate plans for 'world peace'. France, still in a state of domestic flux, with Charles de Gaulle the dominant figure, was not directly represented at the conference, which was hosted by Stalin at Yalta on the Black Sea and lasted from 5 to 11 February.

Solidarnosc (Solidarity), the independent Polish, self-governing trade union that came into being as a freedom movement years later, was to declare the following: "To the people of Poland the term 'Yalta' is synonymous with betrayal. For many the end of the Second World War meant liberation from German occupation as well as the start of Soviet enslavement." The conference was one of extreme frustration for the American and British delegations, which were unable to achieve much beyond peripheral concurrence, essential fundamental detail being held over for later deliberation.

Poland was the main bone of contention at Yalta but with the might of Soviet Russia now virtually astride the entire country the validity of the dictum "Possession is nine tenths of the law" was clear for all to see. Apart from the question of a provisional government, Stalin was adamant that a large tract of Polish territory along its eastern boundary had to be incorporated into Soviet Russia for the spurious reason that it was from that direction that Mother Russia, in time of war, was invaded, as had happened twice in the past twenty-seven years. That such a measure would displace some three million Poles did not seem to matter since, it was argued, Poland would be compensated beyond its western frontier by the accession of an even larger stretch of land at the expense of Germany. That this would, in addition, entail the displacement of approximately eight million Germans and include a major portion of their country's food producing farmland did likewise not appear to be of any consequence to the Soviet leader. Proceedings were furthermore impaired by President Roosevelt's state of health. In fact, as it later transpired, he was already terminally ill.

Another summit was held at Potsdam five months later, after the German surrender, to examine the situation then obtaining and to endeavour to reach an accord on the way forward. But again it did nothing to further agreement on the Polish question, but rather exacerbated it. Other important issues emerged which distracted attention from Poland, even overshadowed it, such as the establishment of Allied zones of occupation, both in Berlin and in Germany as a whole, as well as the ensuing prosecution of the war against Japan. The capacity of the western delegations to assert their beliefs, particularly in regard to Poland, was not strengthened by the death of Roosevelt in April, his place at the conference table being filled by his successor, Harry Truman, nor by the concurrent general election in Britain. Churchill had been confident that he would be returned to office but astonishingly an ungrateful electorate, including the mass of the armed forces, decided otherwise and Britain was represented during the concluding stages at Potsdam by Clement Attlee, leader of the Labour Party. This meant new helmsmen, different approaches and attitudes, and diminished drive. In the final analysis the Soviets held all the aces and, in the words of Churchill, an Iron Curtain descended across the continent, effectively segregating Poland, Hungary, Czechoslovakia, Romania, Bulgaria and Yugoslavia in subjugation to the Russian Bear – these in addition to the eastern Baltic states and East Germany. Austria, Turkey, Greece and Persia were in danger of being engulfed too; in fact, with sizeable withdrawals of American troops and equipment for transfer to the Japanese theatre, continental Europe in its entirety was alarmingly vulnerable. One may conjecture what might have happened during the next few years had not certain developments come into play which must have had a deterring influence on Soviet adventurism, such as stiffening resistance among western leaders, formation of the North Atlantic Treaty Organisation, the dogged determination and triumph of the Berlin Airlift that endured for eight months in 1948 and, of course, the atomic bomb.

The unhappy reality was that when hostilities ended in 1945 the original direct cause, the reason for declaring war, had not been resolved. The restoration of Polish sovereignty and freedom had not been accomplished. It was left to the unquenchable fire of patriotism and courage of the suppressed peoples themselves slowly and bloodily to break the chains of bondage: to men like Lech Walesa who, in 1980, defiantly led the shipyard strike at Gdansk (Danzig) and was awarded the Nobel Peace Prize three years later; and to the passive but profoundly stirring pilgrimages to Poland of Karol Wojtyla, also known as John Paul II, the Polish Pope, gradually to make the rulers realise that the proletariat could not be stifled and subdued for ever. But history bears witness that not until 1988 to 1990, when democracy finally triumphed, when the Berlin Wall was dismantled and the USSR disintegrated, could the guarantees given to Poland by Britain and France half a century earlier be regarded as fulfilled.

From the second week of August 1945 and for several thereafter the universal topic of conversation, the dominant headline in press and on radio, was the atomic bomb. The nuclear age had arrived and, with it, weapons of mass destruction. Fortunately the ability to assemble, construct and deliver the bomb remained, for the time being, with the United States who thus possessed a device which, they believed, could bring the war to an early end. Yet the bomb should never have been dropped, certainly not on densely populated urban areas.

Much play has been made of the contention that the atom bombs saved the lives of perhaps a million American, and half a million British and Commonwealth troops had the Japanese home islands been invaded, as well as millions of Japanese, both combatant and civilian. Indeed precautionary planning for an onslaught and landing on the southern island of Kyushi was begun but it would not likely have been put into effect.

The factual situation was that Japan, by July 1945, was finished anyway. Fleet Admiral Chester Nimitz has described how her cities were being razed in aerial assault by waves of 500 and more bombers from Okinawa and the Marianas. Task Force 37, the most powerful naval strike force in history, consisting of 105 American and 28 British warships, paraded up and down the Japanese coastline, shelling and bombarding towns and installations with near impunity. Her industrial production was grinding to a halt and starvation stalked the land. Japanese territorial conquests had been bypassed and isolated by America's brilliant central Pacific drive and could no longer play a part. Her navy had been all but destroyed, her last and futile naval sortie involving the superbattleship *Yamato*, 63,000 tons, had left the Inland Sea on April 5 (coincidentally the third anniversary of the sinking of *Cornwall* and *Dorsetshire*) 'propelled by the last 2,500 tons of fuel oil left in Japan – just enough for a one-way passage' – a naval banzai charge. She was sunk before reaching her objective.

MacArthur's forces had retaken the Philippines, Slim's 14th Army had liberated Burma, and Japan's last outposts, on Iwo Jima and Okinawa, were in US hands. Her final desperate throw, the kamikaze campaign, had died, her willing 'death and glory' aviators expended. Japan would have had to surrender under the weight of a blockade inexorably applied and ever-increasing conventional bombing. (The massive firebombing of Tokyo on 9 March had killed considerably more Japanese than would either the Hiroshima or the Nagasaki atom bombs.) The need for an invasion of the home islands would therefore not arise; nor should the atom bombs have been necessary. Churchill, too, has affirmed that at that point the defeat of Japan was certain.

But the crux of the argument surrounding the use of the atom bomb lies in the fact that on 22 June Emperor Hirohito told his Supreme War Council that the war must end and thereafter terms of surrender were sought through the Japanese embassy in Moscow. Other 'feelers' were put out through Sweden and Switzerland. President Truman was informed of this while at the Potsdam conference, but he had been aware of these developments even earlier as American cryptographers had broken the Japanese diplomatic code long before. The President could have put the atomic mission on hold there and then by picking up a telephone – after all one does not, or should not, shoot an enemy holding a white flag; one listens first to what the enemy has to say. Instead two Japanese cities, including nearly all their living creatures, ceased to exist in a flash. The bombs, 'Little Boy' armed with uranium 235, and 'Fat Man' armed with plutonium, were carried by B29 superfortresses – the first to Hiroshima on 6 August in *Enola Gay* piloted by Colonel Paul Tibbets, and the second to Nagasaki on 9 August in *Bocks Car* piloted by Major Chuck Sweeney. Churchill had concurred in the drop but should have desisted, and probably thereby stayed the President's hand.

The Hiroshima bomb had been transported by the US heavy cruiser *Indianapolis* from San Francisco to the island of Tinian in the Marianas preparatory to launching the epoch-making strike. Thereafter, on the way to Leyte in the Philippines the cruiser was sunk by a Japanese submarine, with the loss of 900 American lives. Those prone to superstition might draw their own conclusions.

There were other matters which, in retrospect, could have been dealt with differently, such as at the Nuremberg Trials. Accepting that criminals, those who commit murder and other dastardly deeds against humanity, or are materially instrumental in bringing them about must be punished befittingly, one wonders nevertheless whether in some cases retribution was not carried too far. Churchill was later moved to observe that 'moral principles of modern civilization seem to prescribe that the leaders of a nation defeated in war shall be put to death by the victors. This will certainly stir them to fight to the bitter end in any future war, no matter how many lives are needlessly sacrificed … it is the masses of the people who have so little to say about the starting and ending of wars who pay the additional cost'.

It is indeed the masses of the people who are at the core, are the prime participants, and who take the brunt in time of war, those on the home front as well as those locked in combat. They do as they are told, and believe what their news media disseminates – even Churchill has commented that 'in war the truth must often have an escort of lies'. They toil, fight and die for whatever country fate decrees should be their birthplace, their fatherland, or their land by adoption. My maternal grandfather sang as a choirboy in Cologne Cathedral, the twin-towered Gothic masterpiece on the bank of the Rhine, and had he not emigrated circa 1870 I would almost certainly have served with the German armed forces, possibly as a *Matrose Gefreiter* (Able Seaman) and been as much an encumbrance in Hitler's *Kriegsmarine* as I was in the Royal Navy.

It is with the masses of people that the true meaning of war resides – the hardships, horrors, death and mutilation, the comradeship in tranquillity and in peril, the laughter, tears and fears – and threading through all is the yearning for loved ones, family and home, torn apart by the dictates of cruel circumstances. The wartime emotions and sentiments felt by the masses of people tend to find expression in music, in songs of the time, as in Vera Lynn's prodigious repertoire. The same happened in the First World War as in the superb 'Roses of Picardy' ('but there's never a rose like you'), and even the South African War of 1899–1901 brought forth 'Goodbye Dolly Gray' on the British side and the evergreen 'Sarie Marais' from the Boers.

A ballad that emerged only in the concluding stages of WWII was perhaps the most popular of that period. It originated in Germany where it was soon the rage, spilled over in translation to the armed forces of Britain and her dominions, the United States, and probably others. It would be sung in music halls and canteens, and hummed and whistled on route marches. Its haunting melody and lyrics plucked at the heartstrings of every man and woman caught up in the maelstrom of the global conflict. It rang true to life, regardless of what side one was on:

> Underneath the lantern, by the barrack gate
> Darling I remember the way you used to wait
> 'Twas there that you whispered – tenderly
> "If you love me, I'll always be
> Your Lilli of the lamplight,
> Your own Lilli Marlene."

War's end ushered in a dubious peace, changed relationships, new international friends and new potential enemies, menacing confrontations with erstwhile allies, the 'Cold War', 'Communist Bloc', the 'Warsaw Pact', and sabre rattling. In contrast a strong message of encouragement and hope was engendered by the massive American aid given under the Marshall Plan to sixteen devastated European countries, particularly to Germany, just recently a deadly enemy, preventing economic collapse, while a sense of security was strengthened by NATO: the North Atlantic Treaty Organisation.

The central personality in the conflict had undoubtedly been Adolf Hitler, described variably as a genius or maniac, whose meteoric rise from the streets of Vienna to Chancellor and dictator of the Third Reich, unopposed by the largely enthralled masses of the German people, was a phenomenon still defying understanding today. It was only after the show, when the smoke and dust had dispersed and the full extent of Nazi atrocities became known that the ordinary, unsuspecting Germans realised aghast what had lain hidden behind their battlefield bulletins and, in the words of Manfred Rommel, son of the famous Field Marshal, they ruefully conceded that it was better to have lost the war under Hitler than to have won with him.

It has been said that had Hitler, the former corporal, left the prosecution of the war in the hands of his generals and deferred to the advice of genuine military experts, as opposed to sycophants, he might have emerged the victor – if he had not overruled his commander-in-chief, General Brauchitsch, regarding overall strategy on the Soviet front he might have emerged the victor. First and foremost he should not have fallen upon Soviet Russia in the East while Britain was undefeated in the West. Neither should he have allied Germany to Japan, thereby precipitating war with the United States. There were so many imponderables and 'ifs'. If Mussolini had wisely chosen neutrality instead of recklessly thrusting Italy in on the side of Germany when he adjudged the latter to be on the brink of victory, it would have spared the Reich costly involvement in Africa, Yugoslavia, Greece, Crete, Sicily, and eventually in Italy itself. More importantly than the manpower and equipment allocated to those countries, it cost Germany immensely in wasted time, causing Hitler to postpone by several months commencement of Barbarossa, the invasion of Soviet Russia, with the result that his Central Army Group under Von Bock failed to advance the last forty miles into Moscow, the industrial and nerve centre of the USSR, before onset of the dreaded Russian winter which brought all operations to a halt.

And, once again, if the Royal Navy's Eastern Fleet had been destroyed four months later in the Indian Ocean, what would have ensued? It is acknowledged by highest authority, including Admiral Somerville, that the Eastern Fleet was saved from destruction on 5 April by the cruisers *Cornwall* and *Dorsetshire* which, sacrificed as unintended decoys, created a diversion that threw Nagumo's task force off the trail of its prime objective. Given the foregoing, the decisive point at issue is: had the Eastern Fleet not been spared by the intervention of *Cornwall* and *Dorsetshire*, would the logical sequence of events then, to recapitulate, have been the following?

1. Total annihilation of Allied seapower in the Indian Ocean, leaving the same open for uncontested exploitation by Japan and her allies.
2. Invasion and occupation of Ceylon as well as key points in Madagascar by the Japanese.
3. Reinforcements and supplies to North Africa and the Middle East effectively inhibited, leaving Allied forces there to 'wither on the vine' and eventually surrender.
4. German and Japanese link-up in the Persian Gulf, subjugating the entire Middle East.
5. Seizure of the Caucasian oilfields, thereby strangling the Soviet war machine.

6. Collapse of the Soviet Union, whose survival in the northern summer of 1942 was in any case balanced on a knife edge.

7. Transfer of more than 100 German divisions, with armour and Luftwaffe support, from the Russian theatre to the western front, putting 'paid' for the foreseeable future to Anglo-American invasion prospects.

Can it therefore be deduced, on the basis of the above hypotheses, that *Cornwall*'s and *Dorsetshire*'s intervention changed the course of World War II? Indeed did they not by that means validate the subtitle of this book?

Many analysts and sceptics will argue that this representation of events is too simplistic, that other factors would have had a bearing, that such a prognosis is too extravagant. Conceivably so, but in evaluating the possibility I am reminded of the words of the British high-ranking military officer who, as related in the second chapter of this book, impressed on us recruits that 'the smallest fault can cause the greatest calamity' – that a battle, even a war, can be lost because one member of a gun's crew failed to do his job. Other connoisseurs will contend that even if the Soviets were defeated and the consequences depicted did come to pass, all would not be lost. Britain and her dominions would still stand strong and resolute, backed by the world's greatest industrial powerhouse, the United States, who, let it not be forgotten, would shortly thereafter wield the mightiest weapon the world had ever seen, and be sole possessor of this trump card. Would, or should, the United States, to gain ascendancy, unleash nuclear mass destruction on continental Europe? Or optimistically use the atom bomb as a bargaining chip? On the other hand, there is little doubt that the guy on the other side of the English Channel would, given the opportunity, have no such compunction. It is worth reiterating that Churchill adjudged this point in the war's history, the threat to the Eastern Fleet, to be its 'most dangerous moment'.

Another aspect of vital import: if the Axis powers gained mastery on the continent, is the time factor, time available for decisive counteraction. It would avail the Anglo-American coalition naught to sit back undecidedly behind their aquatic barrier enjoying a false sense of security. The resilience and resourcefulness of the German nation was prodigious. Even in the later stages of the war, beleaguered on all sides, blockaded and under sustained heavy aerial bombardment by day and night, she produced in large numbers the V1 flying bomb – the jet propelled 'Doodlebug' – and, more ominously, the V2 rocket designed by Dr Werner von Braun, launched from mobile platforms. Once the rocket was launched there was no defence against it. Eisenhower expressed the opinion that had the V2 been fully operative six months earlier it might have prevented embarkation for the Normandy invasion.

Again, during the last months of conflict Germany was still producing warplanes faster than aircrews could be trained, and was the first to introduce jet fighter aircraft to the warring skies – the Messerschmidt 262 and the Heinkel Volksjachter – which could outpace anything then flying. On the naval front she constructed, in November 1944, only six months before surrender, more U-boats than in any other month of the war, including four 'Walther' types – revolutionary submarines designed by Dr Helmuth Walther, using High Test Peroxide (HTP) to generate steam for turbine propulsion, resulting in underwater speeds in excess of 25 knots.

These amplifications to the strength of Hitler's armoury, on land, sea and in the air, were not to be taken lightly. In fact they each had the potential to add a deadly impact and it was fortunate for the Allies that these innovations were not encountered earlier. In the event, their threat was terminated just in time by the advance of the American, British and Commonwealth armies across France and the Low Countries.

The exceptional standards of German scientific research and production were recognised by both the western allies and the Soviet

Union, and at war's end each scrambled to induce the best German brains to come across and pursue their endeavours in the service of their nation's conquerors, subject to an adequate reversal of allegiance. In this context Helmuth Walther, with many of his subordinates, worked in Britain on the design and production of 'Walther' type submarines for the Royal Navy. The superior performance of this craft was, however, overtaken and exceeded in time by the emergence of nuclear-powered submarines.

More significantly, Werner von Braun, creator of the V2 rocket, was co-opted by the United States, again with hundreds of his team (including a number of former Nazi members) and in due course was appointed to head the American Lunar Rocket Research project, culminating on 20 July 1969 with utterance of the famous words, "One small step for man, one giant leap for mankind". The superbly successful Apollo 11 rocket had carried Neil Armstrong, Edwin Aldrin and Michael Collins to the moon.

Among many others of our former enemies who changed sides after hostilities was Mitsuo Fuchida, who emigrated to the United States, against whom he had struck the first blow as overall air commander of the Japanese aerial assault on Pearl Harbor. He converted to Christianity and became a lay minister. His son and daughter also took citizenship in the USA.

But, as I have again digressed somewhat, allow me to return one last time to the sinkings of *Cornwall* and *Dorsetshire* which, without question, saved the Eastern Fleet from extinction on 5 April 1942, and, in the process, prevented discovery and annihilation of the secret naval base at Port T in the Maldives. Even if none of the other crucial and far-reaching consequences as earlier enumerated materialised, the loss to the British Royal Navy could, by my estimate, have entailed 29 warships, including the *Hermes* and *Vampire* sunk four days later, plus several fleet auxiliaries, with a total loss of life extending perhaps to 25,000 or more. Whether that would have constituted the greatest naval disaster of all time I leave to others better versed in maritime history who might feel inclined to consider the proposition, but certainly it would have been a catastrophe with repercussions that beggar description.

What inestimable debt, therefore, is owed to those aboard *Cornwall* and *Dorsetshire,* the two 'Three Funnelled Bastards', who died. In 2,000 fathoms they lie – no marked grave does them honour, no cross or headstone but the restless sea and a tropical sky, no sound of mourning save the whispering wind and, perchance, the plaintive cry of a wandering albatross.

> *They have grown not old, our shipmates. Age has not wearied them nor the years condemned.*
> *At the going down of the sun and in the morning, we WILL remember them.*

On a gusty October morning in 1945, at about half past eight, I walked towards the bank that I had left almost six years previously, to renew my employment there. The building, I thought, had not changed in the slightest – the same yellow facade and abundant windows. Even the pigeons strutting and preening on the roof and exterior protuberances seemed to be the identical feathered inmates of yesteryear. Everything was quite unaffected by the global turmoil that had raged over those six years and ceased just two months ago. My infinitely puny input had been in the guise of a seaman, an option predisposed at the outset, I recalled, by my dread of poison gas.

These impressions did not bring me peace of mind. I was miserably aware of my shortcomings in the banking environment. Years of absence had dispersed what little knowledge I had had before, and my skills with figures: adding, subtracting, etcetera had, I discovered, deteriorated alarmingly. Banking terminology: bills of exchange, remittances, overdrafts and the rest, had receded into the remotest hideaways of a murky memory. In a few minutes from now I would be deposited among a hundred other banking devotees for whom the Second World War had long since faded into boredom. A few I would remember, but the majority not. I would tag on behind some unfortunate individual sentenced to 'showing me the ropes', feeling gawkish and conspicuous in my new civilian attire, looking sheepish and not knowing my posterior from my elbow (must keep these expressions respectable now that I'm back in 'civvy street').

Peacetime had not, I reflected dismally, unfolded as a bed of roses but, on the contrary, had burdened me with a multitude of new worries... Ah well, at least poison gas was not one of them.

Coats of arms painted on Simonstown dry dock
(right to left - Cornwall, Dorsetshire, Hermes)

THOSE WE LEFT BEHIND

ROLL OF HONOUR – WITHOUT REGARD TO RANK

HMS *CORNWALL*

ADKINS, E A	AMEY, W A
ANDREWS, L T C	ARMITAGE, H V
ARTHINGTON, H	ARTHUR, M E
ASHLEY, E E	AYLING, A D C
BAILLIE, W A	BAKER, H T W
BANNER, D M	BIRD, J M
BISS, G A	BLOGG, F W
BOULSOVER, W	BRADLEY, W
BROCKMAN, F L	BROCKMAN, W C R
BROWN, W F	BUCKETT, L W
BULLIMORE, T E	BURRELL, L
BUTLER, C J A	CASLAKE, J N
CHAVE, W R	COCHRANE, F H
COLEMAN, E	COMER, J
COOK, B N	COWELL, F E
DAWSON, J H	DOLLAN, T
DONOVAN, B E B	DREW, G F W
DUERDEN, C	DUNTHORNE, W L
DURBEE, M L	DURKIN, A M
EDGAR, M L	ELLIOTT, H S

HMS *DORSETSHIRE*

ALLAN, A W	ALLEN, W W B
ALMOND, J	ARMSTRONG, E F
AUSTIN, J	BAILEY, F W
BAMFORD, E C M	BANNISTER, R
BARKER, C	BARRET, J
BELLIS, A	BIDGOOD, W J
BLACKBURN L	BODYCOTE, A J F
BOUNDY, E A	BOUNDY, J
BOUQUET, P Y	BOWRING, S
BRADLEY, J	BRANAGAN, C S
BURDER, A R	BUTTAR, C P
CAINE, R	CALVERLEY, A
CARNE, J W A	CHANTRELL, S G
CLARK, W G	COGILL, K
CONCANON, H B	CONDIE, J
CONNOLLY, D	CONNOLY, E
CONNOR, R J	COOK. A
DARCY, C	DARNELL, H W
DAVEY, W	DAVIS, A E M
DAVIS, H V	DAVIS, I C J

ELSWORTH, I W E
FARLEY, W
FLANNIGAN, A M D
FORREST, J C
FOX, J H E
GASKIN, S F
GILHAM, R T
GOODGER, C F
GRANT, T
HANSFORD, P C
HAYHOE, R A
HENSLEY, E J
HOPPER, C A
HUNT, K G
JACKSON, B T
KEEBLE, L G
KELLY, J
KENNEDY, S
KIRBY, C C
LAMBIE, F M
LANG, R R
LEADBETTER, R
LEWIS, J
LUHN, D
MARRINER, G
MILLAR, J
MITCHELL, A V
MOORE, J A
NEVILLE, F R J
PARISH, K T
PEARN, K H
PICKERING, V
POOLE, L
RAMSEY, W G
READ, A W
ROGERS, E N
ROLLS, G P W
SCHOFIELD, L W
SHARP, F W
SHOEBRIDGE, A G
SMITH, A C
SMITH, J
SMITH, T G

EMBERTON, W H
FEARFIELD, J F R
FLEUTY, R
FOSTER, G
GALLIERS, D
GELDER, K
GODDARD, P
GORE, S J
HALES, W
HARRIS, A T
HEATHER, R C W
HICKEY, E T
HUBBARD, H
IRONS, S W H
JONES, E J
KELK, T L
KENNEDY, G R
KING, M
KNIGHT, R M
LANCASTER, P G
LARMAN, E J C
LEFEVRE, L
LOVELL, C Y
MANTLE, W K
MERRIMAN, C E L
MILLETT, R F
MOODY, J
MORRISH, B C
OSBORNE, C E
PARRISH, A
PHILIPS, R
PLATT, R
POWELL, F G
READ, A R
ROBERTS, J
ROGERS, V R
SARGENT, L W
SENIOR, H G
SHIEL, E M
SHORE, A W
SMITH, A G
SMITH, J W
SOUTER, J

DILLAWAY, S T
DONNACHIE, T M
DUGDALE, F
EADES, W W
ELLIOTT, C F
ELSOM, W J
ESSAM, R E
FERRIS, W A
FLEVILL, T
GARNER, W D
GERRARD, E N
GORMAN, L
GREGG, W A G
GUBB, A G
HALE, W G
HARE, C H
HARRISON, J H
HARWOOD, P
HENDERSON, J B
HERRING, J F
HOGG, R V
HOOPER, L J J
HOWCROFT, F
HUMPHREY, A W
IRVING, T A
JACKSON, W H
JEFFERY, P G H
JONES, W J
KELSHAW, F
KENEALEY, J A
KIDD, W R
LABORDE, E D R
LARGE, E S
LEAT, W R J
LEMPRIERE, F
McATEER, D R J
McGOVERN, P
MARSHALL, W G N
MATTHEWS, W A L
MEADES, A E
MOORE, C J
MOYES, R
MURTAGH, T P

DIXON, H
DONOVAN, J
DUPLEX, J E
EDMUNDS, V
ELLIS, R W G
ERIKSEN, E A
FEDDON, W
FLEETWOOD, E
FRENCH, W H
GARRETT, J E
GIDDINGS, D
GRANT, G H
GREY, D
GULLIFORD, H G
HAMM, P
HARRINGTON, T
HARVEY, G H
HAWKEY, W H
HERRIDGE, W W
HILL, J
HOOKER, G F C
HOTCHKISS, A E D
HUDSON, N
HYDE, A F J
JACK, R W
JARVIE, J S W
JENNINGS, J E T
JORDAN, H M
KENDALL, S F O
KERR, G
KILVINGTON, J F
LAMB, A H
LAWRIE, O
LEGG, S A
LUDBROOK, H
McCORKELL, E S
MANSELL, J F
MARTIN, D
MAY, S
MILLER, G W
MORGAN, E
MULLETT, F J
NEVILLE, N R

SPENCER, S H
THURMAN, W T A
USHER, J G W
WATERS, D E
WATTS, F C
WILLS, E D
WILSON, G W I
STEVENTON, A
TOTTMAN, W C
VALLANCE, W H
WATKINS, W J
WILLIAMS, M
WILSON, A F
WILSON, J

MALTESE

BENNIEI, C
ELLUL, J M
SAMMUT, G
CIOTH, A
PORTANIA, P
VALETTA, L

SOUTH AFRICAN

BATES, J S
COMMERFORD, N P
DU PREEZ, C P H
HANSLO, R F
KENYON, G A B
LAW, E V
MITCHELL, W A
SPENCE, H W
STEPHEN, E R
THORP, E M
VINK, H F
WRIGHT, T H
BESWETHERICK, H C
CRAWFORD, C C
DUTTON, C C
KEITH, K J B
KIRSTEN, M G W
McDAVID, W K
PALMER, W A
SQUIRES, J E
SWANN, L T
VERSFELD, P H S
WILLSON, G F

NAAFI

JAGO, E C E
STUBBING, A H

ROYAL MARINES

BARRETT, C E
GLOYNS, W S
HUDSON, H G
LONG, B W
MODERATE, H T
NOBLE, B E
PERRYMAN, H C
REID, D S
ROBINSON, R W
SIFLEET, E G
WINCHESTER, K A
GARWOOD, A H
GOODWIN, D F
HOWELL, B J
METHERELL, D
MULLINS, S W
O'NEILL, R J
PRODGER, S S
REVERLEY, R H
ROTHNIE, N A J
SMITH, H

SHIP'S CAT

MINNIE

O'BRIEN, J
OSLAND, W G
PASCOE, D J
PAUL, W G
PEARCE, R E
PETRIE, R C
POAD, C A
PRICE, A E
QUIRK, W T
READER, H G
RICHARDS, M K
ROBINS, W J
ROWBOTHAM, M
SAUNDERS, S A
SCOTT, E S
SIBERT, F F
SILVESTER, K G
SMITH, R
STANLEY, H
STRANGE, A E
SUTHERLAND, B
TAYLOR, V J
THOMAS, E E
THORPE, R B
TIPPING, R E L
TURNBULL, R
VAN ZYL, D I S
WARD, D W
WILLIAMS, E G P
WILLIAMS, J
WILSON, D
WOOLEY, E G
WRIGHTSON, C O
ORRELL, L E
PARSONS, E B
PAUL, E D
PEARCE, E T
PEARSON, J E
PILE, S F
PRATT, S W
PRING, N G
RADFORD, W S L
REEVES, W
ROBERTSON, P A
ROBINSON, J A S
RULE, A H
SCOBLE, S J
SHATWELL, W
SIDEBOTHAM, J R R
SMITH, F T W
STAGG, W F
STANNARD, G G
SUGDEN, P W
SWENSON, J W
THATCHER, A
THORNE, H V
THORPE, R B C
TUCKER, R C
TWELIS, A L
WALSH, T
WARD, S H
WILLIAMS, G P
WILLIAMS, W
WOODWARD, J
WOOLLER, G W

SOUTH AFRICAN

BELL, D S
EVENPOEL, A
HOWE, H G
McINTYRE, E G
MILNE, L V
ORTON, C P
SCOTT, W H
WILLET, A A S
BAUCE, A M
GEFFENS, S
KENDRICK, G
McLELLAN, R
MORROW, D F
REDMAN, R A
SEVEL, H
WILLIAMSON, W N

NAAFI

COWEN, H F	LAITY, D
STOTHART, S S	

ROYAL MARINES

ANGUS, R B	BAGNALL, J
BAGWELL, D	BAINES, T D
COCKERHAM, F	COLEMAN, W J
DANBY, H A	DENTON, B J
DUFFY, T P	FARLEY, W
GIBBIN, J	GREEN, T
HALLAM J	HICKMAN, R G
KEAT, A	MACKAY, A L
MERRICK, V	SHELDON, C J
TAFT, L	TAYLOR, H
THURSTON, W J	WILSON, R
WOOD, T	WRIGHT, F S

OLD SAILORS NEVER DIE – THEY SIMPLY SAIL AWAY

PRINTED SOURCES OF REFERENCE

Manual Of Seamanship, Admiralty, London
Jane's Fighting Ships Of World War II, Naval Encyclopaedia
The Second World War, Winston S Churchill
The Great Sea War, Chester W Nimitz and E A Potter
The War At Sea, D W Roskill
The World At War, Commissioned History
World War II – 50th Anniversary Commemoration, Ivor Matanle
Purnell's History Of The Second World War, Basil Liddell Hart and
    Barrie Pitt with Imperial War Museum
Midway – The Battle That Doomed Japan, Mitsuo Fuchida and
    Masatake Okumiya
A Sailor's Odyssey, Andrew Cunningham
South Africa At War, H J Martin and D Orpen
South Africa In World War II, Joel Mervis
The Most Dangerous Moment, Michael Tomlinson
War At Sea – South African Maritime Operations, C J Harris
The War At Sea – Anthology, John Winton
The Rising Sun, Time-Life International
The Fall Of Japan, William Crecy
The U-Boat Peril, Bob Whinney
The Life And Times Of Lord Mountbatten, John Terraine
Turns Of Fate, Ken Dimbleby
In Deep And Troubled Waters, Tony Large

Bismarck, Dorsetshire And Memories, Ray Lock

Rommel, Desmond Young

Wavell – Portrait Of A Soldier, Bernard Fergusson

The Gates Of Hell, Ewart Brookes

Thirty Seconds Over Tokyo, Ted W Lawson

Transcript Of Official Report To Admiralty, James Somerville

On The Sinking Of HMS Cornwall *and HMS* Dorsetshire, Augustus
    Agar, John Fair

*Solidanosc (Solidarity) Independent Self-Governing Trade Union In
    Co-Operation With Ministry Of Foreign Affairs*, Poland

THE PHANTOM FLEET

I once looked out from the Tamar Bridge at the warships down
below,
Ships of the modern Navy, with names I do not know
And as I stood and gazed at them, on the water far below
I saw a fleet of phantom ships and men of long ago.
The RODNEY and the NELSON, the VALIANT, RAMILLIES,
REPULSE, RENOWN and TIGER, coming home from foreign seas.
I saw REVENGE and WARSPITE, ill-fated ROYAL OAK,
So many ships, their names made faint by shell and fire and smoke.

And more I see to harbour come, as though through glasses dark,
The BARHAM and the GLORIOUS, the EAGLE and the ARK.
And then there comes the greatest, the mighty warship
HOOD,
Dark and grey and wraithlike, from the spot on which I stood.
From the cruel North Atlantic, from the Med and Java Sea,
The big ships and the little ships returned for me to see.
There's the HERMES and the CORNWALL, the DORSETSHIRE
and KENT,
The COSSACK and COURAGEOUS, the SUFFOLK and
ARDENT.

But mercifully hidden, are the men, and stilled their cries,
Now I can't see very clearly – must be smoke that's in my eyes.
You don't know Shorty Hasset – he won the DSM,
He still fought on when EXETER was burning stern
to stem.
Where now Dodger Long and Lofty, where now the boys and men?
They are lost and gone forever – will we see their like again?
I thought I saw them mustering, on deck for daily prayer,
And heard "For those in Peril", rise on the evening air.

Then darker grew the picture, as the lowering night came on,
I looked down from the lofty bridge but all those ships had gone.
Those mighty ships had vanished, gone those gallant men –
We'll surely never, ever, see the like of them again.
Anon

*   *   *   *   *

ACKNOWLEDGEMENTS

I owe sincere thanks and appreciation to:

My daughter Karen for pictorial drawings
My granddaughter Irene for constructing diagrams
My granddaughter Karen Jnr for providing publishing information
My son Eugene for correcting English grammar
My wife Stella for enduring the irritating deportment of an
inadequate writer
Commander 'Mac' Bisset (Rtd) of the S A Navy
for invaluable advice
My friend Graham John for photographic reproduction
Especially my friend Atholie Duigan who, during untold hours of
toil and tribulation, transformed a nightmarish manuscript into an
impeccable typescript
Everybody else who, in whatever way, offered assistance and
encouragement.

WALLY MULLER

ABOUT THE AUTHOR

On a personal note I first saw the light of day in January 1921 in the town of Harrismith, South Africa, matriculated at St Charles College, Pietermaritzburg and then, apart from the war years as described in this book, followed a career in banking. After retirement I served for some years in the South African Red Cross. In my spare time I have functioned as husband, father and granddad.

'Tigger' the house cat circa 2008 (and the author)